Beyond the
Ivory Tower

Also by Sir Solly Zuckerman

The Social Life of Monkeys and Apes
Functional Affinities of Man, Monkeys and Apes
A New System of Anatomy
Scientists and War
The Ovary, Volumes 1 and 2 (*edited*)

Sir Solly Zuckerman

Beyond the Ivory Tower
The Frontiers of Public and Private Science

Weidenfeld and Nicolson
5 Winsley Street London W1

SBN 297 00236 8

Printed in Great Britain
by Ebenezer Baylis and Son Limited
The Trinity Press, Worcester, and London

Contents

List of Figures

Preface

I have long held the view that there are powerful built-in constraints to the supposed freedom with which people select the goals of scientific and technological activity. In the essay[1] in which I first spelt out this theme, which is far from being widely accepted, and in a volume[2] in which I tried to illustrate it by reference to the influence science and technology have had on the nature of war, I also argued that whatever the goals which may be chosen, their achievement always entails the risk of unpredictable social consequences. Mainly for these reasons I felt it urgent that the distinction between pure basic research as the first step in the scientific process on the one hand, and what is definable as applied research on the other, should be properly recognised. This still seems to me essential if there is to be any real appreciation of how much, or how little, choice we have in determining our future, and how fast the future is not only being transformed, but also 'set' in this scientific and technological age. As basic scientific knowledge grows and becomes transformed, so does the edifice we build on it, and what is built next is almost inevitably influenced by what is there already. We do not have all the freedom some suppose as we prepare for tomorrow.

I know that there are many who protest an opposite view, and who claim that in this scientific and technological age we are becoming freer than were our fathers and grandfathers, freer and richer not only in a material way, but also freer in the philosophical sense of the term. In the present volume I nonetheless carry my original theme a stage further. What I am particularly concerned to demonstrate is that although the scientist has a special responsibility in deciding what science should be encouraged and what applied – after all he is supposed to have a more intimate understanding of the primary issues which may be involved – the rules by which the scientist operates when he is engaged in the strict exercise of advancing knowledge are not those which regulate action in social and political spheres, and which determine which kinds of science, and what advances of scientific knowledge, should be fostered and applied. The controversies of the open world, controversies which concern social values and action, controversies due to the clash of opposing interests, are very different from those which determine the emergence of scientific or empirical truth.

I list on p. ix those of my previously published essays and articles which I have used, mainly by rearrangement, in illustrating my main theme of the difference between the nature of controversy as it occurs within science, and of that other process of discussion and argument which determines how much pure science to foster, and how much, and what, to apply. I should like to express my thanks to the editors of the various journals in which they first appeared for allowing me to reprint them, even if in a form and order different from that in which they first appeared. The lecture on which I have partly based Chapters 8 and 19 was published in the American, but not the English, edition of my *Scientists and War*.

As a public servant, I should make it clear that the opinions expressed in this book are my own, and that where any – particularly in its second part – might be held to refer, however remotely, to public policy, they do not necessarily reflect the views of Her Majesty's Government.

University of East Anglia
1970.   S. Zuckerman

Essays on Which the Book is Based

'It affords a violent prejudice against almost every science, that no prudent man, however sure of his principles, dares prophesy concerning any event, or fortel the remote consequences of things.'

David Hume: Essay Nine in *Essays Moral and Political*, published in 1741

To Dickie Mountbatten

I
Introduction

The first part of this book illustrates my personal understanding of what science is about, and how it progresses. Such generalisations as I have permitted myself on this topic are based on an extensive practical experience of research and teaching in my own fields of study. The second part of the book deals with the relation of science to public affairs, and of scientists to the machine of government. Here my views derive from many years of 'inside' experience in advising on scientific matters which impinge on areas of public policy. There are no textbooks on this particular subject, and what I have to say touches on only some of its aspects.

The two parts of the book might have been addressed to different audiences, the first to a much more specialised one than the second. Whether or not both will be read by the same reader, I decided to combine them for two reasons. First, my knowledge of what goes on inside science, how scientists work, and about scientists as individuals, has been part and parcel of my education about the impact of science on public affairs, and about the kinds of influence scientists are able to bring to bear on them. My second reason is a more general one. Scientific knowledge hardly ever grows in even fashion, and what is new, and what may prove to be true, does not necessarily drive out what is false but accepted. The advances of science are thus normally characterised by controversy, which theoretically is confined within a scientific frame, except, of course, when vulgarisation, and extraneous considerations, such, for example, as financial reward, make the argument spill over into the world of news and sensation. Controversies in science are also concerned mainly with ideas which precede action, and which may never result in action. For this reason, while they may generate just as much heat, they have a different character from the controversies of the public world, which are inevitably and immediately concerned with conflicts of values and interest, and with action which may affect the lives of hundreds or millions of people. This difference, obvious as it is, needs to be spelt out. There is a danger that its significance is still not widely enough appreciated, or at least that it is being minimised, both by scientists and by some politicians.

Scientists are, of course, involved in the controversies of both worlds, in the private world of science by special right, and in the public world as members of a body politic. Those scientists who feel that they shoulder a special social responsibility, because scientific knowledge is the root of the technological changes which transform the social and political environment, have to decide themselves how to deal with their sense of moral obligation. But they enjoy no special franchise in the public world. Because they are trained, or are assumed to be trained, to search for objective truth, they are not necessarily better able to define the best ways to reach the goals of social justice than are other men. Because some scientists are acknowledged for their special understanding of the nature of the atom or the behaviour of viruses, they are not necessarily political leaders who know best how national goals are to be decided and reached.

On the other hand, in coming to terms with their social con-science, there is nothing to prevent scientists from becoming public servants or politicians or propagandists, and so bringing their views and fears to bear on events. But they have to choose which it is they want to become. To be a propagandist is not necessarily the same as being a politician, and all professional politicians are not members of a government and in control of the machine of government. It is the height of naïveté to suppose – as I have seen it said in a recent public address – that all that scientists need do in discharging what was called their 'first moral or social responsibility' is to 'leave their laboratories occasionally and talk about the political and social consequences of what they are doing.'[1]

Even were it possible for so vast a moral debt to be discharged in so easy a way, these 'consequences' are precisely what scientists have no ready means of foretelling. There would, of course, be no such debt at all if everything scientists did proved a blessing to mankind. The sense of social responsibility always derives from a consciousness of 'bad' technological developments, from those which have potentially disastrous consequences, and not from

2

those which for one reason or other, are rightly or wrongly regarded as blessings. The 'bad' applications of scientific knowledge, or the technological 'blessings' which turn sour, are the ones which are usually uppermost in people's minds when they give a thought to the consequences of scientific advance.

It is still the case that the most outstanding single example of presumed 'scientific sin' remains the knowledge of how to split the atom. This was a scientific discovery in which those concerned at the time saw no possible evil results. But today there are many – including scientists and politicians – who blame science for the peril in which the world stands as a result of the consequential nuclear arms race. Equally there are some scientists who disclaim all responsibility and lay the blame for the development of the bomb on the abstract entity, 'society at large'. Generalisations of this kind are meaningless, and get us nowhere. Only a relatively few scientists were concerned in the development of the bomb; fewer were involved in the decision that it should be developed; and all but none that it should be used. The overwhelming majority of scientists heard about the existence of atom bombs only when the rest of the world did. To take another case – only a handful of scientists have been concerned in those developments of knowledge which have led to the world's population explosion. Few really understand their nature. But all – like the rest of their fellow-beings – have been drawn into the social and political consequences of population growth. Different technological developments, again, result in different kinds of pollution. But not even the applied scientist who is responsible for advances in, say, some particular industrial process, or for producing some new kind of goods for which there is a demand, can tell in advance what will be the social cost, in terms of pollution or some other disadvantage, of his new development. Even when the facts seem plain enough for all to see, there will still be dispute about their significance. The consequences of technological advance, alas, always lie in the future. I remember once having to visit a distinguished American colleague for whose contributions to our knowledge of animal reproduction I had, and still have, the highest respect – he is now dead – to discuss with him a particular development of commercial value for which he was acting as consultant to a large pharmaceutical firm. While this development had already been introduced to the

American market, concern was being expressed in the United Kingdom about its possible side-effects, and a decision had to be taken about either banning or permitting its use. Before seeing him I had discussed the matter in Washington with health authorities and with officials of the Pure Foods and Drugs Administration who, so far as I could make out, shared my disquiet. In the course of two days' talk, my friend made it quite plain that he appreciated that there was cause for concern, but argued forcibly that the danger was being magnified out of all proportion in relation to the benefits which would result from the 'development' – for which he was in large part responsible. There was no shaking his conviction, and this was quite naturally shared by the firm he was advising. His 'bull-point' was that the practice was already allowed in the States, and that the net profit to the firm for what was one of many end-uses of a certain synthetic chemical was more than five million dollars. If any move were now made to ban the development in the USA, the firm could afford to spend up to that amount in legal costs fighting their case – if necessary all the way up to the Supreme Court. Regardless of his personal interest, I have absolutely no reason to suppose that my American colleague was not genuine in his belief that people like myself were exaggerating the danger.

When one talks about the social responsibility of scientists, it is thus carrying naïveté to the extreme to suppose that they speak with one voice and that they share a common conscience when it comes to the application of scientific knowledge. Some scientists were – and many remain – undismayed by the emergence of 'the Bomb'. Some, indeed, still argue publicly for bigger and better bombs. Others, as the Oppenheimer story tells only too well, were appalled when they sensed the likely impact of these weapons on world affairs. But Oppenheimer's conscience was stirred only after he had directed the development and testing of the first bomb. Niels Bohr, knowing what was afoot, was almost alone in his prevision of the postwar international consequences of the bomb, well before it had been proved that the weapon could in fact be made, as well as designed in theory, and well before the bomb was used. But in spite of the opportunity of direct access, Bohr failed to impress either Winston Churchill or President Roosevelt with his fears. Szilard, who a few years before had urged Einstein to use his great prestige with the President in order to get the development of the bomb under way, only started vigorously to oppose its use in actual hostilities – as did a few other scientists who were in the picture – shortly before the weapon was tested. And yet when Peierls and Frisch in 1940 indicated in their short secret paper[2] how to make an atom bomb, they had clearly warned that effective protection against nuclear weapons was hardly feasible, with the clear implication that the new weapon would, if it materialised, transform the character of warfare. It is equally extraordinary that while the lethal effects of radioactive fall-out were immediately appreciated, and the persistence of radioactive contamination understood, hardly one of the distinguished biologists who were 'in the know' gave a thought to the possible genetic effects of widespread radiation – an issue which was one of many that later assumed prominence in the discussions and deliberations which led to the partial test-ban agreement of 1963. And even in these later discussions scientists were far from unanimous in their views about the dangers.*

Scientists are not visionaries – they cannot, as I have so often insisted, and as I argue again in this book, define the nature and magnitude of potential discovery in advance, any more than they can its impact on our social lives. Nor, as I have said, do they constitute a body of men with a uniform social purpose. There are more than a quarter of a million people trained as scientists in the United Kingdom today. In the world as a whole there must be millions who would describe themselves as professional scientists. They all presumably share the same faith in established scientific knowledge, wherever they are and whatever the countries to which they belong. But scientists do not constitute a single profession, like clergymen, or doctors, or lawyers. They are in every profession. And they no more share the same political purposes or passports than do any other body of men. Scratch a scientist, it

---

* According to Mr C. R. Attlee (later Earl Attlee), who was the British Prime Minister at the time the two Japanese towns, Hiroshima and Nagasaki, were effaced by nuclear bombs, not one of the politicians who took the decision to use them was aware of the fact that nuclear explosions differed from the burst of conventional weapons, except in their greater force. 'We knew nothing whatever at that time about the genetic effects of an atomic explosion. I knew nothing about fall-out and all the rest of what emerged after Hiroshima. As far as I know, President Truman and Winston Churchill knew nothing of these things either, nor did Sir John Anderson, who co-ordinated research on our side. Whether the scientists directly concerned knew, or guessed, I do not know. But if they did, then, so far as I am aware, they said nothing of it to those who had to make the decision.'[3]

used to be said, and you draw the blood of any ordinary middle-class man, a man with diverse social views, and often with confused purposes.

The recent establishment in the United Kingdom of a Society for Social Responsibility in Science is the latest of a number of efforts to engage the social conscience of scientists. At least two corresponding British movements in the thirties were swallowed up by the second world war, when most scientists found themselves geared to one general purpose – that of putting their talents to work in the effort to defeat the common enemy. Those social and political problems of the post-war which have their roots in new scientific discovery – those engendered by the Bomb, by population growth, by environmental pollution, by air travel, by computerisation – are immensely more complicated than the problems of the war period, and it would be a tragedy if the good-will which lies behind movements such as the new Society were to run into the sands because of a lack of understanding of the social and political mechanisms by which our actions are regulated. As I have said, scientists have to choose which way they salve their social consciences. Things are not as easy in the political sphere as they sometimes appear. When issues seem crystal clear, and a scientist wonders why the 'right' course of action is not immediately adopted, it may well be that he is unaware of some essential facts which also affect the situation. Unsophisticated propaganda about man destroying himself with his science and technology defeats itself, and hardly gives pause to the developments against which it is aimed.

But in my view nothing but good can come from informed public debate of those consequences of technological developments which are now causing acute concern – in non-scientific as well as scientific circles. The forum provided by the Pugwash meetings in the field of disarmament is an excellent illustration of what can be helpful. These meetings may not have unearthed any new facts or led to any proposals which were not already being canvassed officially in more secret national and international exchanges. But they certainly provided a means whereby more people became informed, and whereby ideas about possible international agreement, however limited, could be canvassed without commitment.

But movements such as these inevitably take scientists from the world of controversy to which they are accustomed as scientists, and where discussion theoretically follows acknowledged rules, into a world of controversy which has few rules and which is bedevilled by ignorance and by the clash of different interests. Furthermore, the ways of this wider world are not the same in different countries. The British system of government is not the same as the USA's, nor that of the USSR, nor that of Western Germany. Scientists who wish to engage in the debate about the applications of science will be frustrated whatever the country to which they belong if they do not know how the particular machine of government which regulates their lives and the lives of their fellow citizens operates. This is something one learns mainly from experience, which is why nothing but good could come from the involvement of scientists in the official world from which social policies emerge.

What needs to be borne in mind at all times, to repeat what I emphasised in an earlier essay,[4] is that we cannot invest pure scientific knowledge with any inherent moral direction. That is imparted by the way science is used. All we can be certain of is that all sides in the continuing world struggle will use science and technology where and how they can in the achievement of their respective national aims. While democracy may be man's answer to tyranny and exploitation, we need to remember that the only form of exploitation which it will never help overcome is the coercion of new knowledge which, by guiding our social lives into certain channels, limits advance in others. The element of the unknown in government increases with every step we are now taking to apply the fruits of science. If the basis of power is being changed, it is less by some governing body, however formed; and more and more by a process of applying scientific knowledge without any real possibility of determining its final consequences. Neither the voice of the majority, nor the voice of those through whom it is expressed, can proclaim the precise lines of the future.

PART I

PRIVATE SCIENCE

2

The Search for Objective Truth

The theory of knowledge is traditionally a preserve of the professional philosopher. It is nonetheless a subject of considerable importance to the working scientist, however slight his overt preoccupation with the world of abstract ideas. Science, as we know, deals only with ascertainable knowledge. But many things which scientists hold to be true are to a large extent conditioned by personal attitudes and idiosyncracies. The line of thought about the general subject of objective knowledge which I myself have always followed when engaged as a scientist in my own fields of scientific enquiry has in recent years crystallised for me in the writings of Karl Popper,[1] which in this particular field of scholarship are, as he tells us, built to a large extent on Alfred Tarski's[2] formal exposition of the 'correspondence theory' of absolute or objective truth. It is on this foundation that I propose to build what follows in this chapter.

By objective truth, which is sometimes called empirical or absolute truth, the philosopher means the enduring 'something' which emerges conceptually from an analysis or interpretation of what we learn through our senses. But since this 'something' cannot be based on all possible experience, the sceptic always has the right to insist that the particular concept which emerges as an empirical truth from a basis of present experience can never be final – it can only be probable. 'The empirical generalisation', as has been said, 'is forever at the mercy of future experience.'[3]

The scientist's answer to this proposition is that the kind of truth empirical knowledge represents, based as it is upon experience, nonetheless constitutes the only kind of truth, as well as the only sure basis, from which to develop his own understanding. Because it is assumed to be predictive in its nature, this kind of knowledge is continually put to the test. If any empirical hypothesis is found wanting, it has to be discarded. On this point I have more than once found it salutory to remind myself of a forceful line from the last of the 'Six Lectures to Working Men' which T.H. Huxley[4] delivered in 1863. 'Every hypothesis', he said, 'is bound to explain or, at any rate, not be inconsistent with, the whole of the facts which it professes to account for; and if there is a single one of these facts which can be shown to be inconsistent with the hypothesis, the hypothesis falls to the ground, – it is worth nothing.' Huxley never tired of emphasising what he called in an earlier lecture which he delivered in 1854[5] 'the utterly conditional nature of all our knowledge', and the dangers of neglecting the 'great process of verification' in deciding what was to be held to be true.

The scientific process is a system of enquiry which combines searching with questioning, and leaps of imaginative understanding with critical disbelief. It constitutes, as it were, a three-dimensional and dynamic structure in which new problems emerge out of the background of others which have already been dealt with by appropriate methods of test, in the full knowledge that eternal verities are not the scientist's business, and that the best which he can logically achieve is to prove an idea or hypothesis false, so leaving the field open to some other explanation.

The objective truth with which scientists are concerned is the truth which corresponds with facts. Subjective truth is of no concern here, presupposing as it does that this kind of truth – to quote Popper – 'is what we are justified in believing or in accepting, in accordance with certain rules or criteria, of origins or sources of our knowledge, or of reliability, or stability, or biological success, or strength of conviction, or inability to think otherwise'.

Such an idea of truth is clearly far too wide and far too arbitrary for the scientist. He becomes isolated if he proceeds on the basis of a series of subjectively held convictions. We have to adhere to the concept of objective truth 'if we wish to elucidate the difference between pure and applied science, between the search for knowledge and the search for power or for powerful instruments.' For, as Popper goes on to say, 'the difference is that, in the search for knowledge, we are out to find true theories, or at least theories which are nearer than others to the truth – which correspond better to the facts; whereas in the search for theories that are merely powerful instruments for certain purposes, we are, in many cases, quite well served by theories which are known to be false.'

One major merit of the concept of objective or empirical truth in science is that its implementation is something in which all can share. There is none of the exclusiveness of subjective truth about it. Inspired and personal knowledge is precious to those to whom it comes, but it does not necessarily follow that others will wish to share it, or accept it.

But having said this, let me immediately add that the path to objective truth in science is rarely charted by a common consent, and then strewn with roses. It is only in theory that some new explanation which may prove to be true in the scientific sense is immediately acceptable. This all depends on the kind of science and on the nature of the scientists concerned. I have been surprised to discover from many reviews of Professor Watson's celebrated book *The Double Helix*[6] that in spite of the vast amount that has been written on the subject, the incorrect idea still prevails that the scientific process is always an orderly one, that one successful scientist pursues the same kind of sequence of logical method as does another, that scientists, as it were, constitute a dispassionate body of men and women who, through training and experience, are all but interchangeable.

This, perhaps unfortunately, is total nonsense. All people who are scientists are assumed to have enjoyed a certain commonality of training and experience – but there, except for two characteristics to which I shall refer, even the theoretical resemblance ends. Some scientists are wide in their interests, others narrow. Some are bright, others stupid. Some are creators, others followers. Some are ready to admit when they have been wrong; others obstinately turn their backs on evidence which weakens their beliefs. Some have even been known to be falsifiers.

The first of the two characteristics which scientists, in theory, share is that they all live professionally in a world of hypotheses, a world which is constantly changing as theories and questions are put to the test either through experiment or some other kind of controlled observation; where hypotheses are found fruitful because they light the path to new discovery and action; or are found defective because the predictions which they generated fail to be borne out by new experiment – and even then not defective in an absolute sense, since the process of testing a false hypothesis may itself suggest a better one.

I had assumed it to be well recognised that hypotheses were not derived in any single way, that sometimes they are carefully formulated as a result of laborious analysis of a problem; that sometimes they constitute no more than hunches and guesses; that scientific enquiry, in short, is usually like some medieval voyage of exploration, with either nothing at all turning up after a week's calm or tempestuous sailing, or some gleaming and marvellous coastline coming into view. But judging by the popular reaction to Professor Watson's book, I was clearly wrong.

There is, of course, as Popper has so clearly argued, a logical sameness about the way all discoveries are made, whether the way was carefully thought out, or whether the discovery came by chance. All discoveries are 'as a rule refutations of theories which were consciously or unconsciously held: they are made when some of our expectations (based upon these theories) are unexpectedly disappointed.' And, as he goes on to say,

science starts only with problems. Problems crop up especially when we are disappointed in our expectations, or when our theories involve us in difficulties, in contradictions; and these may arise either within a theory, or between two different theories, or as the result of a clash between our theories and our observations. Moreover, it is only through a problem that we become conscious of holding a theory. It is the problem which challenges us to learn; to advance our knowledge; to experiment; and to observe [italics Popper's].

In their efforts to advance knowledge, there will always be controversy between scientists as they choose between different hypotheses. But the second theoretical characteristic in which scientists are cast in the same mould lies in the fact that once a new theory has been shown to be valid for the universe of observation to which it relates, by common consent all less valid ones are discarded. There may be several ways in which to worship God, concepts of right and wrong may vary, but scientists – whether or not they speak the same tongue – all operate on the same sets of hypotheses. The structure of the atom and its nucleus is the same in the United States as it is in the USSR and in the Congo.

An endless number of novels – and no doubt some autobiographies in addition to Professor Watson's – could be written about the way the double helix molecular structure of DNA was determined, or about the way the structure of some other complicated molecule was unravelled. There could be an infinite number of musical compositions to sing the glory of these discoveries. But in each case only one molecular formula has proved valid in the end – and all those that had been proposed before the day objective truth dawned, all those which in their day, however brief, also constituted discoveries, had to be relegated to the oblivion which is the graveyard of scientific hypotheses that have failed to account for the facts they were supposed to describe. It is here that we find a real difference between the fruits of creative genius in the arts and in the sciences. One great piece of music does not drive out another, or a new painting black out an old.

Objective truth, in short, emerges from the testing of hypotheses. Hundreds of scholars have said this in a thousand different ways. Medawar[7] has furnished us with a genealogy of this basic concept of scientific methodology, although he has certainly not provided the whole of its family tree. No hypothesis is worthy of the name if it does no more than describe the facts it is meant to comprehend – it must have the generative quality of impelling a new step into the unknown – to test its validity, to show that it is more than a generalisation of the facts which it describes. Every scientific hypothesis must be a statement which to some extent becomes independent of the facts which, when illuminated by new vision, gave it birth.

But hypotheses, as we know, are designed by human beings; and for the benefit of human beings – whether the benefit be intellectual beguilement or material welfare. Human beings differ, and their attitudes to enquiry and understanding differ. It is this aspect of the approach to objective truth about which I propose to write here – basing myself on a variegated and fairly lengthy experience of being both right and wrong in those fields of science, experimental and observational, in which I have worked. But I propose to begin by first pointing to some differences, as I see them, between different branches of science in attitudes to enquiry and understanding, focussing briefly on the two opposite extremes of the physical and the social sciences, in order to provide a framework for a closer consideration of certain classes of biological enquiry.

The physical sciences are by general consent the exact sciences – if any science at all can be graced by that term. If the hypotheses of the physical sciences did not possess the quality of exactness within the framework to which they relate, no one could ever have designed the steam engine, leave alone a nuclear reactor or a computer. The objective truths which we gain about physical phenomena, however they may be derived, must constitute an understanding which provides absolute assurance for future action – whether the action consists of some application of the particular understanding which has practical utility, or whether the further action is the use of the new understanding as a base for a search for new knowledge and a new stage in understanding. By practical utility I mean, for example, the understanding we have of the behaviour of sound waves which has led to the development of seismic techniques which not only provide a means of understanding the nature of the earth's crust, but also helps us locate pockets of natural gas thousands of feet deep in the bed of the North Sea.

The subjective knowledge and attitudes of the flat-earthers neither aid nor hinder anyone but themselves. The objective knowledge and attitudes of the scientific astronomer and physicist, mobilised by the skills of the engineer, make it possible, for all who are competent to learn, to land measuring instruments on precise spots on the Moon, to photograph its dark side, to transmit back to the earth the information gained by means of telemetric devices, which in turn are based on a knowledge of electro-magnetic radiation and of the physics of the solid state; to make observations about the environment of Venus; and endlessly to extend our knowledge of the universe. The recent discovery of pulsed radio sources in far outer space has opened up an incredibly exciting field of scientific enquiry and of mystery. No one has yet explained the amazing regularity with which the radio signals are emitted, but the experts are tackling the problem in a rigorous scientific way, and as a result, a generally accepted explanation will emerge one day, and with it a greater under-standing than we now have of the vast universe of which our own planet is but a speck.

During the course of this process, which may take a very long time, explanations are bound to be proved wrong, that is to say, less useful than others. But a wrong or less useful explanation cannot persist forever in the world of physical science. We have a very interesting example of this before us now. A minority view about what is called continental drift was tossed aside some fifty years ago; today it is becoming the accepted hypothesis by which we explain the vast land movements that have shaped the surface of our globe.

Attitudes clearly affect the choice between closely-matched hypotheses, and as they change, our understanding equally clearly becomes transformed. But in the physical sciences, in the end, there is room for only one understanding – room for only the best hypothesis that can for the time being be advanced to explain the facts, room for hypotheses not coloured by preconception, personal prejudice, or dogmatic belief.

The social sciences lie at the other end of the spectrum of scientific enquiry. We call them sciences. The economist, the demographer and the sociologist try desperately to achieve an understanding of human behaviour which is not essentially historical, but which contains within itself the quality of prediction. But the interaction of vast numbers of human beings within the societies they form seems at present to result in a kind of irrationality, and the irrational is hardly predictable. What, for example, was the nature of the widespread but hidden social and political trouble which was fired in 1968 by the spark of student unrest in France? Why, if the French authorities were right in believing that the 'ship of state' was then proceeding in the right direction on an even keel, was there any surprise? Why are our economic forecasters so often wrong, or if not wrong, why is it that they fail to get their views over to the politician? Why have the warnings of American sociologists about the gravity of the Negro problem so often fallen on deaf ears?

Gunnar Myrdal,[8] the distinguished Swedish sociologist, has recently discussed the problems of objectivity in social research. He points out that the social scientist almost inevitably starts out from a position of prejudice – prejudice derived from the writings he has studied, from past 'moral philosophies of natural law and utilitarianism from which all social and economic theories have branched'; prejudices derived from the influences of the whole social milieu in which he has grown up; the particular nature of his own individual make-up and inclinations. The belief in 'laissez-faire' of some economists conflicts with the beliefs others hold of an interventionist kind; preconceived ideas about the rights and wrongs of human behaviour clash with the actual facts of behaviour. To make matters worse, no one seems able to assemble all the relevant facts from which to conduct a proper analysis of any form of social behaviour. One can speculate about the way the behaviour of primitive man evolved from what we know of the ape in its natural surroundings. One can equate, for what it is worth – not, in my view, very much – the way man satisfies his basic physiological needs of sex and hunger with the corresponding activities of apes, monkeys, dogs or birds. But when one goes further one does so at one's peril. To cite only one example, social concepts such as property, which have evolved differently in different societies, cannot necessarily be equated with forms of territorial behaviour which one finds in the animal world. The vast complex of interlocking activities of men living in modern industrial agglomerations can hardly be discerned and then described fully, leave alone analysed. Objective analyses of social events become confounded by value judgments, and by differing political objectives. And finally – as Myrdal puts it so forcefully – in sociological analysis, 'we almost never face a random lack of knowledge. Ignorance, like knowledge, is steered for a purpose. There is an emotional load of valuation conflicts pressing for rationalisation, creating blindness at some spots, stimulating an urge for knowledge at others and, in general, causing conceptions of reality to deviate from truth in determined directions.'

In the minds of some popular writers, and indeed some social scientists, all this may be overstating the problem. But nonetheless Myrdal is indicating one of the basic reasons why the social sciences progress with so much greater difficulty than do the physical. If scientific method had proved no more successful in the natural sciences than it has in the social, subjects like physics and genetics could never have made the progress they have. Objective truth obviously exists in the social sciences, but it is far more difficult to find, and its achievement necessitates a clear appreciation and admission of the value judgments (or valuations) of the researcher. Concealing them, in the pretence of objectivity, leads only to confusion and delusion – and to writings which mislead because of their presumed objectivity. I agree fully with Myrdal that before he begins his enquiries, the social scientist must stand up and be recognised for the ideals and goals he stands for, consciously or unconsciously. In this he is in a profoundly different position from the physical scientist.

I am not, of course, saying that 'natural' scientists do not have to make value judgments when deciding which explanation corresponds closer to objective truth, for example in deciding between one or other theory about an elementary particle of matter, or about a particular mechanism of inheritance. But these value judgments do not partake of the quality of the ethical or moral judgments which pervade social problems. When they do, as happened, for example, in the celebrated dispute in the USSR between Lysenko and scientific geneticists, chaos results.

The mass of disciplines which make up the biological and medical sciences stand between the physical and social sciences, and to varying extents partake of the quality of both. They range all the way from the precise physical disciplines to the imprecise social sciences – and even beyond them to a world of non-science. The unravelling of the structure of DNA; the knowledge we have of the transmission of a nervous impulse; or knowledge of the reactions which are involved in the acquisition of immunity, are at the precise end of the spectrum of biological sciences. Somewhere in the middle we have a host of problems where tautologies and mysticism often take the place of true hypothesis in dealing with different issues. One example from my own repertoire – and to which I shall return in amplification – is the nature of the mechanism whereby the brain controls, if that is the right word to use, the functions of the anterior pituitary gland, the dominant hormone-producing ductless gland of the body.

At the other end of the spectrum we have the behavioural sciences as they apply to man – psychology, psychiatry, psychotherapy – where understanding is inevitably coloured by the challenge to help those in need, but where at the moment we are dealing with sciences which in general are still in an early, a 'natural-history', stage of their evolutionary development.

We then move right off the register of objective truth into those fields of presumed biological science, like extrasensory perception or the interpretation of man's fossil history, where to the faithful anything is possible – and where the ardent believer is sometimes able to believe several contradictory things at the same time. This kind of biology belongs more to the arena of subjective truth, where personal attitudes to enquiry and understanding become as dominating as are the facts to which they relate, where fashion and what can now only be called pop-science become a far more potent force than scientific criticism in dictating patterns of conventional knowledge.

In the variety of their interests, the biological are totally different from the physical sciences. Indeed, to make them comparable one would have to include among the latter issues like the flat-earth cosmologies. Why, one needs to ask, is this so?

It is all too easy to point the answer. Even the simplest living systems are more complex – by many orders of magnitude – than are the systems of inanimate events which constitute the subject matter of the physical sciences. Complexity, of course, is not an absolute quality, but a matter of degree. Once solved, any highly complex problem in retrospect becomes no more complex than some simpler problem which yielded immediately to scientific analysis. The point, however, is that quite apart from being characterised by a greater multiplicity of interlocking variables, living, including social systems, do not lend themselves to controlled experimental enquiry as easily as do inanimate systems. The latter are much more stable and repetitive from the point of view of enquiry. When one excludes the simple drives of fear, sex and hunger, certain forms of human social behaviour turn out to be particularly intractable to scientific analysis, even when subjected to the most sophisticated varieties of modern systems-analysis, where the aim is to make precise, and to translate into numbers, the issues on which major decisions need to be taken. These situations do not lend themselves to true scientific analysis because when one course of action is chosen, and others rejected, as a result of a piece of analysis, the situation becomes totally transformed. The implementation of the choice makes it impossible to return to the subject to test the situation afresh – which it is always possible to do in a true science.

The complexity of certain kinds of biological problem also becomes disguised by the fact that certain big questions which belong to the biological arena seem on the surface so straightforward. For example, the ordinary citizen might be expected to suppose that the professional biologist could explain to him the nature of life or living matter. It seems a simple question. Can one, again, deliberately alter the hereditary constitution of the next generation? What was Professor Watson of DNA fame up to, one could almost hear our non-biologist citizen say, if this cannot be done? How does the brain work? Isn't it like a computer? If you know what cancer is, why can't you stop it? These are the kinds of problem which the uninitiated see in biology. But the trouble is that few of them can be formulated as scientifically answerable questions.

Unless they can be, confusion results. The questions are too big, and in any event science cannot tackle all questions at one fell swoop. Some questions, moreover, even assuming that we all agree what they are, are not amenable to answer. This may be because our understanding does not penetrate deeply enough, or because the wrong questions have been put. If the questions are not properly faced, or just answered in a kind of scientific 'gobbledegook', an impression of progress may be given. But the progress is both illusory and dangerous. For when people band together to pretend that something has been explained when in fact it has not, attention is diverted from the initial problem, at the same time as followers rush in to build more verbal imageries on ephemeral foundations. There is a lot of misleading triviality in the literature of modern biological science. The pity is that such literature, by feeding on itself, breeds faster than the true.

As I have said, I am basing these generalisations, which concern the nature of controversy within science, on my own variegated experience as an investigator who has worked mainly in fields of biological enquiry. And I propose to illustrate them in the chapters which follow by reference to three examples from my own experience, and from which, no doubt, some of my own attitudes can be deduced.

3
A Story about Mammalian Egg-Cells

My first example relates to the mammalian oocyte or egg-cell, and I propose telling the story as a piece of personal history, in the form in which I set it out a few years ago in an address which I called 'The Natural History of an Enquiry'.[1] The beginning of my tale takes me to the late twenties, when, because of the somewhat obvious observation that reproductive rhythms play a major part in determining the social reactions within a colony of monkeys, I had embarked upon an analysis of the menstrual cycle of these animals.[2] That was the period when the study of reproductive physiology was still enjoying the greatest impetus it has ever received, largely because of the discovery in 1917 by Stockard and Papanicolaou,[3] in the Department in Anatomy at Cornell University, of the existence of a recurring cycle of changes in the cells which line the vaginal canal (in technical language, the vaginal 'epithelium' or 'mucosa'). This cycle, these two workers were able to show, was correlated with cyclical changes which occur in the ovaries and uterus, so that simply by following the rhythmical changes in the cellular nature of the vaginal mucosa it became possible to infer what was happening in the internal reproductive organs without inspecting them directly after a surgical operation. This technique was an enormous advance on what had been possible before, and it was very quickly exploited, particularly by anatomists in the United States, among them Herbert M. Evans, Edgar Allen, George Corner, Carl Hartman and Philip Smith. In the United Kingdom F.H.A. Marshall of Cambridge led the field. The findings and views of these men were a ready guide-line for younger men who sought to add to the body of knowledge in what seemed a fascinating field of enquiry.

In the period about which I am talking the chemical nature of the ovarian hormones, which are now known to everybody in the form of 'the Pill', had not yet been elucidated, nor did we have more than a glimmering of an idea about the way the anterior part of the pituitary gland, which is attached to the base of the brain, and with which I deal in the next chapter, controls the function of the ovaries and testes. My own work began with a general review of what I could find out, both in the literature and by observation, of the reproductive cycle in monkeys and apes, and with an attempt to devise a theory which related the menstrual cycle of man and monkeys with the sexual (oestrous) cycle of animals like the bitch, rat and cow. The animal which I studied most was the baboon, the cyclical changes in whose ovaries and accessory reproductive organs, including external 'sexual skin', I tried to investigate in detail. I followed the rhythmical changes which occurred in the follicles of the ovary, the minute cyst-like structures in which one finds the egg-cell (see figure 1), but I can see no sign in the first papers I wrote on the subject that I was conscious of the fact that doubt had already been cast on what was then the conventional view of the origin of the germ cells. This was that 'every' female mammal is born with a finite stock of germ cells, which she uses up during the course of her reproductive life – unlike the male of the species, which manufactures sperm all the time. This proposition about the origin of the female egg-cells, a process called 'oogenesis', had been elaborated through microscopic and embryological studies, and was associated with the name of a late nineteenth-century embryologist called Waldeyer.[4] But in fact two of the more prominent of American anatomists and endocrinologists, Herbert M. Evans[5] and Edgar Allen,[6] had already launched a powerful attack on the generalisation. Their view, based on what they took to be incontrovertible evidence derived from microscopic ('histological') studies of sections of the ovary, was that oogenesis was a continuous process, and that during each oestrous or menstrual cycle a wave of destruction which eliminated the bulk of the germ cell population of the ovary – a process called 'atresia' – was followed by a wave of regeneration in which thousands more oocytes were formed.

In the early thirties, not long after I had published a paper[7] in which it was said that no evidence could be found that new ova are formed in the adult baboon ovary, I started to study the effects of oestrogen, progestogen and androgen on the ovaries of mature

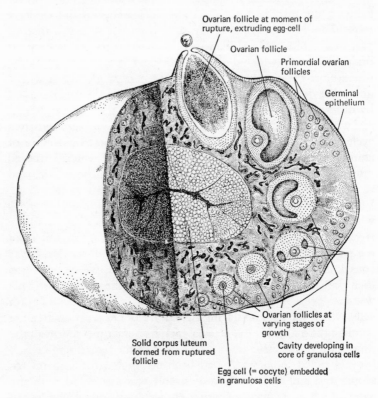

Figure 1. Schematic diagram of an ovary

monkeys. Oestrogen and progestogen were the first two hormones which had been extracted from ovarian tissue, androgen being the hormone which is produced in the testes, and without which, as the next chapter describes, a young male does not develop the secondary sexual characters and behaviour of the adult animal. These experiments showed that all three hormones 'suppressed' the ovaries and inhibited ovulation, although not always in the same way. In 1937 I reported that androgen, like oestrogen and progestogen, inhibited menstruation and ovulation, and suggested that it provided 'a means for securing and controlling temporary sterility'.[8] But in addition I noted that, whereas the treatment suppressed the large follicles in the ovaries, that is to say those which were growing to the point at which one (or more) would, at the predetermined cyclical moment, burst and release the egg-cell it contained, thus making it potentially liable to be fertilised by a spermatozoon, the smaller 'primordial' follicles were not only as numerous as they are normally, but also showed signs of having been stimulated to multiply. From this, I drew the conclusion that while it suppressed ovulation, the injected male hormone had stimulated oogenesis. This conclusion turned out to be wrong, but it also proved to be the starting point of a mass of further work.

Other researches, and then the war, intervened before I could carry this particular story much further. By then I had unconsciously abandoned the Waldeyer view of oogenesis and had, as it were, implicitly accepted the new doctrine of Herbert Evans and Edgar Allen, that oogenesis, like spermatogenesis, was a continuing process which went on throughout adult reproductive life.

My first piece of post-war work on this subject[9] comprised a detailed study of the relationship of the growth of the ovum to that of the ovarian follicle in monkeys which had been treated with either oestrogen or androgen. This was combined with an analysis of the changes which the treatment induces in the proportions of follicles in different stages of development, from which the conclusion was drawn that the diminution in ovarian size which occurs in monkeys after the injection of oestrogen or androgen is not associated with any apparent disturbance in the character of the early growth of the oocytes and follicles. The only 'suggestive' difference which was found was what seemed to be a greater size of the primordial egg-cells in the androgen-treated animals at the beginning of the process of follicular development.

Using what I then incorrectly regarded as a fairly reliable method of estimation, I also thought that the number of healthy young follicles per unit of tissue increased in androgen-treated animals, as opposed to decreasing after oestrogen. While it was clear that there was insufficient evidence to justify a firm conclusion, I nonetheless again came to the view that androgen, unlike oestrogen, had a direct and stimulating effect on the primordial oogonial tissue. At the back of my mind was the thought that this finding implied that one ought to be able to promote oogenesis in a failing ovary, for example the ovaries of a menopausal woman. This notion was more than enough bait to stimulate further enquiry.

In parallel with this work I tried to see what the reaction of the body is to multiple ovarian grafts.[10] From previous work we knew that the increase in size, or hypertrophy, that occurs in the remaining ovary after its partner is removed from the body is not due to any increase in the number of egg-cells, but to enhanced follicular growth, and to the transformation of the large follicles into what are called corpora lutea, the ovarian tissue from which the hormone progestogen can be extracted. This process is called compensatory hypertrophy, and the fact that it occurred had stimulated Lipschutz[11] to postulate in 1925 that the uniformity of the process of follicular development in successive oestrous cycles (i.e. the constancy in the number of follicles which matured) depends, not upon the total number of primordial follicles present in the body, but upon the action of some extra-ovarian factor (which we now know to be the so-called gonadotrophic hormone of the anterior pituitary) which is constant in the magnitude of its effects. What I wanted to do was test this 'law of follicular constancy' in reverse, by seeing whether the number of follicles which matured in an ovary declined if the animal was furnished with more than one pair of ovaries. I then believed that the ovary is a tissue which 'takes' readily in experimentally castrated animals, whether merely replaced as an 'autograft' (that is to say moved from its normal to another position in the body to which it belongs), or provided from another animal as a 'homograft'. We consequently implanted either a pair or three pairs of additional ovaries in two groups of experimental albino rats. The results were surprising. Counts showed that the total number of follicles in all the ovarian tissue in the treated animals, including their own ovaries, was on average significantly less than in a control group. This suggested – again incorrectly as it turned out – that an organ-specific immunological response had been provoked. By 'organ-specific' I mean that the host animal had not only developed a reaction against the foreign tissue introduced into its body, but also some immunological substance which was hostile not only to the ovaries that were implanted but also to its own ovaries. Another of our findings was that oocytes were present in the grafted ovarian tissue in spite of the total disappearance of the original single layer of cells, called germinal epithelium, which covers a normal ovary.

The latter observation reminded me that many years before,

in 1933, I had transplanted the ovaries of two rhesus monkeys from their usual position in the pelvis to a totally unrelated anatomical position in order to discover whether an ovary deprived of its nerve supply could function normally. I remembered that the histological sections had shown that a few oocytes were present in the grafts a year or so after the transplantations were made, even though they seemed devoid of a germinal epithelium. I therefore decided to restudy the sections from these old experiments, and confirmed that the germinal epithelium had in fact disappeared from the grafts, although these contained a small number of healthy-looking oocytes.[12] The conclusion I drew was that oogenesis 'as manifested by the presence of young follicles had not stopped', but that the germinal epithelium might not be essential to the process.

In those days I took the germinal epithelium to mean what it said, and what most people believed – that it was a particular kind of tissue which could germinate new oocytes. In one of the earlier papers attacking the Waldeyer thesis of oogenesis, that a female mammal is born with a stock of egg-cells which she uses up in the course of her reproductive life, Edgar Allen had ostensibly shown that cells of this covering epithelium could become directly transformed into oocytes in the adult animal. Later Everett[13] had reported that in certain conditions the ovaries of mice continued to produce oocytes when transplanted onto the kidneys. This he claimed to occur when the germinal epithelium persisted, i.e. when the ovary was transplanted in its capsule. If the germinal epithelium disappeared through fusion of the ovarian surface with the kidney, i.e. when the ovary was transplanted without its own capsule, oogenesis ceased. The question of neoformation of oocytes in the mature animal thus became thoroughly mixed up in my mind with the problem of the nature of the germinal epithelium.

There was nothing for it but to go on. By this time I was thoroughly confused in my beliefs about the neoformation of oocytes in the ovary – whether Waldeyer was right in holding that the female mammal is born with a finite stock of oocytes, or whether the American anatomists were justified in their advocacy of the reverse view that the germinal epithelium continues to produce germ cells throughout reproductive life. But what I could see slipping away from me fast was the notion that I was going to discover how to regenerate an ageing ovary.

The first thing to do was to recheck Allen's[6] generalisation, which had been echoed by several workers, that both the rate at which the germinal epithelium produces new oocytes, and the rate of destruction of oocytes (the process called atresia), vary according to the phases of the sexual cycle. It was necessary to do this because I was unable to find any paper in which the conclusion appeared to have been derived from a count of all the oocytes in the ovaries. What was clearly wanted was an estimate of the total numbers of oocytes at different times of the oestrous cycle, properly classified into stages of growth. There are nearly always thousands, and at least hundreds, of primordial oocytes in the ovary of an animal during the course of its reproductive life, and only relatively few which have already grown into large follicles. During the process of growth the granulosa cells, the single layer of cells which sheaths the egg-cell or oocyte, multiply until the latter becomes the core of a solid sphere of cells. A cavity then appears in the granulosa, and the whole structure becomes transformed into a cellular cyst called a follicle, to the wall of which the oocyte remains attached (figure 1). Conclusions about the neoformation of oocytes could hardly be drawn from variations in the numbers of large follicles only. It also seemed wise to use only litter-mates in the experiments; we had a suspicion that numerical differences in the numbers of oocytes in rats at the same stage of the oestrous cycle might be due to differences in the genetic strain of the creatures we were studying.

The results[14] were absolutely clearcut. Neither the total number nor the number of healthy oocytes varies significantly with the phases of the oestrous cycle. Whatever variations we found were completely overshadowed by differences in the age and litter-relationship of the animals used in the experiments. Phase differences of a significant kind occurred only in the numbers of those oocytes which were surrounded with two or more layers of granulosa cells. It seemed clear that the American workers had had their attention caught by the latter fact, and that they had drawn from it a far wider conclusion about the continuous formation of egg-cells than could ever be justified.

This new scent had to be followed further. An estimate was wanted of the number of primordial oocytes – that is to say oocytes either with an incomplete cellular cover or with a cover consisting of no more than a single layer of cells – in the total population of oocytes. It turned out that both in monkeys and rats primordial oocytes made up at least ninety per cent, and up to ninety-seven per cent, of the total number of oocytes present in the ovary. Observations about fluctuations in the size of the remaining three to ten per cent of oocytes, on which it was clear that Evans and Allen had focussed their attention, however interesting they were, clearly had no bearing whatever on the question whether oogenesis occurred in the post-puberal animal.

In a carefully controlled experiment,[15] we then eliminated the germinal epithelium of one ovary of a group of rats, and noted that normal and degenerating follicles in all stages of development, and in numbers not significantly different from those in the control ovary, were present up to 469 days after the ovarian surface had been painted with ten per cent tannic acid in order to destroy the covering germinal epithelium. Four hundred and sixty-nine days is a large slice in the life of a rat. This finding seemed to rule out the mature germinal epithelium as an oogenetic tissue, and the result seemed consistent with an earlier and complementary observation that the epithelium persists, apparently unchanged, in ovaries which had been X-irradiated in order to destroy all the germ cells.

The obvious next step[16] was to estimate the numbers of normal and atretic oocytes in rats from which one ovary had been removed. As already observed, the remaining ovary then increases in weight, in fact may double in weight. If new oocytes can be formed in an adult ovary, one would expect the increased weight to be associated with an increase in the number of oocytes. This experiment confirmed an observation reported in 1920 by a Japanese worker named Arai[17, 18], that while the remaining ovary does practically double in weight, and produce as many mature follicles as are found in the two ovaries of litter-mate controls, the number of primordial oocytes remains at the level normal for one ovary. So far as I know, Arai was the only worker before us who had made estimates of the total number of oocytes in the ovaries of any creature; and so far as I know, too, the two papers which appeared in 1920 were the only ones he ever published. Later, in further work[19] in my laboratory, the complementary observation was made that the reproductive life-span of mice is effectively curtailed after removal of one ovary, and that the total number of young they produce is halved.

We then made careful estimates of the numbers of oocytes in rats of different age but of the same inbred strain, and showed, again confirming Arai's less precise earlier observations, that the total number of oocytes decreases with age.[20] The rate of decrease can be generalised in a simple equation which relates the number of oocytes to the age of the rat in days. This finding clearly indicated that either a finite store of oocytes is gradually used up during reproductive life, or that the rate of oogenesis progressively diminishes with age. In the light of all our other findings I felt that the first alternative was the more likely interpretation.

Somewhat later, several pure strains mice of were established in my laboratory. It was a logical step then for my colleague, P.L.Krohn[21, 22], to proceed to an analysis of the ageing process of the ovaries, using the loss of oocytes and of reproductive capacity as criteria; and as a main technique the transplantation of the ovaries of a mouse of one age into an immunologically compatible mouse of a different age. In the course of this work, it was found that the three pure and one hybrid strain of mice which were studied differed significantly in the stage of their ovarian development at birth, in the total numbers of oocytes in their ovaries, and in the rates at which the oocyte population declined in numbers. The strain which lost its oocytes most rapidly was the only one whose ovaries became totally depleted of oocytes long before death – as occurs in women at the time of the menopause.[23] Even though these findings came later, they provided highly important corroboration of the view that neoformation of oocytes does not occur in adult animals.

In parallel with the work which revealed the decline in oocyte numbers with age, I embarked on yet another carefully controlled study in which we[24] divided our experimental rats into four groups. In the first we removed the right ovary and cut away more than half of the left; in the second, we did the same, but painted the bit of left ovary remaining in the body with tannic acid so as to destroy the germinal epithelium; in the third we removed the right ovary without touching the left; in the fourth we removed the right ovary and painted the whole of the left one with tannic acid. The animals were killed 50 to 136 days after operation, and estimates were then made of the total number of oocytes that were present at death, in relation to the numbers in the ovarian tissue removed at operation, corrected for age according to the mathematical relationship our earlier piece of work[20] had revealed. The results confirmed our previous finding that the elimination of the germinal epithelium had a negligible influence on the numbers of oocytes either in the whole ovary or a fragment of the ovary. They also showed that hypertrophy in an ovarian fragment is not associated with an increase in the number of oocytes it contains, any more than such an increase occurs in a single ovary undergoing compensatory hypertrophy.

About this time I decided to repeat the experiment on grafted ovaries which I had done a few years before, since our greater experience had by now impressed on me the imperative need in experiments of the kind on which we were engaged to take litter-relationships and age into account before making any comparisons between the numbers of oocytes in treated animals and in their normal controls. We also thought that in this particular case we ought to study the immunological influence of tissues other than the ovaries. But we failed[25] to confirm our earlier findings, at the same time as we obtained a hint that the ovaries, like the adrenal glands, might increase in weight in certain types of stressful situations. For a time this stimulated another line of enquiry[26] unconnected with the problem of the formation of oocytes, and about which I shall say no more here.

By now I was confident that I had enough data to reinstate Waldeyer's hypothesis, and *ipso facto* to fault the then prevailing belief that oogenesis continued unabated throughout the reproductive life of an animal. In addition to the evidence which our own experiments had provided, I had by this time examined critically all the studies that had been used to support the belief that oogenesis went on after puberty, and felt sure that I could show what their shortcomings were. Some reports, for example that compensatory hypertrophy could occur in an X-ray sterilised ovary or that gonadotrophin could stimulate oogenesis in X-ray sterilised mice, I left for later experimental checking.

In 1951[27] I was invited to expound my heretical views before an international body which included most of the then leading workers in the field of reproduction. Dr Carl Hartman, a prominent American scholar, was in the chair, and I was given an hour to say my piece. Before I began he told me that he had some slides of preparations of recent experiments which demonstrated the stimulation of oogenesis by means of hormones in mature rhesus monkeys, and which either he might show after I had finished, or which I could throw on the screen in order to reinforce the point he thought I was going to make. I had to tell him that the burden of my story was that new egg-cells are not formed after puberty, and that it was for him to show his slides after I had finished if he felt he could refute the conclusion to which my new work led. In the event the slides were not shown. Instead Dr Hartman began the customary laudatory remarks a chairman makes when a speaker sits down by saying that he had listened with attention to my tale and stood there both 'convinced and convicted' – a generous reference to the fact that like myself he, too, had uncritically fallen under the sway of the newer hypothesis about oogenesis. He ended his remarks with the statement that the story I had outlined had convinced him that 'Waldeyer must have been right after all'.

This was handsome support. But it neither meant that those members of my audience who had not worked on the subject had understood, nor that the incorrect story which was now appearing in the newer text-books was going to be altered overnight. Much more work needed to be done.

Among the many points that needed to be checked was an observation in the literature to the effect that the total number of oocytes in the rat increases after removal of the pituitary gland (the operation called hypophysectomy). This observation had led to the conclusion[28] that the pituitary in some way acts as a brake on the process of oogenesis. I put a research student on to the problem, and in a carefully executed experiment he found that oocyte numbers decreased with age in hypophysectomised just as they did in normal animals, but that there was a possible slowing down of the rate of loss of oocytes.[29] Some years later this experiment was repeated[30] in my department on three pure-bred and one hybrid strain of mice. It provided much more precise observations which were fully in accordance with our earlier findings.

From the very moment that I became convinced that Waldeyer had been right after all, and that a female mammal is born with a finite stock of oocytes, and conversely that oogenesis is not a continuous process, I had started to wonder whether the decline in fertility which occurs in mammals as they age is due to a decline in the population of oocytes. In a first experiment[31] to test this possibility, using rats which had been partially sterilised by in a number of fruitful directions which did not bear directly on the main line of my enquiry into oogenesis. This, as I have graded doses of X-rays, it was found that litter size declined in parallel with the reduction in the oocyte population. I then decided to enquire into the same question by examining the relation of age to litter size, and to the proportion of females in a population which are able to breed. It was found[32] that both measures of fertility declined in the three strains of experimental rat we used. This we put down to four interrelated factors, which we found difficult to separate from one another – a decline in the total number of oocytes; a decline in the number which mature and ovulate as the overall population of oocytes falls; a decline in the fertilisable capacity of older oocytes; and a deterioration of the uterine environment with age. At first I was inclined to emphasise the first of these factors – the decline in the numbers of mature oocytes – but later my colleagues Jones and Krohn[33] carried out a number of experiments which suggested strongly that the decline in fertility towards the end of reproductive life is due either to some failing in the hormonal capacity of the ovary, or to a deterioration in the uterine environment, rather than to the loss of oocytes *per se*. This conclusion has been confirmed in some more recent studies in which fertilised ova derived from mice of different ages have been transplanted into the uterine horns of host animals of different age.[34]

About the same time as we started to worry about the question of the relationship of fertility to the numbers of oocytes in the ovary, we embarked upon a quantitative microscopic study of the germ cells in the foetal ovary. Had this work been performed in 1947, part of our early labours might have proved unnecessary. This work[35-39] provided ample evidence that in the rat, guinea pig, monkey, chick and man, the maximum number of germ cells occurs before birth, and that up to sixty per cent of the peak stock degenerates by the time the infant is born (or hatched). The human female is born with a stock of about two million oocytes, of which about half are degenerating. The peak oocyte population in the human ovary, seven million, occurs at the fifth month of gestation. A somewhat ambiguous compliment was paid me by my colleagues when they christened the pre-natal degenerating germ cells 'Z' cells.

From this point on, the search for new facts started ramifying indicated, began with what seemed a very simple idea. It was more than an idea. It was also, as I have indicated, a bit of wishful thinking that with suitable treatment it might be possible to reactivate a failing ovary. My hypothesis, that androgens stimulated oogenesis in post-pubertal monkeys, was wrong. But the process of disproof entailed a crucial re-examination of our basic concepts about oogenesis; and by following one trail after another, by increasingly precise techniques and better controls, it turned out that the prior hypothesis on which my original case rested was itself wrong. I had come full circle, back to the nineteenth century view that oogenesis is a process which – if one sets aside a few exceptional species[40] – is completed soon after birth, so that the female mammal is in fact born with a finite stock of egg cells. By this statement I mean no more than that none of our experimental or observational findings is inconsistent with the hypothesis first stated by Waldeyer.

The real moral of this story is that given the right kind of scientific environment, entrenched views can be swiftly abandoned. I now think that the basic reason why I succeeded on this occasion was the fact that the main protagonists of the theory against which I had accidentally become pitted were few in number, and men of authority who were sufficiently open-minded to reconsider the premises on which they had built their case. No doubt another was that I stood every bit as 'convicted' as was my chairman at the 1951 meeting because of my equally long adherence to the false doctrine of continuous oogenesis. Certainly a third was that it was easily possible to devise experiments to help choose between what proved to be the wrong view and the alternative proposition of a finite stock of oocytes at birth.

My second illustration of the influence of personal attitudes on our conceptions of what constitutes objective truth is a much longer one, and both for this reason and because the story still lacks an end, I propose spelling it out in an historical context and at greater length. It concerns the way the pituitary gland, which is the principal hormone-producing gland of the body, is presumably controlled by the brain.

4

Hormones and Humours

There is a rare and serious disease, called Addison's disease, in which the skin becomes darker and darker in colour – in the classical description, bronzed 'like that of a mulatto' – at the same time as the victim if untreated, wastes away in general weakness. This condition was first recognised and described in the middle of the nineteenth century by Thomas Addison, a physician of Guy's Hospital in London, and its discovery was in effect a major act of creation, as considerable in its time as Crick and Watson's recent elucidation of the double helix molecule which carries the genetic code of inheritance. Addison's genius, which lay in an acute, accurate, and persistent power of observation, reached its fulfilment in the realisation that the symptoms and signs of the illness which bears his name are associated with disease of the adrenal (= suprarenal) glands. These are a pair of ductless glands that lie on the upper poles of the kidneys high in the abdominal cavity. Most big discoveries in biological and medical science begin at the descriptive level, at the level of accurate observation, of discerning classification, and of useful correlation. It was in itself an achievement to generalise as a single syndrome the various signs and symptoms manifested by eleven different patients. It required even more insight to suggest that the disease could be causally related to destruction of the adrenal glands. From the point of view of modern science, however, the essential act of genius lay in the realisation that if this were so, something of the kind we now designate as a hormonal or endocrine mechanism was at play. For there must have been some such idea in Addison's mind, even if his brief writings on the subject are anything but explicit on this point.

When he first reported his observations in 1849, and in 1855 when he published his now classical monograph,[1] there was no clearly stated concept of hormonal action. That emerged slowly during the latter half of the nineteenth century, as a result of the experimental studies and clinical observations of a number of distinguished experimentalists and clinicians. And it did not take the specific shape which it has today until 1904, when Bayliss and Starling[2] elaborated the idea that the different tissues and functions of the body are coordinated by chemical messengers 'speeding from cell to cell along the blood stream'. 'These chemical messengers or "hormones"', as Starling[3] called them, 'have to be carried from the organ where they are produced to the organ which they affect by means of the blood stream and the continually recurring physiological needs of the organism must determine their repeated production and circulation through the body.'

Yet though this conception did not crystallise until the turn of the century, the epoch in which Addison was pondering the significance of his observations was far from devoid of ideas of some such mechanism. It may well be that he was unfamiliar with any of the seventeenth and eighteenth century writings which seemed to suggest – however vaguely – that there were such things as hormones. It may also be – in fact, it is almost certain – that he was unaware that in the very year in which he first reported his observations and his suspicion that the adrenal glands 'may be either directly or indirectly concerned in sanguification' and with 'the proper elaboration of the body generally, or of the red particles more especially', a young experimentalist of Göttingen, A.A. Berthold,[4] had published a short paper in which he had not only reported that the transplantation of the testes of the cock to another part of the body prevented the normal changes of castration, but also correctly concluded that male secondary sexual physical characters and behaviour, which externally differentiate the male from the female, depend on some substance secreted by the testes into the blood. But even if he knew none of this, Addison must have known that his colleague T. Wilkinson King[5] believed that another gland, the thyroid gland, which lies in the neck, stored some material which, passing into the general circulation, exercised 'important subsequent functions in the course of the circulation'. He also must have known that another colleague, Astley Cooper,[6] had studied the effects of the experimental removal of the thyroid, and had enquired into the chemical nature of thyroid fluid. He could hardly have been surprised, therefore, that in 1856, a year after the appearance of his own monograph, the French physiologist, Brown-Séquard[7] showed that pigs, dogs, cats, rabbits, and mice died very rapidly when their adrenal glands were removed, and from this drew the conclusion that the adrenals elaborated some principle which was essential for life. He could not have been surprised, for the simple reason that although his discoveries were made before the dawn of the hormonal theory, as we know it today, they belonged to a period which had certainly not freed itself from the influences of a much older theory of internal secretions. Wilkinson King thought in terms of such an hypothesis, as Brown-Séquard was still doing when, at the turn of the century, he sought to generalise his views on hormonal action, and in doing so merely restated the hypothesis which de Bordeu,[8] a French anatomist and clinician, had put forward in 1775.

Another whose mind flowed in similar channels was Jonathan Hutchinson,[9] surgeon of the London Hospital, who was among the few who set out to confirm and corroborate Addison's clinical analysis of adrenal insufficiency. In his little book on constitutional medicine Hutchinson[10] clearly reveals that many of the conventional physiological conceptions of the nineteenth century took their origin from the old theory of the humours. Clearly these were still in the air when Addison pondered over the strange symptoms and signs of the patients whose adrenal glands had been destroyed by disease.

To say this in no way disparages Addison's share in the development of modern endocrinological concepts. Nor does it mean that there is no real distinction between the old and the new humoral theories. The old theory was formulated in a way which did not call for experimental verification. The new is a predictive or causal type of modern scientific hypothesis. The general proposition that it states demands test; and at the same time it reveals an endless vista of research which cannot but be fruitful both from the point of view of the content of pure knowledge and from that of the aims of clinical practice. Yet there are parallels between the two kinds of theory. They reveal themselves clearly when we compare the difficulties into which seventeenth and eighteenth century physicians got themselves when they tried to explain how the presumed secretions of the brain pass to the pituitary gland, which is suspended from its base, with those which now beset us in our understanding of the functional relations of the latter organ to that minute part of the base of the brain called the hypothalamus, and which modern studies have shown to be of critical importance in the control of a wide variety of the so-called visceral functions of the body.

The old theory of the humours[11-14] derives from the Aristotelian concept that every material thing is made up of different proportions of the four common elements – earth, water, air and fire – of which any one or two are dominant in every object. Each of these four fundamental essences or existences represented the union of two of four primary and opposite qualities (hot, cold, wet, and dry), and corresponding to them were the four fundamental humours – blood, phlegm (or pituita), yellow bile, and black bile (melancholia). When the four humours were in proper balance, the body was healthy. When one humour was unduly strong, illness resulted. The difference in the temperament and constitution of individuals was due to slight alterations in the balance of the humours or to a surplus of any one of them. An excess of black bile, insufficient to lead to manifest disease, produced the melancholic temperament; a non-pathological excess of phlegm or pituita produced the| phlegmatic person; of blood, the sanguine temperament; and of yellow bile, the choleric temperament.

There was also the idea that while the four humours pervaded the body, and determined its state of health and the temperament or 'complexion' (literally 'weaving together') of the individual, each had its principal organ. Yellow bile or choler came from the gall-bladder, and black bile or melancholy from the spleen. Blood arose from the liver, and the brain was responsible for the phlegm or pituita, which escaped into the pituitary body, and thence into the nose. Over and above all this, the Ancients realised that some tissues (e.g. the testes) endowed the body with particular humours or particular qualities.

One of the more useful discussions regarding the cerebral humour is provided by Swedenborg, that extraordinary philosopher-scientist of the eighteenth century, in a posthumous monograph published for the first time in 1882,[15] 140 years after it was written. 'For the purpose of preparing the blood,' Swedenborg wrote, 'the soul has established in the cerebrum an illustrious chemical laboratory, which it has arranged into members and organs, and by the ministry of which it distils and elaborates a lymph animated by the animal spirit, whereby it imbues the blood with its own inmost essence, nature, and life.' He believed that two spirits were produced: one which was elaborated in the 'glandules of the grey substance' and which was contained within the individual nerve-fibres of the cells that make up the mass of the brain (i.e. the 'cerebral cortex'); and the second, a nervous juice which exuded from the capillaries and circulated between the nerve-fibres of the brain.

Like others before him, Swedenborg was exercised about the way in which the essential spirit so formed, or pituita, left the brain. The cerebrum, which is divided into two symmetrical cerebral hemispheres, is the main part of the brain. Deep in each hemisphere is a cavity or 'lateral ventricle' which communicates with a single and smaller cavity, called the 'third ventricle', that lies in the midline near the base of the brain. The 'lowest' part of the third ventricle is called the 'infundibulum', and the part of the brain with which it is connected is the 'hypothalamus'. The latter consists of a mass of nerve cells and their fibrillar extensions, the cells being clumped into discrete groups or 'nuclei', with presumedly different functions. None of this detailed knowledge of

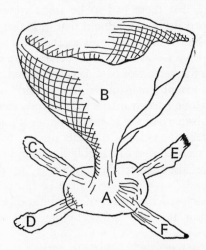

Figure 2. Vesalius's conception of the funnel (infundibulum) (B) through which the phlegm from the brain trickled into the pituitary gland (A). The four imaginary ducts C, D, E, F, carried the phlegm from the gland.

the cellular structure of the brain was known until this century, but Thomas Willis[16] had argued in 1664 that 'the position and structure' of the infundibulum indicate that

> some humour out of the ventricles of the cerebrum is carried into the pituitary gland. For that part is so constituted, that a discharge of humours is effected into its aperture from every angle and recess of the interior cerebrum, and its appendage; and while in the various animals the shape and the situation of the ventricles differ, nevertheless in every one of them all the ventricles, of whatever kind they be, have apertures opening in the direction of the infundibulum. (Figure 2.)

Willis felt that

> there was no room for doubting, that serous liquids descend by this way from the cerebrum into the pituitary gland. . . . If any one takes but a cursory view of the parts which are situated around the ventricles, and if he examines their structure but lightly, he will easily agree with the Ancients, that the excrements of the cerebrum are discharged partly through the infundibulum into the palate underneath, or that in an anterior direction they are cast out through the olfactory bulbs into the nares. *

Tied to the idea that there had to be some connection of this kind, Swedenborg also had no doubt that it, in fact, existed. 'The infundibulum,' he wrote, 'is not only a *vas deferens* or an excretory duct, but it is also a *vas secernens* or a secretory vessel; for those things which in the ventricles have become mixed up, thickened, and in a certain extent amalgamated, the infundibulum separates and filters; . . . [one part] it instils by a fibrous channel immediately into the substance of the gland; the latter it relegates around the gland, between the sides of the sella turcica.' †

Swedenborg realised that the 'highly liquid and refined alcohol of animal nature' about which he spoke was 'utterly beyond the ken of the senses', but at the same time he felt certain that not only did the 'enclosed moisture' of the infundibulum get into the pituitary, but that the infundibulum also transmitted to

---

* nares = nasal cavities.

Willis's own text has been consulted, but the translation is that of Tafel, Swedenborg's editor. Richard Lower (1631-90), Willis's pupil, rejected this teaching, and believed that 'whatever fluid is secreted into the ventricles of the brain and goes from there through the infundibulum does not drip down into the palate but is fed back again into the blood and mixed with it'.[17]

† Sella turcica is the name given to the bony recess in the floor of the skull into which the pituitary gland fits.

the pituitary gland 'a genuine and fresh spirit' of its own.

The invisible opening from the infundibulum into the pituitary, about which Swedenborg had no doubts, disturbed others, and one or two tried to find out experimentally whether, in fact, it existed – as theory demanded that it should. So it was that Vieussens[18] injected a coloured alcohol into the third ventricle. He found that the fluid passed through the infundibulum and stained the upper and lateral parts of the pituitary gland, but that it did not dye its interior. Dismayed though he no doubt was by the lack of a canal or 'sensible perforation' in the lower part of the infundibulum, he nevertheless had to conclude that the latter was probably 'furnished with loose pores and to consist of a substance which is highly fitted for the reception of a certain aqueous humour, and for excreting the same again'.

A few students appear to have followed a different path in their researches into this question. One was Lieutaud, professor of medicine in the University at Aix, and a foreign member of the Royal Society of London.* His observations about the pituita are no more than a historical curiosity; but those he made about what we now know as the hypothalamo-hypophysial connection, or connection between the pituitary gland (= hypophysis) and the base of the brain, are extremely interesting. For it so happens that in the course of his studies he stumbled on what is called today the pituitary-portal system of vessels.

The record of this discovery is in a volume which was published in 1742 under the title *Essais Anatomiques*,[19] essentially a general textbook of anatomy. Its fifth section deals with the central and peripheral nervous system, and in his description of the third ventricle of the brain Lieutaud drew attention to a deep fossa anteriorly whose aperture gradually narrows as it approaches the beginning of the stalk of nerve tissue which connects the pituitary gland to the brain. According to Lieutaud, the stalk, contrary to usual belief, is not canalised, but instead is a kind of cylinder 'two to three lines' thick, formed of a grey substance, and covered by pia mater, the very fine inner membrane which covers the surface of the brain. On the other hand, running along the stalk are very small longitudinal blood vessels which communicate with those of the pituitary gland below.

* He was elected in 1739, the same year as his more renowned fellow-countryman, Buffon.

Hardly ten years had passed before this observation, as well as Lieutaud's general views about the functions and secretions of the brain, were attacked by Theophile de Bordeu, the physician to whom we owe the first fairly clear conception of humoral action.* For Lieutaud the problem of the brain was simple. In designing it Nature had three purposes, and three only: (1) to provide, as it were, a scaffolding for the blood-vessels of the brain; (2) to provide a structure in which the life spirit could be separated out; and (3) to provide an adequate reservoir for this spirit. Would not, he asks, a porous, palpable, or simply spongy mass of moderate density satisfy these requirements? Why, he asks, search further in order to understand the nature of the brain, a secretory organ whose main function is to separate the extremely fine molecules of the ethereal liquid which is the animal spirit? And as for the cerebral nerves, are they not the channels by which this spirit courses from the brain to all parts of the body?

De Bordeu delivered his criticism in 1751.[20] His main theme was that the glands of the body release their emanations as a result of some intrinsic action, in certain circumstances augmented by local irritation or shaking of the body, and not as a result of compression by neighbouring muscles or organs. He devoted a large part of his discussion to the widely held belief that the brain is a glandular organ, and that some vital spirit is directed along the nerves. In the course of his statement, in which he indicates quite clearly that he was no supporter of these views, de Bordeu points out that the three functions which Lieutaud attributed to the brain as a glandular organ could just as well have been applied to almost any organ or tissue of the body. The vital spirit, he remarks, is always shaped by the particular fantasy of the person writing about it; and the arguments of those who are convinced that the brain distils such spirits, or that the nerves, and particularly the olfactory nerves, are a channel for the passage of some cerebral

* The concept is outlined in the sixth part, entitled 'Analyse Medicinale du Sang' of his volume *Recherches sur des Maladies chroniques*, first published in 1775.[8] De Bordeu held that the different organs were related to each other through the spongy cellular tissues of the body, and that in this way the 'humours' of one organ were able to influence the functions of another. De Bordeu particularly emphasised the effect of testicular and ovarian secretions; and the fact that the gonads in some way control the development of secondary sexual characters and behaviour. While one should not deny de Bordeu the distinction of having provided an indication of hormonal action, it would be an exaggeration to say that his writings reveal the precise formulation of hormonal action as understood today.

distillation, are no more probable than the opinions of those who deny them.

De Bordeu was equally unimpressed with Lieutaud's view that the solidity of the pituitary stalk can be easily demonstrated by cutting it in successive sections. The stalk, he found, is too delicate, and is only crushed and torn by such treatment. He admits, however, the existence of axial blood vessels along the stalk, and in doing so leaves the impression that in describing them Lieutaud had implied that they were a channel for the humours of the brain to the pituitary. De Bordeu also states that Riolan[21] had long before noted the same vessels, and that he too, had regarded them as a pathway for the pituita. * Finally, he was unconvinced by Lieutaud's assumption that the axial-stalk vessels communicate with those of the pituitary gland. The ventricular injections which he made to determine the nature of the connection between the base of the brain and the pituitary being indecisive, he ended by emphasising the urgent need for new researches to find out whether the infundibulum was indeed the excretory canal of the brain.

As we now know, Lieutaud and de Bordeu were both right and wrong. De Bordeu was wrong and Lieutaud right in suggesting that the axial-stalk vessels communicate with those of the pituitary below; while de Bordeu was well justified in attacking Lieutaud's conception of the structure and function of the brain, and in doubting that a vital fluid flows from the base of the brain to the pituitary.

The point is that while he was one of the architects of the modern theory of hormones, de Bordeu was a never-tiring opponent of the old humoralism. † His controversy with Lieutaud was inspired less by any fundamental disagreement with the latter's anatomy (which, for its period, was far from bad) than by opposition to his attempt to interpret anatomical observations in terms of an outworn dogma. Those who believed in the old humours had to find a route by which the pituita escaped from the brain – whether through the stalk which connected the infundibulum and the pituitary, or by way of vessels along the stalk.

---

* Jean Riolan the younger (1577–1657). The passage in question occurs in Riolan's *Enchiridium Anatomicum et Pathologicum*, first published in Paris in 1648, and translated into English in 1657. The reference is, however, hardly precise; all that Riolan says is that there are four minute channels on the infundibulum through which some 'serum' is distilled on to the palate and fauces (= back of the nose).

† See Cumston.[22]

Those who did not were suspicious of the whole idea that something passed from the brain to the pituitary. The eclipse of the old humoral theory – the end to which de Bordeu had turned so many of his energies – was finally due to the increasing use of experiment in medicine during the seventeenth century (following Harvey's great discovery of the circulation), and to the emergence of the cellular theory of bodily processes and disease in the nineteenth century. Morgagni, whose labours all but filled the eighteenth century, showed that diseases could be classified according to the parts of the body in which their symptoms occurred, and that it was reasonable to explain them by reference to the associated anatomical changes. His underlying theme was that disease is due to pathological change in specific organs, and not to an imbalance of humours which affect the whole body. From organs it was a relatively short step to the cells and tissues by which they are constituted. In the end it was the cellular theory, the triumph of which we owe to Virchow, and the bacterial theory as developed by Pasteur, Koch, and Lister, which displaced the older humoral theory of disease.

As the old humours disappeared, so too did the need to establish a specific pathway between the pituitary and the third ventricle. And thus it was that the axial-stalk vessels of Lieutaud dropped from view. But the question of a tubular connection between the infundibulum and pituitary continued to exercise successive generations of anatomists. Vieussens's experimental injection of a dye into the third ventricle, which had been repeated by de Bordeu in 1751, was tried again by the brothers Wenzel. During the period 1796–1800 they performed twelve experiments on the human brain, after its removal from the cadaver, and concluded that when any suitable liquid is injected into the third ventricle nothing passes into the infundibulum, and further that the latter is more closely joined to the posterior than to the anterior lobe of the hypophysis.[23]

This last observation foreshadows what we know today—that whatever the connection between the hypothalamus and the pituitary, it is much more intimate in the case of the posterior than of the anterior component of the gland. Wenzel also observed vessels, connecting the pituitary with the infundibulum, which may well have been the same channels as are now called the pituitary-portal system of veins, and which Lieutaud originally described. So, too, did Luschka,[24] who in 1860 described what we might now recognise as the primary capillary loops of the pituitary-portal vessels.

Here and there [he writes] the vessels bulge out, and in the form of loops which are arranged in various ways, they make their way into the interior of the infundibulum, and sometimes their number is so great, that they alone constitute a loose, red substance in the interior. . . . By these vascular loops and the productions which result thence, not only the cavity of the infundibulum is obstructed, but also the proper substance of this organ is crowded out and broken up. [He also speaks of] blood vessels which run in a longitudinal direction, and which not infrequently are enlarged in the fashion of aneurisms.

Luschka, it should be noted, was quite certain that as a rule 'the infundibulum has an aperture only in its upper extremity and in that portion which communicates with the tuberculum cinereum.* . . . Only in exceptional cases the cavity of the infundibulum can really be traced into the pituitary gland.' He also appears to have had a remarkably clear understanding of the anatomical relationship of the tuber cinereum, the infundibulum, and the posterior lobe of the gland. They were, he realised, parts of the same anatomical complex, possessing fundamentally the same finer structure. Even more striking was his observation that 'fine nerve tubes' passed from the infundibulum into the posterior lobe, where they became varicose and broke up. This achieves a particular significance in the light of new discoveries over the past few years, which resurrect, to mystify us once again, the problem of how the brain controls the functions of the pituitary.

* The tuberculum (=tuber) cinereum is a minute part of the lower part of the hypothalamus at the root of the pituitary stalk (infundibulum).

5

The New Secretions of the Brain

The story re-opens in 1895 with the demonstration by Oliver and Schafer[1] that the blood-pressure of an animal rises after the injection of a 'concoction' of the pituitary. Howell[2] soon showed that the effect was due to the posterior as opposed to the anterior lobe of the gland. A few years later Magnus and Schafer[3] found that the posterior-lobe 'hormone' also has a diuretic-antidiuretic action, that is to say a regulating function on the amount of fluid which is excreted by the kidneys. And soon afterwards, Dale[4] demonstrated that posterior-lobe extracts had an 'oxytocic' action, that is to say, that they caused the uterine muscle to contract. Concurrently, numerous clinical observations indicated very clearly that the anterior part of the pituitary also had important hormonal functions.[5] The proof of this was provided in the twenties by the brilliant experimental studies of Herbert M. Evans, Zondek, Aschheim, and others too numerous to mention. These showed quite clearly that the anterior lobe of the pituitary plays a vital part in the control of growth, in the regulation of reproductive processes, and in the maintenance of other endocrine organs such as the thyroid and the cortex (= outer part) of the adrenal glands.

The pituitary gland ('hypophysis' in present-day anatomical terminology), while relatively minute in size (in man it is roughly bean-shaped and its maximum dimension is about 1 cm.), is a highly complex structure consisting of two main lobes. The bulk of its posterior lobe develops in the embryo as an outgrowth of the developing brain, to which it remains attached by the stalk. Together with the stalk and the part of the base of the brain from which the stalk begins, this part of the gland is known as the neurohypophysis, the microscopic structure of which is uniform throughout. The uppermost part of the stalk is the infundibulum of the Ancients, and forms part of the floor of the third ventricle of the brain. The anterior lobe, or adenohypophysis, which is the bigger of the two, develops in embryonic life as a bud of cells from the roof of the primitive mouth and, as it were, grows up to become attached to the lower part, or 'neural lobe' (= processus infundibularis), of the neurohypophysis. The hinder part of the adenohypophysis which comes into contact with the neural lobe differentiates as a third part of the pituitary called the inter-mediate lobe or *pars intermedia*. The latter is usually treated as part of the anterior lobe of the whole gland. Other cells of the upper part of the anterior lobe differentiate as another collection of distinctive cells called the *pars tuberalis*, which form a collar around the upper part of the stalk of the pituitary. The main part of the anterior lobe is called the *pars distalis*. These different parts are shown in figure 3.

The microscopic structure of the posterior lobe did not encourage any of the earlier workers to believe that the active hormones which could be extracted from it were elaborated within it. One powerfully sustained view was that the posterior-lobe hormone was, in fact, produced by the cells of the pars intermedia, and that it passed back into the *neural lobe* and up the pituitary stalk. This interpretation was seized upon by many other workers, and par-ticularly by Harvey Cushing.[6-7] Cushing's belief was that the posterior-lobe hormone not only entered the blood-stream, but that after making its way up the pituitary stalk, it passed through the cellular lining of the third ventricle, called the ependyma, and so entered the cerebro-spinal fluid. This fluid fills the ventricles of the brain and the central canal of the spinal cord. Gradually, however, opinion changed. The next hypothesis to hold the stage was that there are specific secretory cells throughout the neuro-hypophysis, and that these cells are responsible for the secretion of the posterior-lobe hormones.[8] Today the commonly-held view is that the posterior-lobe hormones are secreted by nerve cells of the hypothalamus, particularly by the cells of two nuclei called the nuclei supraopticus and paraventricularis, from which they pass into the neurohypophysis, where they are stored and possibly transformed chemically.

About the secretory powers of the anterior lobe there never was any doubt. Its structure was clearly glandular, and the only difficulty was to reconcile its apparent cellular simplicity with the complexity of its hormonal functions.

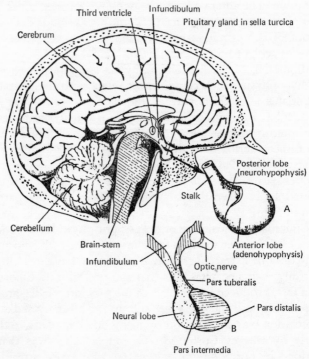

Figure 3. Schematic midline section of the skull and brain to show the position and connections of pituitary gland (A in three dimensions, B in midline section)

By the time we were fairly clear about the distinction between posterior and anterior lobe function, the infundibular region of the brain again entered the picture. It did so first as a result of a series of studies started by Karplus and Kreidl in 1909,[9] which showed that electrical stimulation of the hypothalamus led to a number of autonomic effects (e.g., changes in heart-rate and salivation). These observations were followed in 1913 by Camus and Roussy's experimental demonstration that small lesions in the hypothalamus could cause young animals to remain immature sexually, and to lay on masses of fat.[10] As our knowledge continued to grow, it became abundantly clear that in some mysterious way the hypothalamus – the infundibular region of the Ancients – controlled or modulated the endocrine activity of both the anterior and posterior lobes of the pituitary. Once again the question was, how?

This time, however, the problem was both more specific and more complicated. First it was quite clear that the pituitary consisted mainly of two quite separate endocrine structures – the anterior lobe, and the posterior lobe. Secondly, by now there was precise knowledge of the nature of nervous action; if the pituitary stalk was not a canal for a vital spirit passing from the brain to the nose, at any rate it consisted largely of the fibrillar extensions, called axons, of the nerve-cells of the hypothalamus, which provided an anatomical basis for whatever cerebral control there was of pituitary function (see figure 4). And thirdly – and most important – answers could no longer depend on speculation based on dogma, however hallowed; the hard facts of observation and experiment were needed.

The first problem for which a solution seemed to have been found was the control exercised by the hypothalamus over the secretion of antidiuretic hormone, the hormone which controls the amount of fluid excreted by the kidneys. The explanation seemed simple enough.[11] All levels of the neurohypophysis are connected with the terminations of the axons of cells in two nuclei (the nuclei supraopticus and paraventricularis) of the hypothalamus (particularly the former). Cells in some way concerned with secretion of hormone are present throughout the neurohypophysis, including that part of the floor of the third ventricle, called the median eminence, from which the stalk begins, and all are under the control of the hypothalamus. If the pituitary stalk is divided, the part of the neurohypophysis distal to the section atrophies completely – owing to the interruption of the 'trophic' influence exercised on it by the hypothalamus – and no longer can any hormone, antidiuretic, pressor, or oxytocic, be extracted from it. If the nuclei supraopticus and paraventricularis in the hypothalamus, the two nuclei which are believed to be the primary source of posterior-lobe hormone, are destroyed, the whole neurohypophysis atrophies. A condition, called diabetes insipidus, in which the volume of urine secreted by the kidneys goes up enormously, then supervenes, owing to the cessation of secretion of antidiuretic hormone. Or if the nerve fibres connecting the neurohypophysis with the nuclei supraopticus and paraventricularis are divided, the cells of both nuclei degenerate. The reason why removal of the whole pituitary is only occasionally followed by diabetes insipidus also seemed straightforward; the operation very rarely removes all of the neurohypophysis, and the cells of the part which remains presumably hypertrophy to compensate for the loss of the rest.

These observations and interpretations seemingly provided all that could be asked for in trying to understand the control exercised by the hypothalamus on the kidneys (the diuretic-antidiuretic balance). And since the hypothalamus is a major 'autonomic' nervous centre which is linked, as far as one knows, with all the zones of the brain concerned with the reception of sensory stimuli, they also made it possible to understand how various forms of sensory stimulation are tied up with processes in which posterior lobe hormones are involved. Thus they help to provide an explanation for the effects of emotion on the excretion of urine,[12-14] and also to understand the nature of the nervous pathways concerned in the reflex stimulation of the discharge of milk from the breast.[15] In short, while one might not know exactly how it all worked, there could be little doubt about the general nature of the link between the brain and the posterior pituitary.

If the connection with the posterior lobe of the pituitary seemed, on the face of it, clear enough, that with the anterior was anything but obvious. Here one goes on being confronted by a most bewildering puzzle. First, there is no doubt that the anterior lobe of the pituitary regulates several bodily processes, and that the timing and intensity of its different physiological activities accord with the steps of those processes; or, to put it in the teleological terms used by Bayliss and Starling,[16] that its secretions are regulated by the needs of the body. We know that some of this regulation is effected by hormonal interaction. For example, when, under the stimulus of one of the so-called gonadotrophic hormones of the anterior pituitary which stimulate the ovaries, the latter secrete an excess of their own oestrogenic hormone, the pituitary becomes inhibited, and its gonadotrophic stimulus weakens. But some regulation seems to be of a more direct nervous kind, and is presumably mediated by the hypothalamus. For example, it has been shown that in an animal such as a rabbit, which normally ovulates only after the stimulus of mating, and not spontaneously as women do, direct electrical stimulation of the hypothalamus can result in rupture of the ovarian follicles (i.e. ovulation) provided the experiment is done during the right phase of the sexual cycle.[17] Presumably normal mating starts a train of nervous stimulation which culminates in the 'firing' of the relevant hypothalamic nerve cells. Another illustration of the nervous control of the anterior pituitary is provided by the 'anoestrous' ferret, which becomes oestrous (i.e. comes 'on heat') in the winter months if it is exposed to additional artificial light, in the same way as 'battery-hens' are stimulated to lay eggs, or song birds to sing, in the winter. While the main visual centres of the brain are apparently not involved in the response to light,[18] the primary receptor for the response is the retina of the eyeball.[19] The stimulus is relayed along the optic nerves and then in some unknown way to the hypothalamus before the pituitary is activated.

But – and here is the essential difficulty – few workers believe that the glandular cells of the adenohypophysis are connected by nerve fibres with the cells (neurons) of the hypothalamus, or that there is any other kind of secreto-motor innervation of these cells (e.g. *via* nerve-fibres along the small arteries which enter the gland).[20]

How, then, are the 'reflex' responses of the anterior pituitary controlled?

The belief which now is part of conventional teaching is that the critical anatomical link between the hypothalamus and anterior pituitary is provided by the very axial-stalk vessels which Lieutaud described nearly two hundred years ago. The part they played then was as a channel for the pituita. They derive their present importance from the assumption that they convey some chemical substance, a so-called 'chemotransmitter', from the hypothalamus to the pituitary.

We owe the rediscovery of these vessels, and their first fairly complete description, to Popa and Fielding,[21] who gave an account of what they were the first to call the hypophysio-portal or pituitary-portal system of veins. According to these workers, these veins collect blood below from the pars distalis and pars intermedia of the adenohypophysis, as well as from the pars tuberalis and neural process of the neurohypophysis, and then ascend the pituitary stalk as parallel vessels. Popa and Fielding believed that superiorly, beneath the infundibular recess of the third ventricle, the vessels formed a network of very fine channels which they described as a secondary distributing net. Popa and Fielding were persuaded of the correctness of Cushing's opinion about the direction of flow of the posterior-lobe hormone, and it was their view that the current in the portal vessels was from below upwards, and that colloid material was transported from the pituitary to the hypothalamus. Since then the contrary view has gained ground,[22-24] and most – but not all – observers now believe that the direction of the blood is from above downwards. The secondary distributing net of Popa and Fielding has thus become the primary net, comprising a dense mesh of capillary loops in the pars tuberalis and median eminence above, while the true secondary net is represented by the connection of the main portal vessels with the blood spaces (sinusoids) of the pars distalis of the pituitary below (see figure 4).

It was the failure to establish any clear nervous connection between the brain and the pars distalis of the pituitary that made it necessary to consider the possibility that the pituitary-portal veins are in some way involved in the presumed control which the hypothalamus exercises over the anterior lobe of the pituitary. The hypothesis that has been advanced[20] is that some unknown 'chemo-transmitter' is liberated, as a result of nervous stimulation, in the vicinity of the portal vessels, into whose primary capillary loops it passes. The 'chemo-transmitter' then passes down the longitudinal channels on the stalk into the sinusoids of the anterior lobe, and is so able to influence the secretory cells of the pars distalis.

In the light of the results of sections of the pituitary stalk and of experiments on pituitary transplantation, few will doubt that the portal vessels do play some special part in the 'economy' of the anterior lobe. For example, it is said that pituitary tissue is more likely to 'take' successfully if it is transplanted just beneath the hypothalamus (i.e. in contact with the median eminence), where the grafted tissue can come into relation with the cut stumps of the portal vessels, than anywhere else. Correspondingly, when the pituitary stalk and its vessels are divided (although more vessels are usually divided in this operation than just the pituitary-portal channels), the whole pituitary gland usually dwindles in size. On the other hand, the attractive theory of which the portal vessels constitute the central feature is essentially

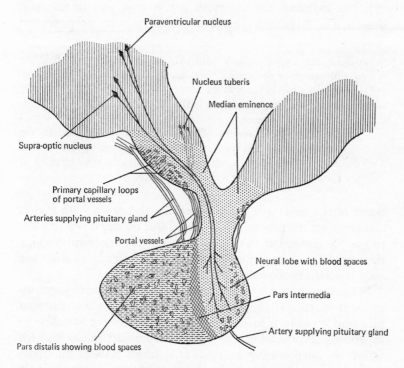

Figure 4. Schematic midline section of pituitary gland and hypothalamus

based on what may be called purely negative considerations.

Moreover, the theory is hardly as precise as the facts which it has to explain. The anterior lobe of the pituitary controls many functions; and we have either to suppose that the gland is differentially activated by different kinds of chemo-transmitter, or that, once activated by a single stimulus, the gland of itself adjusts its secretions according to the needs of the body. If it is the former which is implied, we find ourselves in a maze of contradictory and speculative observation, derived overwhelmingly from experiments of dubious design and inadequate control, and in a field well beyond the area of established fact.[25] If it is the latter, the hypothesis merely transfers the critical problem we are trying to understand – how the reflex functions of the adenohypophysis are controlled – from the hypothalamus to the pituitary itself.

C

If one examines the theory, which is now part of textbook dogma, it is clear that it is made up of three separate propositions:

(1) That the hypothalamus controls, or at least modulates, the functions of the anterior pituitary;

(2) That the only functional and necessary connection between the brain and the pars distalis is the pituitary portal system;

(3) That different chemical substances are produced in the hypothalamus (and because of the specific role assigned to the portal vessels, nowhere else), and that changes in the function of the pars distalis result from alterations in the secretion of these substances into the portal system.

Some fifteen years ago I challenged the theory on both logical and experimental grounds, and argued that no single one of these propositions stood up to critical analysis.[26] My argument remains the same today, but fortified by a variety of observations that have been reported in the intervening years.

In the sense that it implies a specific control of the moment-to-moment reactions and response of the pars distalis, the first proposition, while it may be true, is to my mind not amenable to experimental verification. The changes in pituitary function which follow stimulation or destruction of different parts of the hypothalamus – which is the basis of the proposition – are not only non-specific, in the sense that they are also associated with profound changes in other physiological functions, but are also highly variable in their nature. Moreover because of the minute size of the hypothalamic nuclei relative to the instruments which are used in the experiments, it is next to impossible to confine any experimental interference to specified nuclei. Thirdly, the controls for the experiments are lamentably inadequate. My view remains that if the hypothalamus does in fact control the anterior pituitary, the nature of its influence, whether chemical or nervous – if in the final analysis these are distinct from each other – is hardly likely to be elucidated by the classical approach of stimulation and destruction of groups of nerve cells. Neither technique can be applied with sufficient precision to what are in effect microscopic structures which cannot be approached either with topographic certainly, or without seriously damaging or affecting neighbouring structures.

The same general criticisms also apply to related forms of experiment – which have been equally inconclusive – in which small pieces of pituitary gland or crystalline hormone have been implanted directly into the hypothalamus, or in which alterations in the firing rate of presumed individual hypothalamic neurones have been correlated with changes in endocrine condition, or in which supposedly specific structural changes in the hypothalamus have been presumed, in some undefined way, to reflect its control of the pars distalis.

When we turn to the second proposition, namely that the 'necessary' functional-structural connection between the base of the brain and the adenohypophysis is the portal system of vessels, it is at once obvious that the speculation that hypothalamic chemo-transmitters, if they exist as specific substances, control the anterior pituitary is not dependent upon the belief that they are necessarily transmitted to the gland by way of these vessels. They might, for example, get to the pituitary by a process of simple diffusion through the fluid between the cells of the small region concerned. And here let me observe that experiments in which pieces of pituitary have been grafted in areas remote from the hypothalamus (and upon which a large part of the evidence for the supposed role of the portal vessels depends) could have been interpreted as support for a hypothesis that substances simply diffused from the hypothalamus to the adenohypophysis – had this been the fashionable explanation at the time they were carried out – just as much as they were for the thesis that they were conveyed in the pituitary portal vessels.

My next criticism of the second proposition is that it is by no means certain that the portal vessels do constitute the only connection between the hypothalamus above and the anterior pituitary below. The belief that the anterior pituitary is not innervated by nerve fibres from the hypothalamus is far from proven. There is conclusive evidence that the cells of a part of the anterior pituitary, the pars intermedia, are in fact supplied by nerve fibres.[27] Given therefore that the hypothalamus does 'control' the pars distalis, it is conceivable that the control is an indirect nervous one.

A further criticism of the proposition that the pituitary portal vessels constitute the critical functional connection between the hypothalamus and the pars distalis derives from the fact that this hypothesis presupposes that the portal vessels are distributed only to the anterior and to no other part of the pituitary. If this were not so, the presumed chemo-transmitters would be distributed to the posterior lobe of the gland as well as to the anterior. In fact there is cast-iron evidence that there is a free connection between the vascular beds of all parts of the pituitary gland and of the capillary plexus in the median eminence with the vessels of the hypothalamus.[28] This evidence is however conveniently overlooked in some recent reviews[25] in which the subject is referred to. Indeed the latter have been concerned to attribute to the pituitary-portal vessels an even more specific function than even the accepted dogma demands, but on the basis of experiments which in their technical crudity, when one considers the size of the structures concerned, would be equivalent to some uninformed person smashing an electronic computer with a crowbar, and then trying to explain the way the whole thing worked by examining one of its pieces picked up at random from the floor. Moreover, we are yet to see any analytical study of the flow in the portal vessels which relates in any way to the hydrodynamics of a set of connecting channels that begin in one 'capillary' network in which the pressure must be near zero, and end in another network of vessels where it can be little higher, and in which gravitational and other physical forces might be expected to play a part.

The critical test of the proposition that the normal function of the pars distalis is uniquely dependent on the integrity of the portal vessels, could only be through study of the function of the gland after the vessels had been eliminated, either through the effective section of the pituitary stalk or by transplanting the gland. The hormonal activity of fragments of anterior pituitary tissue grown in tissue-culture could also provide useful evidence. My own experiments on ferrets showed that while the pituitary gland usually rapidly dwindles in size after section of the stalk, due to a clotting process, atrophy is sometimes only partial, and in such cases the gland will occasionally function normally even when completely separated from the base of the brain, and when all possibility of a vascular reconnection had been excluded. There is also clear evidence that the secretion of pars distalis grafts remote from the hypothalamus can alter in response to changes in the level of circulating hormone (this would not be expected to occur if all pars distalis function depended upon variations in the output of hypothalamic chemo-transmitters transmitted through the portal vessels); and also that the cells of the pars distalis are directly sensitive to gonadal hormones. All in all, I fail to see how the second proposition can possibly stand up in the face of evidence with which it is totally inconsistent.

I turn now to the third proposition, namely that the presumed chemo-transmitters which control the functions of the anterior pituitary are specific substances produced by nuclei of the hypothalamus. Let me begin by noting that, at the start, these chemical agents had to be conjured out of thin air, since without them, the speculative hypothesis that the portal vessels constitute the critical functional link between the hypothalamus which exercised control above, and the pars distalis which reacted below, had no meaning at all. Drugs which affect the transmission of nervous impulses have been tested to see if they could directly stimulate the pars distalis, but with variable results, and over the past ten years or so, numbers of people have extracted, or tried to extract, from hypothalamic and other cerebral tissue 'releasing factors' of one kind or another, i.e. extracts which, when injected into an experimental animal, cause the anterior pituitary (pars distalis) specifically to release one or other of its hormones. I hardly need to confess that I have viewed this kind of experimentation – which in any event has resulted in considerable disagreement about the results – with a somewhat critical eye, failing to see how they could possibly show the way by which the hypothalamus exercises its presumed control over the pars distalis, even if the results were either specific to a particular pituitary function, or indeed constant. From the point of view of testing critically a general hypothesis about the control of the anterior pituitary by the portal vessels, the experiments are not only irrelevant; they are also unsophisticated. If there are chemo-transmitters, their existence would no more be dependent on the presence of portal vessels, than the existence of the latter are necessary to give credibility to the idea of a chemo-transmitter control of the anterior pituitary.

And now the whole picture has been transformed by the intrusion into the story of the pineal gland.[29] This is a minute appendage which lies in the midline behind the third ventricle, and to which no modern experimentalist has hitherto succeeded in attributing any function. The picture has also now been blurred by the proposed attribution of a controlling function of the pituitary to certain cells which line the third ventricle of the brain, and which it has long been recognised are different from the normal ependymal cells which line all four ventricles of the brain, and the central canal of the spinal cord with which they communicate. Recent electron-microscopic studies of the monkey show that the ependymal cells which line a circumscribed area of the third ventricle in the region of the anterior (front) part of the hypothalamus connect by long processes directly with the pars tuberalis of the pituitary, terminating either on or near blood vessels, or on the tuberalis cells, which also appear to be innervated by the nerve fibres of a nucleus of the hypothalamus.[30] Both the modified ependymal cells, which differ in appearance between adult male and female monkeys, and the cells of the pars tuberalis, vary in their electron-microscopic structure with the phases of the menstrual cycle. In the case of the pineal the story is that artificial light, which can modify the oestrous cycle of both continuous breeders like rats and seasonal breeders such as the ferret, affects the pituitary by way of the pineal. The rat's pineal contains high concentrations of chemical substances called monoamines, the level of which is apparently affected by artificial light, and some of which may be able to suppress the function of the pituitary. In the case of the ferret it has been shown that the normal response of premature heat to exposure to artificial light in winter is prevented by removal of the pineal gland. The latter receives its extensive nerve supply from the superio cervical sympathetic nerve ganglia in the neck, and their surgical removal also prevents the oestrous response to light.

I do not have the slightest idea how all this is going to add up, or what the physiologists of the year 2000 will believe about the control of the functions of the pars distalis, and about the interrelation of that gland with other parts of the pituitary, for example the anatomically imprecise pars tuberalis, which in mammals has hitherto not been endowed with any function, or with the pars intermedia, which has also not been accredited with any precise role, or indeed with the neurohypophysis, whose physiology is much more clearly understood, as is also its dependence on the nuclei supraopticus and paraventricularis of the hypothalamus. Nor have I any idea about what is likely to be thought of the functions of the pineal, once believed to be the seat of the soul, anatomically in some species a vestige of a third eye, almost generally a cerebral appendage whose microscopic appearance hardly suggests a glandular function, and now a structure from which extracts have been made which do what the presumed hypothalamic chemo-transmitters were supposed to do. Nor again have I any idea about the place where the ependyma of the third ventricle will fit in. Will it turn out that the anterior pituitary is controlled chemically by substances transported in the cerebro-spinal fluid? As I have already said, many years ago Harvey Cushing, that most distinguished of brain surgeons, believed that pituitary secretions made their way up the pituitary stalk to filter through the ependyma into the cerebro-spinal fluid of the third ventricle – but his preparations were later shown to be artefacts. But even if I am alone in my disbelief, what I do know is that the evidence against the speculation that the pituitary portal vessels constitute the critical functional link between the hypothalamus and the pars distalis, which remains the textbook story, is even more convincing now than what it was when I first expressed my contrary view several years ago.

I also know that the whole sad tale provides a perfect illustration of the way *not* to set about testing a simple hypothesis. If one wishes to establish the concept of the critical nature of the portal vessels, then at least one must concentrate on experiments in which the gland is structurally separated from the base of the brain, and on studies of the secretion of cultures of pituitary tissue; and if the function of the gland differs from normal in such conditions, then one ought to determine to what extent the difference is due to the effects of the inevitable damage to the gland which follows stalk section, which relatively speaking is a vast operation on so small a structure as the pituitary. Even so, such experiments would not help decide critically between a view that presumed chemo-transmitters passed to the anterior pituitary by diffusion, and the hypothesis that they were conveyed through the pituitary portal vessels. What does not help at all is to add to an already confused picture a mass of other imprecise observation which is totally independent of the central hypothesis.

The more I have read of work which has been carried out since I levelled my first major criticism on the pituitary-portal hypothesis, the more it has been borne in upon me that most of the people who are now designing experiments to unravel the relationship of the hypothalamus to the anterior pituitary have simply accepted without critical reflection the hypothesis that the pituitary portal vessels constitute the essential structural-functional link between the brain and the gland, as opposed to constituting a purely vascular connection. Even the basic anatomy of the pituitary gland and the hypothalamus, as well as of their blood-supply, is often incorrectly described in what are taken to be authoritative reviews.[25] But standing aside from the battle, I would assert now that the hypothesis that the pituitary portal vessels are the controlling mechanism is probably beyond direct experimental proof; and I would go further and say that the speculation has no scientific value. This, of course, is an isolated view, and not, as I have admitted, the conventional wisdom. But in putting it forward let us remember that another piece of conventional wisdom about the pituitary, now but an echo from a distant past, was that through the gland passed the phlegm, one of the four humours of the body, to percolate through the olfactory nerves to the front part of the base of the skull and so into the nose. We have now abandoned the view that health depends on the balance between the phlegm and the three other humours of the body – blood, yellow bile and black bile. I am prepared to bet that in due course the pituitary-portal theory will follow the humours to the same graveyard of abandoned hypotheses where they now rest.

6

Art and Science in Anatomical Diagnosis

The third and final example which I propose to use in showing how objective truth can become obscured by personal attitudes and by fashion, and how controversy in consequence can multiply within science, deals with speculations about Man's evolutionary origins as revealed by comparative studies of the fossil bones of a variety of ape-like creatures. 'Missing links' and possible ape-men, whether fossil or sensationally reported to be still roaming in some remote part of the world like the Himalayas, or the snowy wastes of Canada, or the unexplored forests of Central Africa or the Amazon, have always been news. But until some forty years ago the palaeontological analysis of the fossil remains of monkeys and apes was pursued fairly quietly and undramatically.* Some fragments, mostly of jawbones and teeth, had been discovered, mainly in India and Egypt, and these had been described without any fanfare, no special significance being attached to them so far as the story of man's evolution was concerned. In that period the limelight was on manifestly 'human' fossil remains, and speculation was confined to such questions as the possibility that modern man, with his smooth and large forehead, had evolved from beetle-browed cave-dwellers such as Neanderthal Man of Europe, or *Pithecanthropus erectus* of Java, or *Sinanthropus* Pekin Man, of China.

Then late in 1924 the fossil skull of a young ape-like creature, to which the name *Australopithecus africanus* was applied, turned up in South Africa in a limestone works in what was then called Bechuanaland, and now Botswana. A new chapter opened in the

* The Appendix provides a brief statement about the general classification of monkeys and apes in what is called the Order Primates of the family of mammals, as well as a short history of these creatures as objects of scientific enquiry.

story of physical anthropology. Professor Raymond Dart, to whom the specimen was turned over for description, had no hesitation – without any apparent prior knowledge of the osteology of the anthropoid apes – in asserting that a unique creature had been discovered which somehow or other was closer to the direct line of human descent than was the family of the Great Apes.

Since then, dozens of other fragmentary australopithecine fossils have been discovered, and with few exceptions, all have enjoyed a similar welcome. The pride of personal possession has been more than a little evident in the finders, with claims about the special hominid status of their fossils often being immediately challenged, usually by workers with a vested interest in some other fossil.

The argument became even more spirited, at least as much in the popular press as in scientific journals, when fossil remains and fragments started pouring out of a goldmine of Primate remains in the Olduvai Gorge in Tanzania which had been opened up by Dr and Mrs Leakey. And since then the debate has often seemed less like a scientific discussion than a public auction of anatomical speculations as to whether one particular fossil specimen is more or less significant to the story of human evolution than another. This is the kind of argument that can go on forever. But it hardly constitutes science, any more than do speculations about the likelihood that living matter as we know it also thrives on one or more planets in one of hundreds of distant constellations in outer space, millions of light years away. That it may do so is certainly a possibility; but it is hardly a scientific question amenable to answer. This is not as it should be with palaeontological analysis regarded as a scientific discipline. Attributing a particular evolutionary significance to some fragment of a fossil should not be a matter for *ex cathedra* argument and pronouncement, but essentially a question for anatomical diagnosis.

'Diagnosis', a term which of course has a wider sphere of reference, is a Greek word spelt in English letters. It means 'to distinguish or to discern', and is mostly used in the world of medicine, where it signifies the attribution of the symptoms and signs of a sick person to some previously defined category of disease. It is also used in a corresponding way wherever the process of discrimination is actively called into play – whether it be in spotting the painter of a particular canvas; in judging whether a glass of wine is this or that kind of claret; or in identifying some species of insect. In short, diagnosis implies the capacity to discriminate, and this in turn presupposes a body of knowledge that has accumulated through experience, that is to say, through learning. Learning could itself be regarded as a process of increasing discrimination, as a process in which the awareness of things which are similar, of what we might call classes of uniform experience, becomes progressively refined and subdivided. So it is that while all of us know what an aeroplane is, some who have had more experience have learnt to tell one aeroplane from another.

In slower motion, the growth of knowledge, as opposed to that of learning, is also a process of increasing discrimination. Galen brought precision to the body of anatomical knowledge which was there before he came on the scene. Vesalius did likewise in his turn, and in the 400 years which now separate us from his achievement, the subject has been even more transformed, largely because we realise, perhaps better than did his generation, that uncontrolled speculation is an expensive luxury in science, and that the more we wish to decide correctly between true and false propositions, the more we have to abide by the discipline implicit in scientific method. Because of this, the area of anatomical reference within which we are now able to discriminate, in which we make our diagnoses on the basis of established or presumed anatomical 'models' – is not only far better mapped and far more extensive today than it was even fifty years ago, but also far more subject to control. We recognise that statements of fact, whether they be based upon simple observation (e.g. dissection), or upon experiment, have to be verifiable. And equally we appreciate that the growth of anatomical knowledge, like that of other fields of natural science, means the continuous testing, refining or rejecting of old propositions and the discovery of new ones.

A dominant interest in the study of comparative anatomy has long been the relevance of anatomical fact to evolutionary studies. Even if we confine ourselves only to the anatomy of the vertebrates, or to that of the mammals, or indeed, merely to the order of Primates, of which we are members, the area of fact which is involved is vastly more extensive than that which concerns the human anatomist interested only in problems of human physiology or human medicine. The bare data of comparative anatomy are never treated merely as a catalogue of the relations of structures in different creatures. By an assessment of differences and resemblances, they are also used to define taxonomic and evolutionary relationships, the underlying idea being that the closer animals correspond in their anatomical structure, the closer they are related from the point of view of evolutionary descent. We now know that this view is far too simple, since relationships which are inferred on the basis of comparative anatomy may not necessarily correspond to true genetic relationships. Nevertheless, lack of other information makes it inevitable that the bulk of our views about evolutionary relationships has to be based on the evidence of structure. Consequently, students of comparative anatomy need to exercise great forbearance, as well as great humility, both in the area of fact and in that of interpretation, simply because the inferences they draw about evolution are in the final analysis speculations – speculations that can only be checked by recourse to the facts from which they are derived.

To a certain extent checks are possible, for while the propositions of descriptive anatomy relate to form and structure, or to form and function, and while very few of them can be tested by experiment, most can be formulated in terms of hypotheses from which one can deduce secondary propositions of a kind which can be tested by further observation, particularly by the use of increasingly precise methods of observation and measurement. But in the final analysis, the answer to the question of human descent always depends upon preconceptions about the way this evolution occurred. For example, no scientist could logically dispute the proposition that man, without having been involved in any act of divine creation, evolved from some ape-like creature in a very short space of time – speaking in geological terms – without leaving any fossil traces of the steps of the transformation.

As I have already implied, students of fossil primates have not been distinguished for caution when working within the logical constraints of their subject. The record is so astonishing that it is legitimate to ask whether much science is yet to be found in this field at all. The story of the Piltdown Man hoax provides a pretty good answer. The essential facts are well known.[1] In 1908 Mr Charles Dawson, a solicitor, recovered from a gravel pit near Piltdown, Sussex, some pieces of a human brain-case. A few years later, he and Sir Arthur Smith Woodward, who was a distinguished palaeontologist at the Natural History Museum in London, found part of a jawbone near the place where the first bones were discovered. Shortly afterwards a well-known French scholar found a lower canine tooth in the same area.

From the outset opinions differed about the significance of the remains. Opinions also differed about the way the fragments of the brain-case should be fitted together and reconstructed; and at least nine different schemes of reconstruction were at one time or another suggested. No one, however, ever disputed the hominid character of this part of the skull, and most anatomists agreed that the brain-box was similar in shape and size to that of a modern man. The controversy which developed was focussed entirely on the association of the human brain-box with an ape-like jaw. Mr Dawson and Sir Arthur Smith Woodward believed that they belonged to the same individual. Professor Sir Grafton Elliot Smith,[2] a scholar of great eminence, had no doubts about this either, writing that 'the jaw and tooth, in spite of their superficial likeness to the chimpanzee's, were definitely human.' In this he was supported by Dr Ales Hrdlicka,[3] a distinguished American anthropologist, who, after examining the original specimen, concluded that

although it resembles in a number of points, the jaws of the chimpanzee, it differs from these in a whole series of points of importance, such as the form of the notch, type of glenoid process, (i.e., the joint of the mandible which fits into a depression, called the glenoid or articular fossa, in the base of the skull), subdued musculature, reduced internal massiveness of body, especially near the symphysis (i.e. the chin region of the mandible), and in the most important characteristics of the teeth, namely height of crown, height of enamel, nature of 'cingulum', and stoutness of cusps – in all of which features it is nearer or like human.

Later on, Dr Hrdlicka[4] made a further statement in which he concluded that 'in both their absolute and relative length, the Piltdown molars, though "connecting" with the teeth of present man, connect more closely with the ancient teeth of Early Man', and that they 'do not connect with the teeth of any of the living forms of anthropoid apes'.

These dogmatic diagnoses of human, and denial of ape-like characteristics in the jaw and teeth of the Piltdown man were endorsed by numerous other anatomists. An absolutely opposing view was taken by Professor David Waterston,[5] the anatomist of Aberdeen University, and then by Mr Gerrit S. Miller[6] of the Smithsonian Institution, Washington. Miller did not question the human nature of the brain-case, but insisted that the features by which the jaw-bone and teeth had been diagnosed as human were merely those which man and apes possessed in common. He pointed out, moreover, that 'the symphysial region of the jaw, the canine tooth and the molars are unlike those known to occur in any race of man', and that their 'peculiarities are such as have been found in the great apes only'. So convinced was he of this opinion that he had no hesitation in suggesting that the jaw-bone be relegated to a new species of chimpanzee which he called *Pan vetus*.

Professor Waterston and Mr Miller soon found their supporters. The distinguished French scholar Marcelin Boule[7] for example, wrote that 'in its general build, as well as in details of its structure, the Piltdown mandible exactly reproduces an ape's jaw, or to be precise, the jaw of a chimpanzee'. Dr W. K. Gregory of the American Museum of Natural History,[8] also endorsed Miller's view, as later did Dr F. Frassetto,[9] an Italian student, who decided, however, from a comparison with apparently the jaw of a single orang skull, that the Piltdown mandible had the characteristics of the orang's mandible – not the chimpanzee's. Dr F. Weidenreich,[10] a distinguished German anthropologist, shared much the same opinion, but was somewhat more forthright. In his view the Piltdown skull should be 'erased from the list of human fossils. It is an artificial combination of fragments of a modern human brain-case and orang utang-like mandible and teeth'.

In addition to forthright statements of this kind, there were a number of students who took a somewhat intermediate position. Among them was Sir Arthur Keith,[11] one of the best known of English anatomists of the time, who recognised ape-like features in the front part of the mandible in association with essentially human molar teeth. Sir Arthur was thoroughly aware of the difficulty of taking a firm position, but in 1939[12] declared that all the studies he had made of the remains since 1915 had convinced him more firmly than ever that 'skull and mandible are in harmony, and form parts of the same head'. Sir Arthur implied that he was driven to this conclusion on anatomical grounds, and not because of the difficulty in believing that sheer chance had brought together in the same deposit the brain-case of a man and the jaw of an ape. Here he differed from other students who felt themselves impelled to attribute the mandibular and cranial fragments to the same creature, against their better anatomical judgment, simply because the remains were found in such close association. Even Frassetto, who believed that the jaw was identical with that of an orang, nevertheless felt that this association meant that the jaw was a human mandible which only 'accorded' with the orang type.

No doubt the whole subject would have been allowed to rest, each school of thought sticking to its beliefs, if it had not been for the renewed interest taken in the remains by Mr A. T. Marston,[13] a dental surgeon, who in 1935 discovered the Swanscombe skull, a fossil type which resembles modern man more than do the beetle-browed cave men of the Ice Ages. Mr Marston was convinced on purely anatomical grounds that the Piltdown jaw and isolated canine tooth were those of an ape, and his suspicions had been raised by the fact that the Piltdown remains had been dipped in potassium bichromate in the mistaken belief that this treatment would harden them. About the time his interest was thoroughly aroused, Dr Kenneth P. Oakley,[14] of the British Museum, had started to try out a fluorine test for the age of bones which had originally been suggested by Middleton in 1844, and by Carnot in 1893, and which is based on the fact that the fluorine content of bone increases with geological age. Dr Oakley was aware of Mr Marston's interest, and suggested in 1952 that the test should be applied to the Piltdown remains in order to see whether the cranium and mandible were of the same age. His first results showed that the fluorine content of the cranium and mandible was the same, and at the same time suggested that the remains were not as old as had always been believed. On the assumption that both mandible and cranium were genuine fossils, he was therefore ready to believe that they had been derived from the same individual. The recent exposure of a possible fraud was based on a second study[15] which was stimulated by a suggestion made to Dr Oakley by Dr J. S. Weiner, that the cranium might be genuine, but that the jaw-bone might have been 'planted'. Further and more sensitive tests were made, and their results suggested that the fluorine content of the cranial remains is greater than that of the mandible; that the reverse holds with respect to the nitrogen content; and that the iron oxide, to which the Piltdown fragments owe their colour, penetrates the cranial fragments deeply, whereas it is quite superficial on the mandible. It is now suggested, therefore, that the Piltdown mandible is a deliberate hoax, the idea being that someone had got hold of the jaw of a living ape – the species is undecided – broken it carefully, filed down the teeth, stained it, and 'planted' it. Dr Weiner, Dr Oakley and Professor Le Gros Clark, the authors of the memoir in which the story is told, write that 'the faking of the mandible and canine is so extraordinarily skilful, and the perpetration of the hoax appears to be so entirely unscrupulous and inexplicable, as to find no parallel in the history of palaeontological discovery.'

Be this as it may – what of the distinguished anatomists who were absolutely certain that whatever resemblances the jaw might have to an ape, the specimen was really human? What of the ability of these anatomists to diagnose human anatomical characteristics? What of the credulity of those students who have been only too ready to follow the authority of great names? How comes it that as late as 1950, the late Dr Robert Broom,[16] whose capacity to assess what is a human and what an ape-like characteristic in a bone or tooth is almost the mainstay of the contention that the South African australopithecine fossils are hominid as opposed to ape-like creatures, could have written that he had 'scarcely any doubt that the Piltdown mandible belongs to the same individual as the associated brain-case', and that the 'simian shelf in the lower jaw is probably not an indication of close affinity with the anthropoids, but a specialisation due to evolution parallel with that of the modern apes'? And is this chapter in our knowledge of the Piltdown jaw firmly closed? Mr Marston[17] did not agree that the mandible was definitely planted. Nor did he believe that the molar teeth had been filed down to indicate a particular pattern of wear; nor indeed, that they had been filed at all. He was also unprepared to believe that the faker went to the extent of deliberately filling the pulp cavity of the canine with radio-opaque material.

One implication of the story, as I see it, is this. Accepting that the jaw-bone was deliberately planted and faked, the faker must have known more about primate anatomy than all the highly distinguished anatomists he deluded. He knew enough to take them in not once but repeatedly. And presumably he knew which features to fake so as to confuse them most. If he knew as much as this, why did he not satisfy his ego more simply by becoming the foremost physical anthropologist of his day, or for the period in which he fooled so many distinguished anatomists? And if he did not, was his just an acute knowledge of human nature, and a cynical suspicion that whatever the anatomical knowledge of the authorities he fooled, they were likely to be misled by the publicity value of a missing link? What really was his motive? I shall return to this point later.

This is one implication of the story. But the most important moral to which it points – as I see it – is that the diagnostic value of marginal anatomical characters can be very easily over-emphasised. If this were not so, it is inconceivable that some of the things that were in fact said about the Piltdown fragments could have been said.

The tendency to over-value such presumed diagnostic characters emerges equally clearly in the story of another fossil known as *Hesperopithecus*, the name given to a Primate genus to which a fossil tooth was assigned in 1920. It is a much shorter story, for the dénouement came more swiftly than in the case of the Piltdown remains. Mr H. Fairfield Osborn,[18] a prominent American palaeontologist, who first described the specimen, gained the immediate impression that the tooth was that of a Primate – of an ape which could have been closely related to the origin of the human stock. Sir Arthur Smith Woodward challenged this view,[19] believing that the tooth was more like that of a bear, but Drs W.K. Gregory and M. Hellman,[20] two of Mr Osborn's colleagues, and who were regarded as among the world's leading authorities on the teeth of the Primates, endorsed his contention, stating that the tooth's 'nearest resemblances were with Pitecanthropus and with man rather than apes'. Drs Gregory and Hellman[21] then went into the matter again, and in general reaffirmed their previous statement, but with a slight difference, for while Dr Hellman was still inclined to the view that the closest resemblance of the tooth was with the fossil human type called *Pithecanthropus*, Dr Gregory altered his opinion and stated that 'the prevailing resemblances . . . are with the gorilla-chimpanzee group'. But the assignation of the specimen continued to be challenged, and a search was made for further material in the area where the original tooth was found. More teeth were discovered, and as their number and that of other remains multiplied, it became evident, as Dr Gregory[22] himself was the first to admit, that the original tooth was not that of any Primate, but that of a fossil peccary. And it remains the tooth of a fossil wild pig to this very day. The moral here is that the correction was not made on the basis of what can be called internal evidence, for Dr Gregory appears to have had no doubts about the primate affinities of the original tooth. His diagnosis was amended because the additional material was clearly peccary in origin.

Another example of mistaken interpretation concerns *Sinanthropus pekinensis*, Pekin Man. When this group of human fossils was discovered, Professor Davidson Black,[23] who was responsible for the first official descriptions of the remains, recognised that in some ways they resembled both Neanderthal Man and *Pithecanthropus erectus*, the species of low-browed man which Dubois had discovered in Java in 1891. He nevertheless took the line that all these hominid fossils differed 'from one another in points of size, proportions, and detail, to a degree amply sufficient to proclaim their generic distinction'. His view that they belonged to different genera of men was accepted by most students. Professor Elliot Smith then suggested that I should review the subject independently. This was in 1931. As a result, and with much diffidence, I came to the conclusion that there were discrepancies in the commonly accepted classification, and that either *Sinanthropus* and *Pithecanthropus* should be placed in the same genus, or alternatively, that the accepted classification of all extinct *Hominidae* should be revised.[24] At first little attention was paid to this dissenting view, which Elliot Smith himself accepted, but today – largely as a result of the advocacy of the late Dr Weidenreich, who took over the description of the Pekin fossils after the death of Professor Black – *Sinanthropus pekinensis* is no longer its old self, but *Pithecanthropus pekinensis*, and it is generally recognised that the Chinese and Javanese fossils should be regarded as variants of the same early human type.

Diagnosis, as I have said, means comparing a new thing with an existing array of 'models' that have been built up in one's experience. How such an array becomes constituted, it would be impossible to say. A particular book is recognised by its size or colour; by its position on a shelf; by the pattern of printing on its spine; or by a slight tear or stain. And two individuals might recognise the book by reference to very different diagnostic signs. The total *gestalt* by which an object becomes identified may, in fact, mean a constellation of innumerable items. But however one's reference models are developed, the first step in diagnosis is practically instantaneous, whether it be that one immediately recognises a similarity between the thing which is being diagnosed and one's models; or whether one suddenly imagines that the new object is something completely different. In the kind of anatomy which I have been describing, a student gets hold of a fossil bone, and he immediately says to himself: 'This is like something I already know – or this is something very different.' Where there is any possibility that the fossil may fall into the class of so-called missing links, the likelihood is that any small divergences will become exaggerated. They become essential diagnostic features. That, alas, is part of the price we still have to pay for the publicity, and publicity-value, which attaches to the term 'missing link'. The fundamental difficulty – and here I repeat what I have written more than once – is that the descriptions of possible human or hominoid fossils that have been provided by their discoverers have almost always been so turned as to indicate that the remains in question have some special place or significance in the line of direct human descent, as opposed to that of the family of apes. Before the 'exposure' of the fake about the Piltdown remains, I wrote[25]:

It is so unlikely that all Primate fossils could enjoy this distinction that, in the circumstances, an outside observer might well imagine that an enterprising anatomist would find little difficulty in substantiating a claim that an artificially fossilised skeletal fragment of any one of the living great apes had a greater relevance to the story of Man's evolution than to that of the skeleton of which it was a part.

Now that the Piltdown exposure has occurred, it is clear that I did not exaggerate.

Dr G.M. Morant[26] long ago pointed out that the eye often emphasises a cranial divergence 'which tested numerically is found to have no mark of racial differentiation at all.' Dr Morant was concerned to show that the Chancelade skull, a fossil human skull of no great age – relatively speaking – could not be differentiated in any measurable character from the modern Eskimo.

Sir Arthur Keith[27] refused to accept this view, or the biometric methods which led to it.

> Anatomists like Le Gros Clark and myself [he wrote] applying the ancient methods employed by zoologists in the recognition of species and varieties, have come to a positive verdict. We are guided by anatomical characters. We can assess their value for purposes of race identification by the unaided eye. For example, if we are asked to determine whether a given skull is that of a New World or of an Old World monkey, we first examine the teeth, the orbit, and the ear, and therein find certain marks which guide us to the racial identity of the skull. Calipers could not help us. It is so with the identification of any given human skull. Certain marks determine our verdict.

And the particular 'mark' which determined Sir Arthur Keith's view in the instance which occasioned this expression of opinion was the fact that the nasal bones of the Chancelade skull, as judged by a photograph before they were broken off, were more prominent than is usual in an Eskimo skull. Alas, this mark belongs to the same family as those which also determined his view that the Piltdown jaw-bone and skull belonged to the same individual.

But even so, there is, as Sir Arthur's remark implies, both art and science in anatomical diagnosis. The moral is that when one is diagnosing, too much art tempered with too little science can sometimes be highly dangerous. This applies not only in the field which I have been discussing, but also in that of the Fine Arts, where corresponding problems of diagnosis often arise. Here, too, there have been numerous hoaxes, and many books have been written on the subject, both in order to provide a warning for unwary collectors, and as exercises in human psychology. The motives of the faker appear to be many – honest emulation of something admired; the blind pursuit of an accepted style; and, as in the case of Van Meegeren, whose Vermeer's and De Hoogh's were remarkable contributions to the world of faked art, unsatisfied ambition and the desire to score off unsympathetic critics. But all these motives are secondary to the desire for profit, even if the better part of the profit has often failed to reach the author of the fake.

Where in all this does the Piltdown faker fit? – here, of course, we follow authority in accepting the diagnosis of a deliberate fake. He could hardly have done what he did for financial profit. Was it just a wish to expose what he held to be pompous authority? Was it a desire to discredit people who believed in evolution? But whatever the motive, the game misfired because – let us admit it – anatomists were in fact deluding themselves about their capacity to diagnose marginal human and ape-like characters in bones and teeth.

How are we to ensure that we are not fooled again? There can, in fact, be no final assurance. But this can be usefully said: each new fossil specimen is a representative of a population of unknown size, and each specimen is defined by an arbitrary number of characters. The specific terms by which they are designated are, however, in a sense abstractions, and the different constellations of characters which we use to designate different species may overlap to varying extents. When an anatomist sets out to 'diagnose' a new fossil, what he should, in fact, be trying to say is – 'these are the characters by which I define this specimen; this is the way constellations of similar characters vary between overlapping species of an ape – living or fossil – that have already been defined; and in my view this new specimen is closer to this than that constellation of corresponding related characters.' The essence of the problem is that each species, fossil or living, is a highly varying entity, and that the entities overlap. The new specimen would be something which fitted somewhere into a three-dimensional succession of creatures, of which time would be one of the dimensions. But where exactly it fitted, would depend – again judging by past experience – partly on guesswork, and partly on some preconceived conception of the course of hominid evolution.

Those anatomists who believe that the eye can recognise critical differences in marginal cases have been proved wrong so often that the immediate diagnosis which the unaided eye provides should always be regarded as something suspect, and merely as a working hypothesis which requires critical test. The comparative anatomy of fossil Primates is a study of size and shape, and to a large extent both are measurable. Measurable quantities can in turn be compared by various statistical techniques, and especially by methods of multivariate analysis. These can help one to check impressions of similarity or dissimilarity, and by so doing they provide some leavening of science to the art of diagnosis in this particular field of study. The only additional way in which serious mistakes in the assessment of the relationship of fossil Primates are likely to be avoided, so far as I can see, is by exorcising any tendency to assurance in these matters. And by remembering that all evolutionary interpretations of the significance of similarities and dissimilarities between fossil bones are conditioned not only by imperfections in our anatomical knowledge – in our capacity to diagnose correctly – but also by the fact, to which I have already referred, that the evolutionary inferences we base on structural comparisons are in the end only speculations.

7
African Cousins

The first Australopithecine fossil skull came to light when I was a pre-medical student in South Africa. I well remember the excitement the discovery caused. The newspapers were full of it, and I still have a folder of contemporary cuttings in which the specimen was described and the importance of South Africa extolled as the cradle of man. In the small world in which I lived it was as though a South African had miraculously landed on the Moon. At the time I had already, almost without realising it, embarked on a career as a scientist, and was making a study of the changes which take place during growth in the skull of the baboon, a process which transforms the small gentle face of a young creature into the long-snouted fierce face of the adult animal. I had also begun a more general anatomical study of the whole animal, and out of interest had accepted a suggestion of Dr Haughton, then the senior palaeontologist and geologist in the Museum in Cape Town, to 'develop' from their limestone matrix fossil baboon skulls, some of which, if I remember correctly, were in a near-perfect state of preservation, and which did not seem to me to be significantly different from the specimens of existing baboons I had been studying.

In those days there were only two Chairs of Anatomy in South Africa, a recently created one in Witwatersrand to which Professor Raymond Dart had just been appointed, and a somewhat older one in Cape Town, which was then occupied by Professor M.R. Drennan, under whom I had begun my anatomical studies. Towards the end of 1925, Professor Dart was in Cape Town as an 'external examiner' and he took the opportunity of discussing his 'find' with Professor Drennan. I do not remember being asked to take part in their talks, but I still recall my astonishment when, as I was sitting at my bench chipping bits of limestone from a fossil baboon skull, I was shown the skull of a young gorilla – at the time one of at most two or three skulls of young apes available for study in Cape Town – and asked my opinion as to whether it was the skull of a chimpanzee or gorilla. It seemed remarkable to me that while the pundits had no difficulty in diagnosing that the ape-like young *Australopithecus* was a unique creature, and totally different from the family of existing apes, they could be uncertain whether a young skull was that of a gorilla or a chimpanzee. At the time, I knew, of course, that Professor Drennan, while interested in the comparison of the skulls of different human types, had never – at any rate not until then – studied subhuman primate skeletal material. Professor Dart's work had also not yet carried him into that field of research. From that day to this I have been interested in the claims that have been made about the original *Australopithecus*, and about the related fossils which have followed it into the light, in particular those whose more recent discovery in East Africa we owe to the Leakeys, who have for so long and so assiduously explored the fossil fields of Tanzania.

Over the years my interest has been less in the merits of the claim that the creature which *Australopithecus* represented (or creatures, for several genera and species were soon defined) was more man than ape, than in the anatomical statements on which it was based, and which with the help of colleagues in my former Department in the University of Birmingham I proceeded to test in a series of comparative anatomical studies. This work still goes on actively, and several reports of what we have found have now been published. But such is the strength of fashion that I do not believe that our observations, which have frequently failed to confirm what has been claimed anatomically, have yet succeeded in denting a single one of the generalisations that have been made over the last thirty years about the Australopithecines. Once Dr Robert Broom,[1] one of the group of wise men who had never doubted 'that the Piltdown mandible belongs to the same individual as the associated brain-case', had endorsed with his authoritative voice the original assertions of Professor Raymond Dart,[2] and as soon as Professor Sir Wilfred Le Gros Clark[3] added his support to their views (at the start he was a 'disbeliever' or at least an agnostic), a host of lesser known anatomists and anthropologists fell into line, and the Australopithecines automatically became members of the same family, the Hominidae, as ourselves, and not of the Pongidae, in which the living apes are classified. As Le Gros Clark[4] sums up the situation:

'It is now generally agreed that *Australopithecus* is properly to be classed as a genus of the Hominidae, for although the size of the brain had not advanced very much beyond the maximum so far recorded for anthropoid apes, the morphological details of the dentition, and the structural adaptations in the pelvis and other parts of the skeleton for an erect posture and gait, make it clear that the genus had already advanced a considerable distance along the evolutionary trends distinctive of the Hominidae (and quite opposite to the trends which were followed by the anthropoid ape family).'

More than this – not only have the ape-brained Australopithecines, in accordance with present convention, become members of the human family; it is also claimed that they were users of tools and that they possessed a rich culture of bone and other implements (e.g. Dart[5]). It is all this that is 'generally agreed'. Perhaps it would be more correct to say that it is all this which has become part of current dogma. But I myself remain totally unpersuaded. Almost always when I have tried to check the anatomical claims on which the status of *Australopithecus* is based, I have ended in failure. I propose telling only part of the story here – partly because most of it is rather technical, and some not a little tedious.

Let me begin with the Australopithecine brain-case, which from many a published statement one would imagine implied a bigger brain than those of the living apes we know (e.g. in the language of Le Gros Clark[4] the brain-case had 'not advanced very much beyond', i.e. if words mean what they say, it had advanced at least a little bit beyond, that of living apes). If there is any evidence for this belief it has certainly never been published. The volume of the brain-case (i.e. 'endocranial volume') of the Australopithecines in those specimens where it can be ascertained with any degree of assurance (which is the only indication we have of the size of brain of these fossil creatures) is comfortably within the range found in extant great apes.[6-7] All the values that have been made available fall easily into the range for gorillas. Presumably because they would have liked the facts to have been different, some physical anthropologists and anatomists (e.g. Le Gros Clark[4]) have therefore argued that the weight of the brain relative to that of the body may have been greater in the Australopithecines than in extant apes. This proposition is supposedly put forward to imply that whatever the absolute weight of their brains, the fossil creatures had enjoyed a higher 'cerebral status' than do the apes. So far as I can see, this argument has no significance at all. The brain/body weight ratio varies enormously in the Primates, and what is more, is far higher in some monkeys than it is in man.[8] Furthermore, the ratio is very much higher in immature apes, monkeys and children than in adults. No one would suggest that this implies that a process of cerebral degradation occurs in apes and men as they grow to maturity. The short answer is that we know all but nothing about the significance of brain/body weight ratios, and that the only positive fact we have about the australopithecine brain is that it was no bigger than the brain of a gorilla.*

The claims that are made about the human character of the australopithecine face and jaws are no more convincing than those made about the size of its brain. The australopithecine skull is in fact so overwhelmingly simian as opposed to human (figure 5) that the contrary proposition could be equated to an assertion that black is white. So in deciding whether *Australopithecus* was more man than ape, we have to look to details, and particularly to focus on those features which are indicative – or held to be indicative – of the way the head was carried on the trunk. Was *Australopithecus* a large-jawed animal? Did it have temporal muscles, the muscle of mastication which covers the side of the skull between the eyes and ears, and which is attached below to the jaw bone, of the relative size found in the great apes, or in this respect was he like man? Was its skull of the heavy simian type, so that, as in the living apes, it had to be supported on the vertebral column by a powerful neck (nuchal) musculature? And relative to its long axis, how was the skull balanced on the vertebral column? Can we relate these cranial features to other skeletal characters which might give some indication of the posture of the Australopithecines? In short, did they carry themselves like apes or like men?

The claim that the Australopithecines carried themselves like men was originally made on the basis of the presumed forward position of the *foramen magnum* (the big aperture in the base of the skull through which the brain continues into the spinal cord in the

---

* A recent paper by Holloway[9] shows that even the previously published figures for the size of the Australopithecine brain, on which the above comment is based, 'were highly overestimated'.

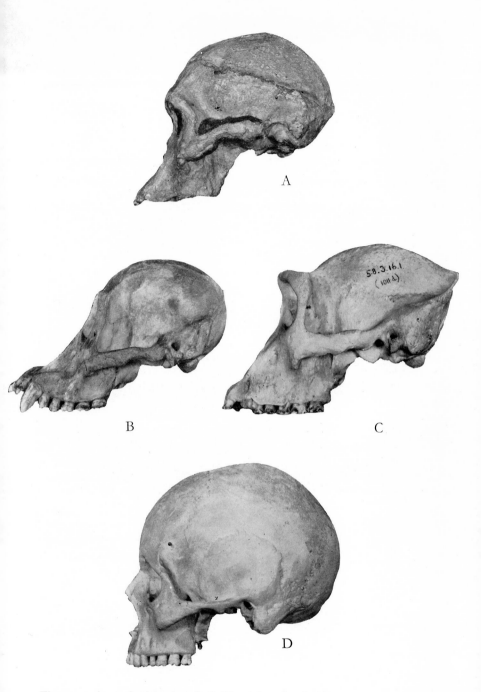

Figure 5. Australopithecine skull ('Sterkfontein 5') (A) compared with skulls of modern man (D) and the great apes, (orang-utan (B), and gorilla (C)) all to same scale. (p. 97)

ertebral column) in the first australopithecine skull that was ever discovered – the Taungs skull. In creatures which walk on all fours, the foramen is near the hinder end, and in man about the middle of the long axis of the skull.

As long ago as 1925 we were told that relative to the long axis of the skull, the foramen was much further forward than in apes, and closer to the position one finds in man. The point was later elaborated by Le Gros Clark[10] by reference to three indices, which he regarded as correlated, and which described first, the relative height to which the area of attachment of the nuchal muscles, which support the head on the spine, extended up the back of the skull ('nuchal area height index'); second, the height of the brain-case above the eyebrow ridges ('supraorbital height index'); and, third, the position, in relation to the long axis of the skull, of the occipital condyles, the two processes which lie at either side of the foramen magnum, and by which the skull articulates with the first of the neck vertebrae ('condylar position index'). These three 'indices' are shown in figure 6. This study suggested to Le Gros Clark that the numerical value of each of these indices in the one australopithecine skull in which they could be estimated with any assurance, was human and not simian, the comparison being made with figures derived from the study of about ninety skulls of adult chimpanzees, gorillas and orang-utans. But no values for the three indices in human skulls were given in the report of his enquiry.

In a study[11] of a far more extensive series of specimens than Le Gros Clark had measured, which was carried out in my own laboratory, we confirmed Le Gros Clark's conclusions about his 'nuchal-area height' and 'supraorbital height' indices. On the other hand, we found that the condylar position index in the australopithecine skull was very much closer to the ranges we found for apes than in three human types we also studied. This seemed to us to dispose of the claim that the australopithecine skull was balanced as in a human as opposed to an ape skeleton.

But in believing this we were more than a little optimistic. There are references in the literature to our agreement with Le Gros Clark's statements about the first two of his indices (e.g. Robinson[12]), but nothing is ever said about our discordant findings with respect to the position of the occipital condyles. We then decided to study the changes which occur after birth

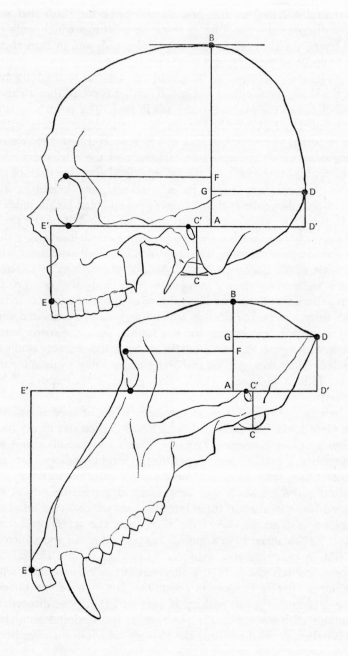

in the relative position of the foramen magnum in men and apes, for by this time four australopithecine specimens had become available – two adult and two immature – all of which provided a useful indication of the position of the foramen relative to the front and back of the skull. We found that while the general pattern of growth change in its position was the same in man as in apes, the extent of the change was less in man, this finding apparently correlating with the fact that after the eruption of the milk teeth, the face grows relatively less in relation to the brain case in man than it does in apes. At the same time we found that the values of the index in all four australopithecine skulls fell within the range for apes and well outside that for the human skull. The fossil sample was clearly too small to provide any precise indication of the age changes which occur in the position of the foramen magnum, but it was clear enough that during the period of years in which the permanent teeth erupt, the face of these extinct creatures grew more in accordance with the pattern that applies to existing apes than to man.

When he introduced his three cranial indices, Le Gros Clark[10] held that they were related to 'a common factor – the poise of the head in relation to the vertebral column . . .'. 'Taken in

---

Figure 6. Cranial indices in human compared with baboon skull:
Baseline ('Frankfurt horizontal') passes through lower margin of socket of eye (E′) and upper margin of earhole (C′)
A = point on baseline where line projected at right angles hits B
B = top of vault of skull
C = lower margin of occipital condyle
D = level of hindmost point of skull
E = front of upper jaw
F = level of eyebrow ridge

$$\text{Nuchal area height index} = \frac{100 \text{ AG}}{\text{AB}}$$

$$\text{Supraorbital height index} = \frac{100 \text{ BF}}{\text{AB}}$$

$$\text{Condylar position index} = \frac{100 \text{ C}' \text{ D}'}{\text{C}'\text{E}'}$$

combination,' he wrote, 'they appear definitely to place the australopithecine skull outside the limits of variation of the large anthropoid apes and to indicate a rather remarkable approximation to the hominid skull'. In his view they were measurable features which 'evidently related to erect bipedalism', i.e. to an upright gait.

To this conclusion our own findings clearly say 'no'. First, they do not reveal any high degree of correlation of the three indices. And second, and more important, it is difficult to see how the numerical value of the 'condylar position' index gives much of an indication of the way the skull is balanced in apes. Indeed, in spite of the very considerable age differences which occur in the value of the index in apes, there are no clearcut, or indeed obvious, differences in the way young and old apes carry their heads on their bodies.[13]

The only other worker of whom I know who has taken up the point about the relative position of the occipital condyles is Biegert.[14] On the basis of an extensive study of a wide range of Primate genera, he also concluded that the position of the foramen magnum is independent of the nature of a Primate's posture and locomotion.

While these findings about the position of the foramen magnum have, to the best of my knowledge, not been controverted, equally they have not made any impact on the conventional story that is told about the Australopithecines. Some related observations of ours did, however, stimulate attention.

There are at least three specimens of australopithecine skulls (*Paranthropus*) which possess a well-marked 'sagittal' crest in the mid-line on top of the skull. Such a bony crest, which is formed by the fusion in the midline of the two temporal lines which mark the upper limit of origin of the temporal muscles from the two sides of the skull, is never found in human beings, but occurs in the great apes (figure 7) and in many species of monkey, as well as in a host of other long-snouted mammals – for example dogs. When present, it is almost inevitably associated with flattening of the lowest part of the back of the skull. The flattened area is called the nuchal plane. This is capped above by a horizontal bony ridge called the nuchal crest (figure 8). A nuchal plane and crest are indicative of the presence of a relatively powerful set of neck muscles, which in a four-legged creature, or an ape with a heavy snouted face, which shambles along with its knuckles on the

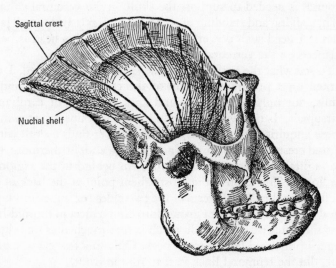

Figure 7. The direction of pull of the temporal muscle in the adult male gorilla

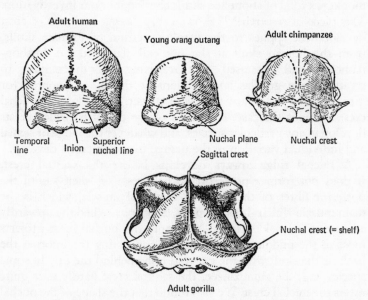

Figure 8. The formation of the sagittal and occipital crests

ground, is needed to support the skull on the vertebral column. Man, walking and standing upright and with relatively small jaws, does not need such powerful neck muscles, as his head is better balanced on the vertebral column.

To see what the australopithecine sagittal crest implied, I embarked on a preliminary study of the crest in several hundred skulls, not only of monkeys and apes, but also of carnivores, marsupials, bats, insectivores and other groups of mammals. These enquiries showed that one hardly ever finds a skull with a sagittal crest if a nuchal crest is not present, and, furthermore, that the sagittal crest usually begins to form behind in the region of the 'inion'. The inion is the most salient point at the back of the skull where the nuchal crests of the two sides (or 'superior nuchal lines' when these have not grown into crests) meet in the mid-line. It is the point on one's skull which is first touched as one slips a finger up the mid-line of one's neck. Only in a few cases, e.g. in bats, did the temporal lines start to fuse in front.

I then embarked upon a more detailed study of the development of the crests in great apes, in the gibbon, and in certain species of monkey, a total of about 800 skulls coming into our investigation. This piece of research[15-16] showed that the same process of crest development applies to the whole spectrum of Primate skulls, from the human skull at the one end, flat-faced (i.e. 'orthognathous') and possessed of a relatively smooth cranium, to creatures like gorillas and baboons at the other, snouted (or 'prognathous') and furnished with powerful sagittal and nuchal crests. This is the case, regardless of the extent to which crests develop in any particular species, and whatever the range of sexual and individual variation in the degree to which crests develop.

A nuchal ridge always develops before the sagittal crest. It does not form a powerful nuchal crest (or 'shelf') until the posterior fibres of the growing temporal muscle, which is the main muscle which shuts the jaws, have approached the upwardly advancing nuchal muscles. As a rule, the nuchal crest projects most in the middle third of the arc connecting the inion at the back of the skull with the mastoid bone behind the ear. In some species, e.g. the chimpanzee, the sagittal crest hardly ever quite meets the nuchal crest. We also found that the shape of the nuchal plane varies between and within species. In some it is flat, in others convex.

The conclusion we drew, therefore, was that unless the Australopithecines were the one exception to a process of cranial growth common to all known Primates, it followed that the existence of a well-defined sagittal crest in certain of the fossil specimens presupposed that these same skulls had been furnished with a powerful nuchal crest – a region of the skull which unfortunately was either deficient or missing in the fossil specimens. If, on the other hand, it was going to be argued that the Australopithecines had been an exception, it would follow that the bony arrangements which fitted the lower jaw to the skull (their 'temporomandibular apparatus') did not follow the pattern characteristic of existing Primates, including man. Since this seemed an almost ridiculous proposition, we concluded that the existence of sagittal crests in the Australopithecines implied that they had carried their heads like apes and not like man.

This conclusion was far from welcome to the protagonists of the hominid status of the Australopithecines, and was quickly challenged. For example, Robinson[17] immediately asserted that whatever our findings and conclusion, a nuchal crest had for all practical purposes been lacking in the australopithecine fossils which had a sagittal crest (and in which the posterior part of the latter had been broken away). He quickly corrected himself with a further statement[18] to the effect that sufficient of the hinder part of the skull was in fact present in two specimens to show that the animals had been furnished with a nuchal crest, but that this was drawn out into a ridge which reached a maximum height of only 6 mm. in one specimen, and 3 mm. in a second. Since these figures were smaller than what he thought occurred in the apes, they presumably made our findings more acceptable.

But not for long. The next step in the tale was an argument that the nuchal crests which were present in the australopithecine fossils had not been formed as in other Primates through the opposing pull of the posterior fibres of the temporal muscles on the one hand and the upwardly growing neck muscles (nuchal musculature) on the other. In the analysis leading to his conclusion, Robinson[12] differentiated what he called a 'simple nuchal crest', caused, it was held, by the pull of a single muscle, from a 'compound crest' which develops when two muscle masses approach each other sufficiently closely to meet, even if still separated by a bony up-growth. A compound crest comes about

D

85

from the fusion of two simple crests. 'Each muscle involved in effect produces a simple crest, but as they are applied to each other, not two but only one crest results.' Robinson's argument was that because the superior nuchal line and the inferior temporal line seemed to be separated on the fossil specimens, the nuchal crest found in these creatures could not have been formed in the same way as the corresponding crests in apes and monkeys. A crest of the kind he had managed to define in the fossils sometimes occurred, so he claimed, in man. He therefore concluded that 'the distinction between the known prehominines (i.e. Australopithecines) and the known pongids (i.e. apes) is "absolute" in this respect and can be seen on any two skulls, whereas that between prehominines and hominines is statistical and depends on having representative samples of each group.'

This attempted separation of simple and compound nuchal crests has no more anatomical significance than there is scientific meaning in the differentiation of absolute as opposed to statistical differences in the cranial characters of the Hominoidea.

The plain fact is that it is anatomically inconceivable that the posterior fibres of the *temporalis* muscle had not grown backwards during the process of skull development in the Australopithecine skull, and so exerted stresses in the cranial bones in a direction in general opposed to those generated by the nuchal and associated musculature. This process of growth occurs not only in monkeys and apes, but also in man, as can be seen in any careful dissection which displays the relationship of the posterior fibres of the temporalis muscle and its covering sheath of fibrous tissue ('temporal fascia') on the one hand, to the insertion, on to the superior nuchal line, of the neck muscles called the sternocleido-mastoid, *splenius capitis* and *trapezius* on the other. What is more, the picture which Robinson provides of the temporal line and the nuchal line in the skull (S.K. 46) on which he based most of his argument, is no different in kind from what one can see in the occasional specimen of extant apes.

When I first drew attention to what seemed to me to be the most likely conclusion that should be drawn from the occurrence of sagittal crests in the Australopithecines, I suggested[15] that if the creature had indeed been an exception to a general growth process which occurs in all Primates, including man, it would follow that its temporal muscle and the movements of its jaws would also have been exceptional. Since nothing should ever be regarded as impossible, I set about testing this hypothesis by examining the nature of the 'mandibular apparatus' in man, apes and Australopithecines, with particular reference to statements that the type of wear shown on the premolar and molar teeth of the fossils followed the human pattern, as opposed to what was presumed to occur in the great apes (cf. Le Gros Clark[10]; Robinson[19]). The contentions of these workers were that the Australopithecines, like man, were able to grind their teeth by rotatory movements of the jaw, whereas such movements were restricted in apes and monkeys, as in carnivores, because of a presumed interlocking of the large canines when the jaws were in apposition, which made it impossible to do more than move the jaws up and down.

These statements appeared to be based only upon a theoretical assessment of the movements of the mandible in dried skulls. In order to get some real information, we set about recording the order of appearance of the degree of wear on all teeth of about 500 gorilla, chimpanzee and human skulls. Our observations showed that the order in which the facets of wear on the cusps of the teeth appear is more or less constant, and that there is practically no difference in the order of coalescence of the facets of dental wear in apes and man, and particularly in the wear of the molar and premolar teeth. If, therefore, the pattern of wear in man is due to his ability to grind his molar and premolar teeth, it followed that the ape must be able to do the same – a conclusion contrary to what Le Gros Clark and Robinson had stated, but a simple fact which anyone can confirm by visiting a zoo. The possession of large canines certainly does not preclude an ape from moving his mandible sideways.

Once again an answer consistent with what we had found before had come up. It seemed impossible to us not to conclude that the Australopithecines possessed temporal muscles built on the same plan as those of other Primates, and no reason at all to suppose that the posterior horizontal component of the muscle had developed according to a pattern different from what one finds in Primates in general. But, again, our observations about the wear of teeth failed to make any impact on the conventional story about the poise of the head and the size of the jaws. The general belief continues to be that the Australopithecines did not possess a powerful nuchal musculature; and the presence of sagittal crests is dismissed as of no consequence.

I have been no more successful in my efforts to contribute to what is known about the limb and pelvic bones of the Australopithecines, and particularly in my efforts to check the anatomical observations on which is based the claim that the creatures walked and ran upright. I do not propose going into the detail of the many studies which I and my research colleagues embarked upon to this end. Our published results have failed more often than not to confirm the numerous *ex cathedra* statements that have been made about the anatomical characteristics of the australopithecine pelvis as compared with the corresponding one of the great apes and man.

The pelvis is made up of two large innominate bones and a smaller triangular bone called the *sacrum* (figure 9). The innominates form its sides and meet in front at what is called the *symphysis pubis*. The triangular *sacrum* fills in the pelvis behind, and the two innominate bones articulate with its sides. The innominate

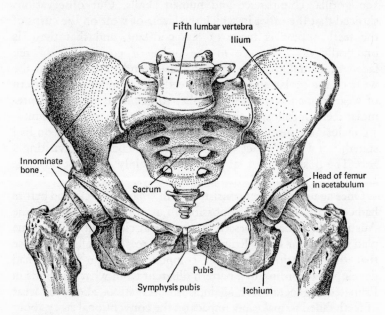

Figure 9. Human pelvis

itself is made up of three bones, the *ilium*, the *ischium* and the *pubis*, which are distinct in foetal life and in young children. The three meet in a circular cavity called the *acetabulum*, which is the socket for the head of the femur. Most of the ilium forms the upper flared part of the innominate bone, constituting what is called the false pelvis. The pubis and ischium are much smaller bones. The pubis is in front of the ischium, and both lie below the ilium, forming with the sacrum what is called the true pelvis. In our first studies of the pelvis,[15] we had at our disposal a cast of the most complete australopithecine innominate bone that was available. This was kindly given to us by Dr J.T. Robinson, who also provided a series of measurements of the actual specimen which he took between points we had defined as a check on the accuracy of the cast. Our comparative material consisted of thirty foetal and new-born human innominate bones, forty-three adult human bones, ninety-four innominate bones of the great apes, and a varying number of innominate bones of monkeys and baboons.

From the start our results did not accord with conclusions that had been based on observations made with what Keith had called 'the unaided eye'. It turned out that the angle of twist between the main plane of the ilium and the ischio-pubic part of the inno-minate in the australopithecine cast corresponded to that in the four-footed macaque or cercopitheque monkeys and baboons, and was well outside the range for apes and adult men, although close to the limits for a new-born baby. It also transpired that the angle of twist in man was usually less than in apes, in spite of the fact that in man the main muscle of the buttock, the *gluteus maximus*, is seemingly disposed more to the back than to the side, as it is in apes (which have wide but not projecting buttocks). From this and other observations it seemed difficult not to con-clude, therefore, that the gluteus maximus in the Australo-pithecines was a muscle which pulled the thigh sideways at the hip joint (i.e. 'abducted' the thigh), as it presumably does in monkeys and apes, rather than being the powerful extensor of the thigh on the trunk, as it is presumed to be in man, thus helping in the maintenance of the erect attitude.

These findings raised still more doubts in my mind about the claim that the Australopithecines were bipeds, like man, and a new study was, therefore, launched in my old Department in

Birmingham, in which we are aiming to show how nine features in the innominate bone vary between different groups of Primates. The particular characteristics we are studying were selected on the basis of an appraisal of the mechanics of the pelvis in quadrupedal Primates, that is to say animals like baboons, which move on all fours, in Primates which swing by their arms in the trees, for example gibbons, and in man with his upright gait. The characters we studied reflected the way the innominate bone becomes modified for these different types of locomotion. So far, we have accumulated data for 350 individuals belonging to twenty-eight genera of monkeys and apes. We have also collected corresponding data for thirteen different genera of the more primitive suborder of Primates (the Prosimii) which includes creatures like the lemurs (see Appendix).

One of the features we have studied is a further measure, more direct than the one we used in our first study, of the extent to which the iliac blade faces either backwards ('dorsally') or sideways ('laterally'). On this occasion, we focussed our attention on the areas of attachment of the *gluteus medius* and *gluteus minimus* muscles, two smaller muscles which lie deep to the gluteus maximus, and which in monkeys and apes, and depending on its position at the time, extend (straighten) or medially rotate (twist inwards) the thigh at the hip-joint. In man, they abduct it (that is to say pull the thigh sideways from the trunk; they are also believed to rotate it inwards a little). Our findings leave little doubt that, in this respect, *Australopithecus* resembles not *Homo sapiens* but the living monkeys and apes. In the Australopithecines the muscles could hardly have abducted the thigh and helped keep the pelvis in balance, which is a necessary condition for the human type of walking. This conclusion seems inescapable in spite of the fact, as defined by yet another of our indices, that the lateral expansion of the hip bone ('the 'iliac blade') of *Australopithecus*, which is so frequently featured as one of its most conspicuously human characters, makes the front end of the crest of the hip bone ('the anterior superior iliac spine') lie somewhat more to the front than is usual in the subhuman Primates.

We have also examined such features as the position of the *acetabulum* in relation to the main axes of the innominate bone, i.e. its maximum width (or 'dorso-ventral' axis) and its maximum length (or 'cranio-caudal' axis), the degree of its separation from the sacro-iliac joint, and the relative position of the latter. These measures are related to the way the weight of the trunk is transmitted to the legs in the bipedal or quadrupedal positions. In some of this group of characters *Australopithecus* agrees with *Homo sapiens* and differs from monkeys and apes. In others it falls in a position intermediate between man and the subhuman Primates. Another dimension we have examined describes the length of the body of the ischium relative to the innominate as a whole. This measure is much greater in quadrupeds than it is in man. A longer ischium gives a good mechanical advantage to the hamstring muscles at the back of the thigh as they contribute to the 'power stroke' in locomotion. In this feature, *Australopithecus* is completely unlike man, and identical with monkeys and apes.

More recently we have been using an advanced form of multivariate analysis called 'canonical analysis', which the electronic computer makes possible, in the comparison of the dimensions of the corresponding bones of the fossils and living Primates.[20]

This study has shown that when the nine pelvic variates to which I have referred (p. 90) are examined in combination, man is clearly separated from the subhuman Primates. Within the latter, there is some measure of differentiation between prosimians, monkeys and apes. *Australopithecus* lies between man and the subhuman Primates, the closest members of the latter being the great apes. When the four variates relating to the relative position of the sacro-iliac and hip joints are combined, man is, once more, clearly separated from the subhuman Primates; but here *Australopithecus* lies much closer to *Homo sapiens* than to other living Primates. On the other hand, when the analysis is restricted to the five variates relating to the disposition of the abductors and extensors of the hip joint, there is, again, a clear differentiation between man and the subhuman Primates; *Australopithecus* is similar to monkeys and apes, contrasting with man. Similar results emerge when corresponding analyses are carried out including only the great apes, *Australopithecus* and man.

There are still many problems to be solved in this analysis, and I exclude neither the possibility that we may have failed to pick the best set of pelvic angles and indices which are appropriate for the purpose of differentiating those characters which set a quadrupedal apart from a bipedal pelvic bone, nor the chance that some of the differences which have emerged between the innominate bones of living Primates might in part be attributable to what is called allometric growth (i.e. differential growth of the parts of the bone during the course of development). Equally, although we can group our measures according to the various functional complexes which they seem to describe, we do not yet know to what extent they are interrelated, mechanically or statistically.

Comparative quantitative studies, first of the size and form of the related muscles, and second of the patterns of electrical response they produce when they contract ('electromyographic patterns') which they produce in different living genera of Primates, have also now been started. These, along with analyses using photostress and photoelastic techniques to define the stress distribution in the bones, will, we hope, show which bony features are likely to be of the greatest significance in relation to posture and locomotion.

A parallel study of the shoulder bones which has been taken nearer completion by a former research student of mine, C.E. Oxnard,[21] now working in America, has provided a more clear-cut result than has our study of the pelvis so far. As background he studied the shoulder-blades (*scapulae*) of forty-one different genera of monkeys and apes, on the basis of nine particular dimensions chosen after extensive anatomical studies of the shoulder muscles in relation to the movements which characterise locomotion in the creatures concerned. The canonical analysis was designed to indicate the degree of separation from each other of what constituted forty-one 'clouds of points' plotted in a nine dimensional space. It would clearly be impossible to attempt such an analysis without a modern computer. The results of the analysis correctly grouped those species with corresponding habits of locomotion, but also indicated man's unique position in being the only living Primate which never uses his arms as a normal aid in locomotion.

The human shoulder [to quote Oxnard] finds its nearest analogues among those of arboreal forms, and its simplest evolutionary pathway from that of the orangutan specifically. This does not suggest that the human shoulder evolved from that of an orangutan; the morphological, genetic, and biochemical data all point to the gorilla and chimpanzee as being genetically closest to man among living forms. But it does suggest that the presumed common ancestor of man and the African apes may well have been an animal that lived in trees and which used its shoulder in a manner reminiscent of that of the orangutan. Certainly it would seem, on this basis, unlikely that the human shoulder had ever passed through a stage relating to knuckle-walking functions such as are displayed in the terrestrial chimpanzee and gorilla.

Unfortunately there are no fossil remains of the australopithecine shoulder girdles in a sufficiently complete form to permit of their comprehensive analysis by the same methods. Three of the nine chosen dimensions are however known from fragments of a scapula and a clavicle, and a comparison is possible by assuming that in their missing dimensions the fossils resembled in turn each of the existing forms of Primate tested in the background study. This addendum to Oxnard's analysis showed that whatever the missing dimensions may have been in the fossil creature, the likelihood was that the latter resembled the orang utan far more than it did the terrestrial chimpanzee or gorilla. At the same time it was 'virtually impossible', to quote Oxnard's own words, for the australopithecine shoulder girdle to have been similar to that of man. Since publishing the results of this study he has shown that a different and new form of analysis of the data called 'neighbourhood limited classification', which is based on a mathematical concept totally distinct from that which underlies canonical analysis, leads to basically similar conclusions about the separation of different Primate groups in accordance with the way they use their shoulder girdles when moving.[22]

In the light of past experience I look forward with interest to seeing whether these newer and highly precise findings will in any way weaken the general acceptance of the pronouncements of Dart and his supporters that the Australopithecines were creatures which walked and ran upright, and coursed wild animals across the plains with the help of primitive weapons. For my own part, the anatomical basis for the claim that the Australopithecines walked and ran upright like man is so much more flimsy than the evidence which points to the conclusion that their gait was some variant of what one sees in subhuman Primates, that it remains unacceptable.

The fault for my failure over the years to impart any word of caution to the accepted dogma may well be mine. Even though the observations I and my colleagues have reported have not been refuted by scientific study, they could well be less important than

D*

we ourselves supposed. This is an obvious possibility. But I do not think that it is the main reason for our failure. Where I went wrong was in supposing that, in the field of anatomy I am talking about, facts such as we have been collecting could stem a tide of opinion based on *ex cathedra* statement. We were not the first to make this mistake. Professor Waterston made a similar error, as I pointed out earlier on, with respect to the Piltdown skull, and so too have others, about other fossils. The unscientific and doctrinaire character of the whole of this field of study is well epitomised in the observation of an enthusiastic supporter of the conventional australopithecine wisdom, who in a recent note supporting this school of thought writes:[23] 'Scientific discoveries and hypotheses must arise from some element of inspiration, and *their value is not diminished because they are unverifiable*' (italics mine). It would perhaps be unfair to suppose that all members of the school to which he belongs subscribe to this conception of scientific method, or if they do, that they would be so candid in declaring their faith.

Equally it would be a form of exaggeration to say that the present phase of the study of human evolution, as revealed by the fossil record, provides a model to be followed in scientific enquiries. The position will, I hope, one day change for the better since fashion cannot always override rational criticism. Given that they do not bow down to the voice and weight of outworn authority, I have every confidence that a younger school of anatomists, if they still find the problems interesting, will set about resolving them in ways which are more scientific and enduring than those that were pursued by my own generation and by those – including Keith – by whom we were taught. But I must confess to a lingering fear. So much glamour still attaches to the theme of the missing-link, and to man's relationships with the animal world, that it may always be difficult to exorcise from the comparative study of Primates, living and fossil, the kind of myths which the unaided eye is able to conjure out of a well of wishful thinking. Perhaps 'always' is too strong a word. Let me instead say it will continue to be difficult until the day dawns, not too far ahead, when no recruit to anatomy finds in the mathematical techniques of multivariate analysis a greater mystery than the myths he is able to create without them.

8
Convention and Controversy

I said earlier on p. 13 that the path to objective truth in science is rarely mapped by common consent, and then strewn with roses. What I have written in the preceding four chapters might make it seem that, far from being adorned with roses, it is always beset with pitfalls. Such an impression would however be wrong. What I have done is choose deliberately as illustrations of my main theme, not those of my own studies which have been marked by orderly agreement, but three fields of work in which controversy has always been brisk, and of which the first lent itself to precise answers, the second to no useful answer at all because the question had been incorrectly put, and the third to no answer, because while the question remains real enough, no unequivocal answer would ever be possible. But, having said this, I have to add that one always encounters obstacles when one searches for objective truth, and that the main one is always, as it has always been, the prevailing dogma. It is because of this that the health of science demands the continuous testing of any new doctrine which science itself may create. 'Sooner or later – insensibly, unconsciously – ' wrote Osler,[1] 'the iron yoke of conformity is upon our necks; and in our minds, as in our bodies, the force of habit becomes irresistible.' Irresistible, and one might add, also commanding.

William Harvey's first public demonstration of the circulation of the blood, in 1616, was not greeted as the fabulous discovery that it was, but, in his own words, was regarded as 'a crime' because he had 'dared to depart from the precepts and opinions of all anatomists . . .' '. . . I tremble lest I have mankind at large for my enemies,' he wrote, 'so much doth wont and custom, that has become as another nature, and doctrine once sown and that hath struck deep root and rested from antiquity, influence all men.'[1] Of course few discoveries have so colossal a transforming influence on the body of accepted wisdom as did William Harvey's;

and equally, life for dissenting scientists is far less dangerous today than it was in his time or in that of Galileo. But the dead hand of convention is always there, and has always to be guarded against.

And so too, as I hope I have succeeded in showing, is the confusion about what constitutes objective truth in the sciences. My main theme so far has been that understanding in the biological, as distinct from the physical sciences, as well as the nature of enquiry in some of these sciences, in practice swings between the opposite poles of objective and subjective truth. To illustrate this proposition I could have used examples other than the personal ones which I chose, and which I have spelt out in detail. Indeed I am sure that my own experience is in no sense unique, and that it merely reflects what is generally and implicitly appreciated, even though my broad proposition would not normally be acknowledged in some scientific circles. It is mere pretence that all scientific talk today partakes of the character of objective truth.

I am referring particularly to what can still be called the 'natural sciences'. Scientists know what they are, and know how they have been built up with the years. They also know how new 'sciences' are born. If it were ever to become the case that the 'occult sciences' became scientific, or that water-divining became a science, they would do so only because scientific methods of enquiry had made them so. Primitive man found his minerals by following outcrops of rock back into the earth, having first learned that some other material, a metal – gold, copper, or tin – for which he had found a use, could be extracted from the rock by smelting. He learned to recognise the rocks he wanted by particular characteristics which he could discern by eye. Today the geologist uses not only the eyes with which he is born, but also new eyes that have been furnished through the advances of science – magnetometers, Geiger counters, boring equipment and so on. He uses scientific methods of observation and analysis to build a corpus of knowledge which not only 'explains' the past and present, but also foretells part of the future. That is the only way a science can be created, the only way areas of human interest ever become transformed into bodies of knowledge consisting of propositions which have the dual characteristics of effective stability and predictive value.

The tidal wave of interest which is now carrying science along has made little difference to the nature of the individual research worker. Usually we still see him growing up in a university department where his first field of enquiry would have been greatly influenced by the work, however narrow or however wide its intellectual scope, that was going on around him. To some extent, he, therefore, begins as a victim of fashion, in the same way as did his teachers before him; and to an extent which will vary with his own powers, and particularly with his capacity for truly original thinking, he will continue as such, if he carries on as a research worker at all. A far-reaching advance in the laboratory in which he may be working, whether it happens to be in his own or in a related field of interest, may turn the direction of his enquiries. So, too, will some new major development in another laboratory.

He cannot predict when success will crown his efforts. A lot of his work will turn out to be plain hard slogging – but no less fascinating for that – whether he is researching in some esoteric branch of natural knowledge, or directing his energies to advancing some obviously utilitarian field of applied science. What the pure scientist basically wants and needs is the assurance that he will be allowed to give full rein to his curiosity without being harried, until the moment comes when he himself thinks his ideas have either flowered or run into the sands, and it is time to change direction, or give up research.

Whether a scientific discovery proves to be far-reaching or trivial, it is inevitably an act of creation. What matters to the scientist, as Koestler[2] so eloquently puts it, is 'the emergence of order out of disorder, of signal out of noise, of harmony out of dissonance, of a meaningful whole out of meaningless bits, of cosmos out of chaos'. Few can enjoy this kind of revelation – which indeed applies to any field of creative activity – or derive from it any sense of fulfilment, without trying to communicate it to others. This is so even though communication is not inevitably associated with acceptance. Something which is new is always opposed to something which is old; and often acceptance of the new is less dependent on either its intellectual force or its potential practical value than on the strength of the conventions and vested interest which sustains the old. At the same time, most of the new things which are discovered, the new explanations which are devised, paradoxically become the very ideas which a new revelation will sweep away tomorrow. The recognition of error, the admission of error, and the elimination of error are as much, therefore, a part of the process of science as is the controlled experiment.

This I believe to be easier in fields of biological study which approximate most closely to the physical sciences, and where the influence of personal idiosyncrasy and of prejudice, however powerfully it may operate at the start of an enquiry, inevitably becomes erased when understanding takes the shape of objective truth. Whatever the speculations, whatever the personal rivalries between the workers concerned, whatever the hunches, right or wrong, and whatever the way in which light dawned, the moment Crick and Watson published their picture of the molecular structure of DNA, we moved into a new era of objective truth in which the beliefs of the preceding era no longer counted. Unfortunately in some fields of enquiry, and, as I have shown, in some in which I have worked, the likelihood of objective truth ever emerging seems remote, and what we go on accepting as knowledge are arbitrary views coloured by the varying attitudes of different minds.

This, as I have suggested, is because of the complexity of the problems concerned in relation to the possibility of controlled enquiry, and because, strangely enough, it is often the most difficult problems which seem to translate themselves into the apparently simple questions, about which discussion can proceed unhampered by the rigid disciplines of experiment and statistical enquiry. In these burgeoning days of science, when each year sees thousands more researchers at work, it becomes vitally important that we understand what this means, and also when science ceases to be science. If scientists fail to do this, they should not be surprised if a general disillusion, which in these troubled days is already beginning to attach itself in the popular mind to the concept of the growth of scientific knowledge, spreads even more quickly than it is doing now.

Obviously much that appears in the name of science outside the biological fields I have been discussing is also pretty poor science, and sometimes misleading science. In a recent Presidential Address to the Royal Statistical Society, Dr Frank Yates,[3] whose contributions to his own subject provided techniques for the development of many other fields of science, reviewed the present state of statistical research and commented sadly on the way things are going. He tells us that it often happens that one statistician publishes a theoretical paper which is either irrelevant to statistical theory in general, or is based on unrealistic premises. This stimulates a second and then a third writer to publish further thoughts on the same lines. And this 'results in our statistical journals being cluttered up by vast amounts of rubbish which stimulate students to work on further investigations on the same lines'. These are strong words, and it is salutary to hear them stated with authority about any branch of science. But they certainly have a wider relevance.

For the more science becomes trivial in the sense Dr Yates was illustrating, and the more it is pursued outside the framework of objective truth, or is allowed to overlap that framework, the faster does the nature of the controversy which is inherent in the growth of any scientific knowledge change. With so much science in the air, areas of interest or discussion become treated as scientific whether or not they are subject to the real discipline of scientific method. We live in an age of more and more science, and also, alas, more pseudo-science. This is one of the unfortunate facts of our time. It, too, certainly does not help provide the best conditions for scientific progress. The public is led to believe that anything is science if it has numbers in it, or demands slide rules, or is carried out by people with a PhD; and equally that anyone who writes about what is believed to be a scientific matter is necessarily a scientist.

Certain areas of biological enquiry have an immediate impact on human welfare, and are now of critical importance because their outcome is much conditioned by the reciprocating attitudes of the researcher on the one hand, and of an anxious audience on the other. The business of organ transplantation in man is one such area. At the present moment it is so sensitive an area that almost all discussion is characterised by emotional overtones of one kind or another. These overtones do not aid the search for objective truth. The corruption of the scientist's understanding of his discoveries, due mainly to popular oversimplification, often becomes another factor which helps divert attention to the wrong issues, or imparts unnecessary emotional overtones to the right ones. For example, the unravelling of the structure of DNA showed the way to the breaking of the genetic code. But in spite of what we read in certain popular works, it has not provided us with a means of controlling, through what has been called chromosomal 'surgery', the genetic structure of our offspring – at any rate, not as yet. The popular conception of what constitutes space science is another such area where misleading ideas abound – but I shall not elaborate here on this point.

The kinds of issue which I have been discussing multiply and magnify the controversies which are inherent in the growth of science. But controversy in science serves no purpose except where it relates to the search for knowledge which potentially can be categorised as objective truth. Scientific controversy needs to be self-contained in the sense that it should be concerned only with differences of view about what constitutes the best kind of understanding of the facts at issue – in Popper's formulation it should be concerned with the search for the objective truth which accords most closely to the facts. As soon as scientific controversy starts spreading to matters which are extraneous to the problem in dispute, and to irrelevancies which become introduced either deliberately or fortuitously, the likelihood of it being resolved starts receding. In particular, when scientific enquiry steps out of its own ground and treads into the area of value and moral judgments, it starts to become something more than science, and something which then begins to partake of the controversial character of economics, or even of politics.

Tradition has it that economists can never agree among themselves when it comes to debate about economic policy, whereas scientists, as scientists, always tend to agree about methods of analysis and about the solutions to their problems. I have referred to Gunnar Myrdal's view of the difficulties which face the social scientist. Fritz Machlup[4] has given four other reasons for the particular difficulties which face the economist. First, economists when they tackle a problem are straightaway confronted by differences in semantics. The established rules of scientific method are there to help the scientist over that obstacle. Second, economists are apt to differ from each other in logical approach. Here again the scientist ought to be protected by the rules of the game. Third, economists are very prone to differ in their factual assumptions. Once more the advantage is to the scientist. And finally, economists differ because of differing value judgments associated with the aims of different courses of action – the particular point which Myrdal stresses. *

* A penetrating analysis of the difficulties which beset economic predictions is provided by de Jouvenal.[5]

There are some who are sceptical, but I live in the hope that these differences between the social and the exact sciences are merely a reflection of the fact that the latter are further advanced in their formal evolution than is, say, the subject of economics. There is probably no logical reason why, in time, economists should not be provided with the basic scientific framework and apparatus of working which will be able to impose the necessary discipline on subjective and wishful thoughts, as is now possible within the body of science.

But at the moment it remains true that it is only when we come to value judgments that in theory the scientist is exposed to the same blaze of difficulties as the 'social scientist', with the added disadvantage that because the scientist is always expected to agree with the body of scientific fact, it is also expected that there will be a single scientific point of view on matters which are external to the facts themselves.

It is in this respect that controversy in science differs from controversy in fields which are characterised by action. A scientist who specialises in the immunological problems which concern the transplantation of kidneys or hearts can give his view about the likely outcome of such operations. But when it comes to saying whether organ transplantation should be carried out, he treads into ground where the non-specialist also has a say, even if the latter's opinion is not fortified by more than a secondhand appreciation of what terms like 'immunological tolerance' mean. Some astronomers, again, might question whether the examination of stones from the moon's surface will tell us not only about the moon, but more, as is claimed, about the origin of the solar system of which our earth is part than we can deduce from the more intimate knowledge we already have of our own planet, reinforced by the information we have gained through indirect methods of astrophysical observation. While acclaiming the magnitude of the technological achievement of landing men on the moon and of returning them safely to earth, and the incredible courage of all space travellers, they could legitimately doubt whether the effort will result in any commensurate increase in basic scientific knowledge. But it is another matter when it comes to arguing whether manned space exploration should or should not be encouraged. Here they only have one vote among many.

The controversies which bedevil decisions about the application of scientific knowledge spread beyond the confines of science, and the rules which guide them, if they can be dignified by such a term, are totally different from the precise methods which should govern true scientific controversy. In short, science is one thing; but its application through technology rapidly slips into the field of politics. As I have insisted, the scientist has as much right to express his views about technological choice, and about its possible consequences, as has the next man. But the authority a scientist can command within the private world of science does not extend, as such, into the political world where decisions are taken about the application of the fruits of knowledge, and where decisions are taken about the extent to which public resources should be devoted to the promotion of basic science. In that world a different kind of authority prevails. There, and quite understandably, we move into a world in which subjective truth also has a major part to play.

PART II

PUBLIC SCIENCE

9
Science and Politics

When a revered public figure dies, a respectable interval usually passes before his house is marked by a plaque or, as in France, before a street is graced by his name. So it is with the stages of history. Regardless of the vast expansion of education and know-ledge in the past few decades, no one yet calls the second half of our century 'The New Age of Enlightenment'; nor, in spite of the apparent riches it has garnered, is it hailed as a new species of Golden Age. But however it may be viewed by future generations, we ourselves can see it only as a more tumultuous era than any man has known before – an age of atom bombs and of population explosion; of space exploration and of tormented nationalism; of immense new wealth and of widespread hunger. We live in a period of uncontrolled and accelerating change, an age in which technology has raced ahead, and in which hallowed social values have tumbled. Economic aid to underdeveloped countries is out-stripped by military aid. Inadequate famine relief and fabulously expensive space rocketry march together. The most powerful state which the world has ever known, equipped with all the arms which modern technology can provide, finds itself pitted in seem-ingly endless conflict against a nonindustrialised opponent whose poverty in weapons is made up by a determination not to yield. We live in an age of paradox: an age in which the politician – to paraphrase a recent British prime minister – has been straining after the scientist and technologist, and in which the latter have been trying to understand the social consequences of the innova-tions to which their work has led. The world is clearly living through a period in which the aims of politics and the outcome of scientific endeavour sometimes appear to clash.

The great social changes of our times derive from the spread of education, from the proliferation of old and new media of com-munication, and from a background of political philosophy which itself is constantly transmuted as economic conditions alter. It is to factors such as these that we look when we seek the origin of the forces that have led, for example, to the end of colonialism and to the rapid multiplication of independent sovereign states over the past two decades, and to the world-wide diffusion of European concepts of social justice. But when we look at the major social problems of the post-war years, we can see that they have come about less as a result of clear-cut political decision than automatically from the uncoordinated application of scientific knowledge. By multiplying the ends of production and by transforming the processes of production, science, using the term in its broadest sense, has transformed the politics of our times.

Many believe that we would be better able to control the speed and the directions of the growth of science if we knew more about the way it grows, and about the ways it affects social and economic affairs. Others do not share this optimistic view. They do not believe that a more detailed understanding of the way science has led to technology, and technology to production and wealth, would necessarily help the efforts of the politician to spread happiness and peace. But the proposition, nonetheless, contains two important admissions. The first is that scientists do not know much about the natural history of scientific growth; the second is that scientists, as well as non-scientists, are poorly equipped, if indeed equipped at all, to predict the social and political repercussions of the applications of science and technology.

Until recently, these were matters with which relatively few people concerned themselves. Today they are commonplace. In order to improve the organisation and promotion of scientific activities, and in a presumed effort to understand the part which science and technology play in social and political change, the governments of practically all countries have appointed science advisers and advisory councils of independent scientists, and all industrialised countries – and also many underdeveloped countries now striving to develop their own industries on very primitive foundations – are intensifying their scientific and technological efforts. Ever since the end of the second world war, twenty-five years ago, we in the United Kingdom have been spurred on to increase the numbers of professional scientists and engineers in our working population, and to ensure that adequate resources go to research and development. This we have been encouraged to do by successive governments, basically because of a belief in the simple proposition – perhaps too simple a proposition – that both national security and the competitiveness of manufacturing industry, particularly in export markets, depend primarily on their scientific and technological backing. As a measure of the success of this effort to increase the volume of our scientific resources, the working population of British scientists and engineers has now reached the record figure of 350,000, some three times what it is estimated to have been twenty years ago, and the amount of money which is spent annually on what is broadly called 'research and development' (R and D) is about one thousand one hundred million pounds, compared with an estimated fifteen million pounds or so just before the start of the second world war. In the United States the most recent phase in the development of the nation's scientific potential has been even more aggressive. The volume of national resources which are devoted to research and development has until recently increased at a fantastic rate. The federal government now provides nearly twenty thousand million dollars for research and development (much more than Britain's total expenditure on education and defence together), of which the bulk is spent by the Department of Defense, the National Aeronautics and Space Administration and by the Atomic Energy Commission. The scientific effort of the Soviet Union has also been greatly intensified over the period. So, too, has that of France, Germany and Holland, and of almost every other industrialised or industrialising country.

While some scientists still live and dream in ivory towers, the figures leave no doubt that the bulk of science and technology has moved to the public arena; and the move has been as swift as its effects have been far-reaching.

At the turn of the century, science in the United Kingdom was pursued with relatively little support from public funds. Politics also went its way almost unaware that its preoccupations were going to be increasingly affected by the advances of scientific knowledge. When the government of the day decided to take an interest, during the period of the first world war, it did so in the gentlest way possible. Research councils, which are at the heart of the British form of scientific organisation, were created to ensure that adequate resources were made available to scientists to pursue their independent researches. The Haldane Committee, which was set up in 1917 to enquire generally into the responsibilities of government departments, and to advise how the 'exercise and distribution by the government of its functions could be improved', provided the blueprint for government action in relation to science.[1] It recommended that the responsibility for our national research institutions should be placed 'in the hands of a Minister who is in normal times free from any serious pressure of administrative duties', and who was 'immune from any suspicion of being biased by administrative considerations against the application of the results of research'.

Lord Haldane and his colleagues would seem to have laboured in the belief that in normal circumstances the results of scientific enquiry were not applied for useful purposes. The minister chosen for the task was the 'Lord President of the Council', who by tradition is never head of a department of state with executive functions, and the recommendation soon developed into a presumed principle of scientific independence, which clearly helped the 'pure scientist'. But its effect was to create a series of autonomous research councils which pursued their work in quasi-isolation, and whose activities in the medical, agricultural and industrial fields did little to influence the policies of those government departments which were concerned executively with related technological matters. In consequence, and contrary to what the Haldane Committee had intended, a vertical division developed between research council and university science on the one hand, and the executive activities of government departments on the other. This separation inevitably became associated in the United Kingdom with a widespread belief that the kind of work which was carried out in the universities and under the banner of the research councils was intellectually more exacting and worthy than the kind of scientific and technological work required and pursued by government departments and in industry. Science, not application, was what counted.

Surprisingly, the nation-wide mobilisation of scientists and engineers in the second world war, and their considerable practical achievements, induced little permanent change in this attitude, or in the basic nature of our scientific organisation. It did, however, point to the need for some central advisory council which would be charged, in the words of the Barlow Committee[2] of 1946, with advising the Lord President of the Council 'in the exercise of his responsibility for the formulation and execution of Government scientific policy'. It was for this reason that an Advisory Council on Scientific Policy came into being at the beginning of 1947. One of the first problems which it debated was the place of science in government, and in particular the respective functions of government departments, of the research councils and of outside bodies in carrying out research.[3] The Council was divided in its views on this important matter, but a compromise was reached on two general principles: first, that departments of state with executive responsibilities should be responsible for identifying problems requiring research, stating their order of priority and deciding where to carry out the work, and how to apply the results; and, second, that the research councils, and particularly the old Department of Scientific and Industrial Research, should continue to initiate background research where they thought fit, free from administrative control of the executive departments and from considerations of day-to-day expediency.

The Advisory Council on Scientific Policy, which continued in existence for seventeen years, was never inhibited in its efforts when it discussed problems in which no other body had a particular vested interest – for example, questions such as the growth and deployment of scientific manpower, the scale of financial support for basic research, and matters concerning certain aspects of our overseas scientific relations. But throughout its existence it not surprisingly found itself impotent, and often baulked, when it came to advising either about the use of scientific and technological resources in executive departments of state, for example, the Defence Departments, or about the programmes of the research councils. In spite of these inhibitions, it observed in its final Report[4] that the overriding issue by which it had been exercised during its seventeen years of life was the scale and balance of the national civil scientific effort. While it had failed to discover any way of deciding what proportion of any country's gross national product should be devoted to the advancement and exploitation of science, the essential task which it therefore passed on to its successor body, given that such a body was going to be provided with something approaching executive rather than just advisory responsibility, was to determine how much money should be devoted to science and technology, and the clarification of the priorities and criteria by which to decide how to divide the cake of our national scientific resources. This valedictory note was no confession of failure; it was merely an indication of the magnitude of the problems that needed to be solved. For it was plain to all that whatever the position which had prevailed before the start of the second world war, the United Kingdom no longer possessed the resources to engage freely over the whole front of science. Some fields, such as aerospace technology and high-energy physics, were moving well out of Britain's national reach.

The way in which the old Council became transformed into its successor bodies, the Council for Scientific Policy on the one hand and the Advisory Council on Technology on the other, and the time this took, were determined first by the recommendations of the 1963 Committee of Enquiry into the Organisation of Civil Science[5] and, second, by the departmental changes introduced by the Labour government when it took office at the end of 1964. Overshadowing the enquiries of the 1963 committee was the soaring cost of certain branches of science. But the two essential questions to which it addressed itself were: first, the fact that the various agencies which were concerned with the promotion of civil science were not interrelated in a coherent and articulate pattern and, second, that the arrangements for apportioning resources between agencies were insufficiently clear and precise. The committee was asked to concern itself with questions of function, not of structure, and was not asked to advise on the adequate exploitation of science and of scientists by Departments of State with executive functions. The recommendations which it put forward were in the end wrapped up in the changes which flowed on the one hand from the creation at the end of 1964 of a Ministry of Technology, which was immediately given responsibility for the larger part of the biggest of the old research councils, the Department of Scientific and Industrial Research, including several of its research stations; of the National Research Development Corporation, a body which had been established in 1946 in order to help the private inventor exploit promising projects – such, for example, as the hovercraft; and of the Atomic Energy Authority; and on the other, from the shaping of the Department of Education and Science to its present pattern, which includes responsibility for most of the old research council structure (medical, agricultural, science, natural environment and social sciences) as well as the University Grants Committee. These initial changes, made in accordance with the Science and Technology Act of 1965, were taken a considerable step forward when the Ministry of Technology took over, at the beginning of 1967, most of the functions of the previous Ministry of Aviation, and so became provided with the apparatus to help chart, and indeed determine, the future of a significant section of that part of British manufacturing industry which is based on advanced technology.

An inevitable change in the central advisory structure for science followed these transformations of ministerial responsibility. A Council for Scientific Policy was established to advise the Secretary of State for Education and Science in the formulation and execution of that part of government scientific policy for which he is responsible, but as the Council recognised in their first Report,[6] their mandate was restricted to basic science, both nationally and internationally. At the same time, the Minister of Technology set up an Advisory Council on Technology, but a council without executive powers, to help such affairs of his Ministry as were brought to its attention. And finally, and partly because the scope of these two advisory bodies relates to separate and limited parts of the whole field, in the same way as there is a vertical separation between the two departments to which they report, a Central Advisory Council for Science and Technology was established in order to help advise the government as a whole on the most effective use of Britain's scientific and technological resources, whether in the civil or defence fields, or in the public or private sectors.

10

The Scope for Advice

The objectives and value of the counsel given by committees of independent advisers varies according to the circumstances of the moment and the executive responsibility of the authority which is being advised. This point may seem obvious, but it needs to be made because the issue has been greatly confused by writers who attribute to advisory councils, as well as to scientific advisers in general, far greater powers than they in fact possess. Even committees which are charged with the straightforward direction of programmes of basic research are far more limited in the exercise of a corporate wisdom than is often supposed. They can make judgments about the degree of support work that may be proposed to them should receive. But encouraging or discouraging proposals is almost all they can do in the field of basic research, and even in that of invention. Committees discovered neither the atom nor penicillin, nor did they invent jet engines or zip-fasteners. As C.E.K. Mees, an Englishman who for many years was vice-president for research of the Eastman Kodak Company, once put it, even if too vigorously:

the best person to decide what research work shall be done is the man who is doing the research, and the next best person is the head of the department, who knows all about the subject and the work; after that you leave the field of the best people and start on increasingly worse groups, the first being the research director, who is probably wrong more than half the time; and then a committee, which is wrong most of the time; and finally, a committee of vice-presidents of the company, which is wrong all the time.

It is not without interest that we owe the resurrection of this adage to the Rand Corporation, a United States institution which is mostly associated in the public mind with the evolution of formalised processes for so-called decision making, and with rigid procedures for controlling research and development expenditures in the defence field.

Devising research programmes is not, however, the level at which the new advisory bodies of the British government (the Central Advisory Council for Science and Technology, the Council for Scientific Policy, and the Advisory Council on Technology) operate. Their concern is primarily with general matters, such as the volume and scale of our national scientific resources, and with the criteria which determine, or which should determine, the way they are used. All experience has shown that this task is hemmed in by as many constraints and pitfalls as the difficulties which Dr Mees had in mind when he spoke in 1935 about research itself being directed by committees. It is these constraints which determine the limits of so-called 'science policy' when conceived of as a course of action which is laid down by bodies of independent scientists.

The point is well-illustrated by the problem of increasing the numbers of professionally trained scientists and engineers. The original stimulus for embarking on this course in the United Kingdom came from the Barlow Committee[1] of 1946, and was based on the very reasonable assumption that the problem of post-war reconstruction, and of maintaining, leave alone raising, our standard of living, depended upon a very rapid increase in the numbers of professional scientists and engineers in the working population.

Starting from the acceptance of this recommendation, a vast national programme was initiated to expand our universities and to up-grade technical education in general. This course of action was spurred by the advocacy of a succession of advisory committees, including the Scientific Manpower Committee[2] which was established in 1950, and which was somewhat more successful than industry itself in 'guesstimating' the latter's likely future demand for qualified manpower, and by its successor body the Committee on Manpower Resources for Science and Technology, which was established in 1965. In 1939, just before the second world war started, the level of output of qualified scientists and engineers in Great Britain was of the order of some 5,000 a year. Today it is 26,000. But while scientific advisory councils have been successful in urging the government to provide the resources necessary to allow of this vast rate of increase, they have been far less successful in determining what kind of subjects or what kind of science students take up. Moreover, in spite of much propaganda, they have not been very successful in raising to the desired level the proportion of the brighter boys and girls of school-leaving age who go in for science and technology. Regardless of national needs, hundreds of university places in departments of pure and applied science, and especially departments of engineering science, remain unfilled. This issue dogged the old Advisory Council on Scientific Policy in the same way as it does the present Council for Scientific Policy.

If their achievements have fallen short of the mark in these latter respects, the advocacy of these two Councils, coupled with pressure from the universities and Research Councils, was, however, highly successful in persuading successive governments to multiply the financial resources made available from public funds for science and technology, from pure research at one end of the spectrum, to development and production at the other. The propaganda which emanated from their efforts also undoubtedly helped to encourage private industry to intensify its own efforts in the field of research and development. In financial terms the results have been spectacular. In 1939 the total amount of money available in the United Kingdom for research and development was, as I have said, little more than fifteen million pounds. Today, industry alone is devoting five hundred million pounds to R and D which, even taking inflation into account, certainly means a very considerable increase. On the other hand, both the old Advisory Council on Scientific Policy and the present Council for Scientific Policy have learnt from experience that the money which is made available by government for pure research is only with considerable difficulty reapportioned between one field of potential discovery and another. New money can be allocated, but it is not easy to take resources from, say, the Medical Research Council, and give it to Agricultural Research. The controversies which beset the search for objective truth within science may be different in kind, but they are certainly no more intense than those which attend exercises of this kind.

No one need doubt that the advocacy of advisory councils was largely responsible for the fact that the amount of money made available for pure research has grown over the past ten to twenty years at a much higher rate than that of any other sector of public expenditure. But the situation is changing, and it now seems to be generally accepted that the rate of growth of the resources made available for pure science in the United Kingdom has to slow down. The claims of pure science for additional resources need to be judged within the same framework as claims for other national cultural activities. Scientists, however, can always make the special plea – and can be relied upon to do so – that without the new knowledge provided by pure science, there would be no new science to apply in all those fields of activity – manufacturing industry and agriculture for example – which help determine the rate of economic growth as a whole. The counter-argument, of course, is that new scientific knowledge is available to all, regardless of its national source, and that it is never as essential to provide pure science with such massive support as scientists customarily insist.

The demands of scientists for an ever-increasing share of public expenditure would be more difficult to resist if our 'scientific investment' over the past twenty years could have been shown to have resulted in a dramatic alleviation of our national economic ills. They would also prove more difficult to resist if the increase in the rate of growth of our scientific resources had not been associated with a so-called 'brain drain', which could be taken to imply an over-production of scientists and engineers, and with the emergence of an increasing 'technology gap', by which is roughly meant the gap between the general technological and industrial power of the United States compared with that of European countries, and which cannot be simply related to the numbers of professionally trained scientists and engineers in the country.

That the scale of the brain drain has almost certainly been exaggerated does not matter in this context. What matters is that large numbers of scientists and engineers who have been trained at great expense in the United Kingdom do not take up jobs at home which could help improve the national situation. Instead they choose to go abroad, in particular to the United States, in the hope of better status, higher salaries, lighter taxation, the promise of greater opportunities and of less frustration. Without doubt most of these hopes stem from the fact that the United Kingdom does not, and cannot, deploy such lavish resources as the United States in order to satisfy the appetites, and release the potentialities, of all our science and engineering graduates.

Diagnosis of the causes of the brain drain, which is only part of a much wider process, is relatively simple; it is the therapy which constitutes the problem. The term itself is something of a misnomer. In general, educated men throughout the ages have always moved from areas of lesser, to areas of greater opportunity, where they expect to find better resources with which they can apply their talents. And there have always been areas of greater and lesser opportunity, both between countries and within countries. Culture has never spread evenly over the earth. We lose people to the United States; but we absorb large amounts of professional manpower from countries like India and Pakistan. Japan welcomed the scientific and technological culture of the West, in an age when it was taboo in China. In South Africa some parts of the population enjoy all the fruits of western civilisation, while others live as primitive hunters and graziers in a Stone-Age culture. The United States refers to the movement of people from poorer to richer states as its internal brain drain. Before a monetary value was placed upon professional training, no one bothered about these things. No one noticed when a scholar from one country moved to another. It would have been thought odd if he did not. We accepted as natural that men like Rutherford and Florey should leave the countries of their birth to build up schools of science in England.

But there is always a shortage of the best brains, and in a period when scientific manpower as a whole is generally held to be in short supply, not surprisingly a different view is taken about the brain drain.

The imbalance between countries of greater and lesser opportunity shows itself in other ways, every bit as important as the brain drain itself. One country's wealth inevitably throws into relief another's poverty. Every year in Britain we absorb into our hospitals, universities and industries, large numbers of professionally trained Indians and Pakistanis. But at the same time we give technical and financial aid to these countries, so that it becomes a moot question – as it is in the United States – whether what we give is as valuable as what we take. But beyond this lies another issue. We are not only increasing the numbers of professionally trained manpower in this country; we are also exhorting them to exploit their talents in manufacturing industry in order to improve our competitive position in overseas markets.

We seek for innovations others have not devised, for the invention of new kinds of capital equipment, for the development of new products which overseas markets will absorb. In so doing we cannot avoid damaging the economies of poorer countries. For instance, jute is one of Pakistan's major exports. But in its end-uses jute is in immediate competition with certain synthetic substances which we manufacture for packaging materials and other end-uses. The better our chemical industry performs in this field, the worse, therefore, for Pakistan, so long as it remains under-industrialised.

The brain drain is part of an age-long international multifaceted problem. Advisory councils might perhaps suggest measures which can minimise our own losses of trained manpower, but they cannot stop the differential growth of technologically based industry in the world at large, any more than so-called science policy can show how the widening gap between advanced and underdeveloped countries can be narrowed. The basic problem is that of enhancing opportunity where it is missing; and its solution is in the field of politics, not science. The concepts of the Common Market and of its reflection, a technological community of Europe, are concepts which carry with them the promise of wider and greater opportunity for the exercise of scientific and engineering talent. But they are not scientific; they are political and economic concepts. Scientific advisory councils and science policy have, as such, little to contribute to their formulation.

11

The Criteria of Science Policy

At the present moment the amount of money from all sources which the United Kingdom spends on research and development is very nearly three per cent of our gross national product, a percentage which is practically the same as that of the United States and higher than that of any other country except, perhaps, the Soviet Union. This money is divided between basic research, applied research and the prototype engineering development work which leads on to production, in the proportions of approximately ten per cent, twenty-five per cent and sixty-five per cent. But the actual pattern of distribution between different fields of science and technology has been determined not on the basis of an up-to-date assessment of needs, but through a series of unrelated decisions taken in the past, many of them hardly explicit. Advisory councils, such as the old Advisory Council on Scientific Policy and the present Council for Scientific Policy, have dealt mainly with the amount of money which goes either to pure basic research or to objective basic research, the first constituting those enquiries which are carried out in order to increase scientific knowledge without any social or economic purpose in view, and the second those kinds of basic research which are deliberately undertaken in fields of recognised technological importance. Deciding the resources required for 'development', that is to say the amount of money and manpower which should go to projects like a supersonic freighter or a hovercraft, is a responsibility which has never come within their purview.

The criteria for assessing the relative merits of projects which fall into these two categories are necessarily different. In the case of objective basic research, the assessment of value has to take account of the social and economic purpose of the research, and of its cost, as well as of its merit from the point of view of scientific quality. Where pure basic research is concerned, judgments can be based only upon an intellectual assessment of the quality and promise of the proposed work. Experience has shown that there is no objective way of deciding how much money should go to this kind of science, any more than it is possible to say that this branch of pure science should necessarily get greater support than that. Biologists grumble that nuclear physicists get too much, and the latter are wary lest one day space scientists bleed away their resources. Moreover, every group of scientists can be relied upon to argue powerfully that without additional support their particular branch of science will wither away, with dire consequences both to science and to society at large. There is no end to value arguments of this kind.

Most scientific and technological work in government is, however, carried out not by bodies like research councils, advised by committees of independent scientists, but by departments of state charged with executive functions. The resources which these deploy in the fulfilment of their responsibilities, whether these lie in the field of health, or defence, or transport, are decided as matters of national policy, within the aggregate of resources which ministers collectively decide can go to public expenditure without prejudicing the general economic strategy of the country. In theory, and to a considerable extent in practice, it then becomes the responsibility of the minister concerned to decide what proportion of the resources which he has been allocated should go to the research and development necessary to underpin the activities of his department.

There is, or should be, an immediate parallel here with industry. The primary purpose of the research and development which is carried out by, or for, manufacturing industry is not to increase the body of scientific knowledge, but to secure and maintain a high rate of productivity through technical innovation, to develop new products, and eventually to make greater profits. The resources which are spent on public services, such as health, agriculture, or defence, are directed to corresponding utilitarian, if not necessarily commercial, ends. Thus the criteria which determine the allocation of research and development resources for defence are held to be based upon an assessment of the needs of the armed services for equipment to carry out their defined tasks. The services and their technical advisers determine their research and development priorities, and whatever the short-comings in the way they are implemented, it is generally recognised now that expenditure has to be controlled by rigorous procedures, beginning with the formulation of an operational requirement, and leading through a feasibility study and project study, to final production – given that the project can be realised within the limits of time and resources, and that what is being sought will still fill a justifiable need when it comes to fruition.[1]

Broadly speaking, the same kind of control should apply to applied research and development in all fields of public expenditure. Priorities need to be set on the basis of criteria which are partly technical, partly economic – but hardly ever clear-cut. The technical criteria relate to the feasibility of the project under consideration, to its level of technological sophistication, to the time it will take to complete the development, and to the likelihood that the project will be successfully completed in the face of competition from other countries. The economic appraisal demands as thorough an examination as possible of the financial costs of the project, of its expected financial return if sufficient capital is available to exploit it expeditiously and, in the case of the United Kingdom, of its impact on the balance of payments. The same kind of considerations apply, of course, to major industrial research and development projects and to projects which are carried out in collaboration with other countries.

None of this highly controversial kind of work falls within the ambit of independent advisory councils, for the good reason that in the case of industrial projects responsibility lies with industry itself, and for projects which are supported out of public funds, with the particular minister concerned. Yet the problem of improving the efficiency of all activities which lead to economic growth, and in particular the efficiency of manufacturing industry, nevertheless lies at the heart of 'science policy'. This was one of the basic arguments behind the post-war, and the continuing, call to multiply the numbers of qualified scientists and engineers. Those who are concerned with the formulation of science policy must necessarily have an interest, therefore, in the problem of applying the fruits of scientific research, even though they may not be directly concerned with the way this is done.

But here we are faced by the paradox that twenty-five years after the Barlow Committee used this argument to spur the British government into action in this field, and in spite of any amount of literature on the subject, we still know very little about the true significance of research and development to economic growth. Of course, we all accept that if there were no new scientific knowledge to be exploited, the processes and products of manufacturing industry would soon become fixed in their present mould. Equally we know that broad international comparisons of research and development expenditures tell us very little that is significant about economic growth. For example, the United States and the United Kingdom stand high in the league of countries which devote resources to research and development, but their rate of growth has been remarkably low in comparison with that of Germany and Japan – two countries which have spent relatively little overall on R and D, and practically nothing on R and D for defence. If we want to learn from comparisons, it will be necessary to undertake case studies of corresponding industries, or, indeed, of corresponding firms in different countries; to the best of my knowledge, this has not yet been done except in a very elementary way.

Other factors which have to be taken into account when considering the causes of economic growth are, of course, the productivity and educational level of labour, economies of scale, and qualities of management and marketing. Some estimates suggest that the knowledge which is gained through research and development, when translated by way of technology into innovation, contributes as much as fifty per cent to the economic growth of advanced technological countries. Others put the figure much lower. Analysis of statistics both in the United States and the United Kingdom also shows that most of the money available for research and development, whether from government or industrial sources, is spent by a few large undertakings. For instance, in the United States, four giant companies alone account for a quarter of the total United States research and development expenditure, that is to say, for more than five thousand million dollars of R and D. In the main, the companies concerned are producers of aircraft and missiles, computers, radar and other electronic equipment, and, to a lesser extent, chemicals and machinery. Relatively little R and D is carried out in more conventional sectors of industry. From these analyses we also know that the large companies concerned employ more professional scientific manpower than do others in *all* sectors of employment, not just in R and D, and that they are usually powerful in overseas markets. The five United States industries with the strongest research effort account for over seventy per cent of the nation's export of manufacturing goods, although they are responsible for only some forty per cent of the nation's total sales of such goods. Companies such as these begin to enjoy what is virtually a monopoly position for their goods in world trade.

But when we have done with observations such as these, we always seem to come back to the point that, other than the United Kingdom, most European countries experienced greater annual increases of output per man-hour during the post-war years than did the United States. Does this mean, as some would argue, that the strength of a country's own R and D effort and the source of the technical information which it uses, have no particular relevance to the problem of economic growth? Japan, we are often reminded, has produced few innovations in the field of plastics but, nonetheless, is second now to the United States in their production, partly through the purchase of technical know-how, and then through the operation of partly-owned subsidiaries of overseas companies. Or does it mean that these countries enjoyed their high rate of growth because they started at so low a level after the second world war?

What we can be sure of is that money spent on applied research and development, the results of which are not carried through to production, is money which is in effect wasted, and that in judging the potential value of an R and D programme, it is essential for those concerned to assess lead-times and likely cost in relation to the resources the company commands, and the commercial returns which may result. This means, as several recent writers have pointed out, that it is necessary to differentiate between the scientific and technological work which leads to invention and that which is necessary to bring about the successful marketing of the end-product. This point is neatly illustrated by a much-quoted official report on technological innovation issued by the US Department of Commerce.[2] The authors were fifteen prominent Americans convened by the Secretary of Commerce, all of whom could claim some form of direct experience either of major research and development projects or of manufacturing industry. On the basis of their own practical experience, they differentiated between the process of invention, which they defined as the conception of an idea, and that of innovation, which they saw as the process by which an invention or idea is translated into something of economic value. Professor Quinn[3] had the same notion when he talked of technology as constituting two phases of operation, first, one in which knowledge is 'created for practical purposes', and second, a stage when that knowledge is 'used and transferred for practical purposes'. As he aptly put it: 'a crude lathe in the hands of a skilled man can represent a sophisticated technological system' whereas 'the most advanced computer in the hands of a savage jungle tribe is likely to simply be a rapidly rusting hunk of junk'.

The authors of the American report to which I have referred soon discovered that such data as were available for their enquiry mainly concerned the amount of money that was going, or was said to be going, to research and development, and that there were few figures which gave the cost of the complete process of innovation. A series of case studies was, therefore, made and it turned out that, on average, research and development accounted for only five to ten per cent of the total cost; engineering design, ten to twenty per cent; tooling and manufacturing engineering, forty to sixty per cent; start-up manufacturing expenses, five to fifteen per cent; and start-up marketing costs, ten to twenty per cent. Basic R and D thus accounts for only a very small part of the efforts made by scientists, engineers, managers and market specialists in getting value out of new discovery. Obviously the inventive phase, if we can so call the stage of R and D, is vitally important, but its value, on the basis of this analysis, will not be realised by a firm unless it has something like nine times the resources which it devotes to R and D to spend on the rest of the process of innovation and production. Big, well-endowed companies which operate in accordance with technologically based management techniques will always be at an advantage. If they have been successful in diverse fields of production, and have already established close contact with markets for other goods, they will be all the more likely to hold their own. The 'technological gap' about which we hear so much seems to be due less to differences in technological knowledge than to differences between European and corresponding American firms in the part of the innovation process which comes after the research and development has been done. British expenditures on research and development in advanced technological industry – aircraft, electronics and so on – are high in relation to those of most countries. The reason why they have not brought in their train all the rewards we should like is almost certainly that the bigger American firms against which they compete are better geared than we are to achieve commercial value out of what is discovered in the laboratory. They are better geared in the sense that the personnel they employ in all parts of the business are more technically orientated than ours, that they command greater financial resources than we do, and that they have a greater assurance of markets than we have.

These generalisations, which have been endorsed in an independent study[4] carried out in this country, cannot be made the basis of action just through the advocacy of advisory councils of independent scientists to different government departments. If they so decided, such bodies could, of course, recommend that less money be made available for basic research, and more for generalised scientific and engineering education, or that the former should not be reduced and the latter increased. But, as I have already said, widespread propaganda for people to go in for a scientific education has failed so far to fill all the places that have been made available in our universities for this purpose. And I am not sure that other forms of major advice about basic research or engineering education would have any greater immediate impact on Britain's economic prospects – and it is immediate impact with which we are so critically concerned.

In the case of government departments which are concerned with technological matters, the responsibility for advising how resources can be used to best effect lies more at the door of the technical staff which the departments employ for the purpose than that of independent advisers. Their task is always a formidable one, even when they have full access to all matters relating to the objectives of the departments to which they belong. Scientists and engineers who are members of departmental staffs almost inevitably fight for departmental interests. For example, the ill-fated British TSR 2 aircraft project, which in the end was judged to be making too great a demand on public resources in relation to the military need it was designed to fill, was necessarily supported by those scientists and engineers in the Ministry of Aviation whose business it was to see that the project did not fail for technical reasons. To this extent, it could be claimed that they were supporting the vested interest of the Royal Air Force, which was the potential consumer. But it was their business to do this. Equally it could be said that independent scientists who felt that the project represented an unjustifiable strain on our resources lacked the necessary forum where they could make their views felt. There is always a difficulty in resolving conflicts between departmental views and views which may be held outside. Dr Skolnikoff,[5] now at the Massachusetts Institute of Technology, and previously a member of the staff of the US President's Special Assistant for Science and Technology, has published an interesting article on this point, with particular reference to the difficulties of getting an overall scientific point of view to bear on United States foreign policy. According to him, the State Department's complete dependence on outside technical information, that is to say, on information provided by other departments, and by external advisers employed by these departments, means that on important issues of foreign policy the United States government is 'at the mercy of the technical judgments' of men who were concerned only with their departmental interests. He illustrates this conclusion by the difficulty which the State Department experienced in dealing with the numerous arguments put forward by scientists who were opposed to the conclusion of the test ban treaty. 'Each new technical concept for evaluation put forward by the agencies concerned appeared as a major problem, and the Department was unable to evaluate the practical feasibility of the concepts or their importance in the basic political equation' – which was achieving a treaty. Another illustration which he gives was the follow-up of President Kennedy's proposal in 1962 that the United States and the Soviet Union should co-operate in the expensive field of space technology. Naturally enough the agency which took the responsibility for putting forward proposals was the National Aeronautics and Space Administration (NASA) 'whose technical judgment of the feasibility of certain classes of projects was inevitably affected by its own objectives, its concepts of what contributed most to American foreign policy, and its preferences with regard to international co-operation'. Whatever the State Department may have wished, NASA 'was ensuring that US–Soviet co-operation in space would be minor, involving little political risk

E*   125 but offering correspondingly little chance for political gain'. Every country conducts its business in its own way and in accordance with its own kind of political organisation. In the Soviet Union the work of the Academy of Sciences is articulated with that of the State Committee on Science and Technology, and its members are paid by the State. France has its General Delegation for Scientific and Technical Research (DGRST), which reports to a committee of ministers. In the United States there are several executive and advisory agencies with one central presidential body – the President's Scientific Advisory Committee, which is chaired by the President's Special Assistant for Science and Technology. The deliberations of this committee extend into all fields of government, military or civil. In general it has been more concerned to see that scientific knowledge is applied and new technology developed than to assure the growth of science itself – a task which it leaves to the National Science Foundation, the National Institutes of Health, the National Academy of Sciences and several other bodies. Because the President's Committee has the widest possible remit, it has concerned itself with federal expenditures for technical developments in both the civil and defence fields. In the words of one of its members,[6] because of its past performance, the President's Committee serves 'as critical adversaries of agency planners, to be convinced by them, so that it may provide to the President objective unbiased advice with respect to the quality and magnitude of on-going programmes and the plans of the science-using agencies and of inter-agency arrangements'.

The new Central Advisory Council for Science and Technology which has been established in the United Kingdom has the responsibility of 'advising the Government on the most effective national strategy for the use and development of our scientific and technological resources' – which means that it is not debarred from commenting on departmental programmes of research and development. This responsibility will clearly be more readily discharged in the field of public expenditure on science and technology. But clearly since the latter affects the deployment of all our scientific and technical resources, it will also need to direct attention to the way resources are used in the private sector. Even if it is too soon to say how successful the Council will prove in practice, the responsibility is there.

I turn now to the question of science policy. Most of us think we understand what is meant by the phrase 'foreign policy', 'housing policy', or 'educational policy'. On the other hand, many of us – and I amongst them – find it difficult to use the term 'science policy' with any precision. The bulk of the scientific activity of the country, whether measured in terms of manpower or money, proceeds independently of the deliberations of advisory councils on science policy. It takes place either in the laboratories and workshops of industry, or in government laboratories which are necessarily, and in my view rightly, controlled departmentally. Over the years, the preoccupations of the independent scientists who have been concerned with science policy in the United Kingdom have, therefore, focused on our educational programmes, on the resources available for basic research, and on schemes for international co-operation of the kind that the European Space Research Organisation (ESRO) and the European Organisation for Nuclear Research (CERN) represent. These matters relate to only a small part of the deployment of our scientific and technological resources, even though they are fundamental to the rest. They are the general problems of science. But the bigger part of our scientific activities, with which advisory councils concerned with policy cannot deal executively, is the part that produces the economic resources on which all else depends, as well as the problems which continually confound the world of politics.

These matters are inevitably in the public arena, and decisions about the deployment of our scientific resources must in the end inevitably be political. Advisory bodies can only advise. In the British system of government the power of decision rests with the minister concerned, or with the government as a whole, or with the boards of companies. Although we are learning fast, the scientist, as we stand today, not only does not have the responsibility for public decision, but also still lacks the apparatus with which to predict the repercussions of technological developments. Since the scientist is in the public arena only as the expert worker and adviser, it is his employer, whether it be the government or the board of an industrial company, who commands his service and who has the responsibility for action. The decision whether to accept or reject his advice is the employer's, and his only. If the scientists who now advise feel that this is not good enough, they will, as I have already suggested, have to decide in what other way they can discharge their 'social responsibilities' – whether as propagandists, as members of a government machine, as politicians – or at least as leaders of industry.

12

The Technological Foundations of Society

Technology is a catch-word of our times – an immensely important word, but a catch-word all the same. Whatever people may understand by the term, they have learnt that it is technology which is transforming society at an ever-accelerating pace. They are told that the recent landings on the moon epitomise 'America's technological century'; and are warned that an ever-widening technological gap separates the United States and the USSR from all other countries of the world. They are reminded day-in, day-out, about Britain's shortcomings in technological innovation; about our past failures to grant technologists the esteem they have long been accorded in the societies of the two super-powers; and by this time – unless the message has been too shrill – all must surely recognise that unless science is put to work through technology, Britain will be denying itself an essential ingredient of industrial health and economic growth. Speeches are made; endless articles and books are written about these things, and the nation has taken urgent steps to put matters right. The newspapers are flooded with advertisements for applied scientists, engineers, computer programmers, and managers; we have a Ministry devoted to technology; the merits of a scientific and technological education in universities and colleges are continually stressed and encouraged; and the British professional engineering institutions have organised themselves in a federal council to help them speak with one voice.

Contrary to what many may have been led to believe from all this upsurge of activity, the only thing that is novel about the word 'technology' is the new emphasis we place on it. Technology has always been with us. It is not something outside society, some external force by which we are pushed around. It is one of the main roots of man's social, political and commercial life; and it will always be that. Even the cry about Britain's technological backwardness relative to other countries merely echoes a message that was drummed out ceaselessly in the latter half of the nineteenth century. Today, of course, we mostly use the term to signify the organised exploitation of scientific knowledge, particularly new scientific knowledge, to make things people need or want, or are persuaded they want, as they strive for an ever better material life. Nuclear energy, colour television, satellite communications, antibiotics and computers, are among the fruits of this kind of technology. We welcome without hesitation the transforming influence these things are exercising in our social lives, in the same way as our forebears of the eighteenth century accepted what one might call the fruits of the protoscientific technology of the industrial revolution.

Before this particular revolution, a pre-scientific technology had been at work, for thousands and thousands of years, and had been responsible for shaping the basic forms of all our social institutions. The invention of stone implements, of the spear and bow, the discovery of the wheel – which in turn led not only to the primitive lathe but also to the potter's wheel – the emergence of smelting and metal working, the discovery of the weaving of fibres, the domestication of animals and the cultivation of plants – all these and other major technological advances were steps along which human society slowly and painfully evolved. Without organised agriculture man would never have ended his nomadic life as a hunter and food gatherer. Had he not done so, fixed habitations would never have come about. Permanent village life would have been precarious if pots had not been invented to store food, water and oil. Co-existence in settlements demanded social rules to which the members of the group adhered in peace. The social life of the village opened the gate to intellectual exchange, to trade, to specialisation of labour, and through larger settlements, to urbanisation. This social and economic revolution took thousands of years. But at all times the culture of early society reflected its technology, in the same way as the fruits of technology continuously enriched society, both directly and indirectly, providing a basis for man's earliest scientific knowledge, and for his art. In a very genuine sense society and technology are therefore reflections of each other. The accidental sequence and acceptance of discoveries and invention – of stone implements, of fire, of the primitive hut which liberated man from the cave, of the first plough and hoe – not only determined the emergence but also the shape of society. Where culture spread by contact, society repeated the form it had already taken. And where culture was indigenous, it often took a different shape.

In the interaction of technology with society, there is, in short, nothing qualitatively different between the situation in which we find ourselves today, and that which conditioned the emergence of neolithic settlements some ten to fifteen thousand years ago, and of industrial cities in the latter half of the eighteenth century. But there is a vast quantitative difference, of which the accelerating pace of technological change today is only one aspect.

Another and much more important one is the fact that the major technological changes of the latter half of our century are far more pervasive and widespread, and have a far more immediate influence, than those of any previous period of human history. During my youth in South Africa I was taught that the indigenous Bushmen, more numerous then than the handful who now survive, still lived in accordance with the Solutrean stone culture which had faded out in Europe by about 15,000 BC. Until the second world war, the industrial revolution of the eighteenth century had hardly begun to touch the communal life of the better part of Africa, of South America, and of vast parts of Asia – nor, until the war's end, did the telegraph or radio really disturb the life of the native in those parts of the world. Indeed, it was years before the British industrial revolution spread to, or even significantly influenced life in many European countries.

But in the course of our century, and particularly during the past thirty years, culture has diffused so fast that hardly any new thing which has emerged in the advanced industrialised societies of the world has not had an immediate impact, or a potentially immediate impact, on the remaining dark corners of the globe. Even the primitive naked tribes of the remote highlands of New Guinea, who until four to five years ago were cut off from all contact with other peoples, have now been exposed to the industrial culture of the West. The transistor radio is everywhere. So are dried milk and fire-arms. The technical advances of industrialised societies spread willy-nilly. Even the fear of nuclear war is something which is not confined to the nuclear powers and their allies; were it ever to erupt, its direct and indirect effects would spread over the whole globe, giving a new and tragic dimension to the concept of one world.

Most pervasive of all cultural developments are those measures of public health which, by reducing death rates, particularly among infants, have led to so dramatic an increase in net reproduction rates, and in consequence to so sharp an increase in population size, as to result in violent political strains in vast areas of the world. Advances in medical knowledge and associated technological developments have all but eliminated the communicable diseases which held populations in check. It was an Austrian chemist who discovered DDT, and it was another European who found that this chemical compound killed the Anopheles mosquito. But the consequent elimination of malaria transformed the demographic and political future of Ceylon – to mention only one country which had had nothing to do with either discovery, but which was immediately caught within the net of its consequences.

Another new facet of the interaction of society and technology lies in the scale of the major technological developments of today. Over the thousands of years of man's existence, most technical developments were minor improvements of previous practices. Sometimes, of course, these had the most phenomenal effects. It was, for example, the final touches to the agricultural revolution of the neolithic period which resulted in the village and urban environment in which man's intellectual capacities found their first major opportunity of flowering. But today, the technological changes which make news are the big and glamorous ones. In the most advanced industrial societies the electronics, aerospace and chemical industries attract the greatest support, and it is mainly their development which is widening the so-called technological gap between nations. Colour television, computers, guidance systems for ballistic missiles, advanced aircraft, satellite communications, petrochemicals, pharmaceuticals and synthetic pesticides and herbicides – these are the developments which attract investment, not the more conventional industries which minister to the basic needs of ordinary life. The spotlight is now on advanced technology. And advanced technology moves fast – to repeat that well-worn adage of the defence scientist, 'if it works, it's obsolete'. The positive effects of the developments of advanced technology are pervasive, reaching over the whole world, and their negative effects, due to the fact that they lap up the available investment resources, are equally pronounced. The landing of men on the moon telescoped time, but left behind hundreds of millions in continuing squalor.

The spread of culture over the globe has, of course, seldom, if ever, been an even or orderly process, and the clash of different cultures out of phase with each other has never failed to result in trouble. For all its achievements, for all the benefits it provides, our own technological age, to repeat what I have said in an earlier chapter, is perhaps more unstable and politically unsettling than any that have gone before. The world today is in turmoil, turmoil due to the decolonisation which marked the end of one phase of culture-contact; turmoil due to the consequential, and over-compensating, growth of nationalism; turmoil because the exploitation of technology, while it creates riches, is intensifying the disparities of wealth between nations, and sometimes within nations; turmoil because the efforts of vast populations to better themselves economically are nullified by high net reproduction rates; turmoil because environmental pollution spreads as a direct consequence of modern industrialisation and urbanisation. Nowhere does it seem possible to reconcile the effects of rapid technological change with the social institutions and attitudes of the past. The tribal past of Africa fights with its political aspirations of today. Black and white are in conflict. The Church of Rome fails to adjust to the realities of population growth. As the United States reaches out to the stars, its cities fall apart in racial conflict and physical neglect. The orderly economic and social advance of the USSR, as seen by its rulers, is put at risk by the dissident voice of liberalism, and is threatened by an arms race with the West. Europe remains divided, while we in the United Kingdom painfully adjust to the fact that we are no longer in the first league of military and industrial powers, and to the realisation that we shall have to go on striving in order to maintain our standards of living in the face of increasing competition in world markets for manufactured products.

The overriding problem of our times, and this applies the world over, is how to learn to adjust social attitudes and institutions to conform with the demands, and the new dimension of risk, which modern technology has brought in its wake. The Luddites who in the latter part of the eighteenth century saw themselves dispossessed by the machines of the industrial revolution were pitting themselves against a visible and urgent threat to their immediate well-being. The strains and stresses of our day are due to a technological threat which is far less concrete, and much more pervasive. No one can deny that the advances of technology add to the variety of our intellectual experience and to the richness of life; that they also add to its duration, and to the decrease of its burden. But the present phase of technology has burst upon a world whose institutions, both national and international, seem unready. Nuclear power, instead of being a boon, appears as a threat overhanging all mankind. Companies compete with each other on the basis of new technology, both within and between nations, and sometimes end by destroying each other. The proved technical possibilities of increasing and distributing food supplies at a rate, and with an efficiency, adequate to meet the needs of hundreds of millions of undernourished people, fails to be realised. Instead of bringing wealth to all, modern technology seems to enrich the few. The individual wants to enjoy its fruits, but organised labour fights against the changes which are generated by new methods and new systems of production.

No wonder, therefore, some ask whether technology has not achieved a momentum of its own, whether it has become unmanageable, whether it is not in danger of becoming a Frankenstein monster which will destroy us all. The answer is that these things need not happen. Technology is what we ourselves make of scientific knowledge. Unlike scientific knowledge itself, which flowers in the open and spreads through the world as fast as the media of publication allow, and which we can never reject, we can use new technology or reject it as we choose, in spite of the fact that it usually emerges in the competitive environment and secret shadows of commerce and defence. The challenge before society is to use technology in a way which is not only compatible with our own political aspirations, but which lessens rather than increases tensions between nations, and which does not threaten the physical environment of man's future. These, of course, are the central problems of government; and to govern is to choose. Technology and applied science are in the sphere of politics, and the problem inevitably boils down to the questions – how to choose, and who is to decide, which technological possibilities out of a seemingly endless series should be fostered?

Most of the immediate concerns of politics, by which I mean here the processes of discussion and compromise which determine social policy, do not seem to lie in the sphere of technology. Some do; for example, a decision to embark on a new aircraft project or nuclear reactor which commits vast resources that have to come from the tax-payer. At second or third remove, practically all the issues of politics, even those which lie in the domain of the public services, have a technological base. We would not want new roads or new airports if technology had not improved the means of transportation. We would not seek new television stations if TV had not been invented. We would not press for better health services if the hope of better health had not been stimulated by developments in medical and pharmaceutical science. We would not insist on more and improved schools if increases in knowledge and in teaching techniques had not stimulated a greater demand for education. Even our foreign policies are in part shaped by our access to raw materials from overseas, and by the technological competence of our competitors in overseas markets. Technology is, in short, part of the substance of politics and government. And the question, both in the public and private domain, is always – what technology, which technological projects to support?

There would be no difficulty in providing an answer if resources of trained men and money – and time – were unlimited. In such abstract circumstances all bets could be covered. But this is what resources never are in any country of the world today, including the United Kingdom. Britain may once have been in the forefront of technological advance, and it may once have been able to command the resources that were necessary to exploit all the technological developments it wished to foster. But this no longer applies. Choice is as much the keyword in the public sector which underpins all our activities, as it is in the private sector of industry and commerce where negotiable wealth is produced – and where choice and controversy also march together.

The nation generates only a finite amount of resources a year, and the government of the day can withdraw only a part through taxation in order to pay for the communal services it provides – for social security and health, for roads and education, for defence and houses. What it apportions to each is determined by the inter-action of numerous conflicting political pressures. But whatever else, the government must leave enough resources to the private sector to cater for personal consumption and for investment in profitable and socially desirable enterprise, whether it be in commerce, manufacturing industry, or farming. As a nation Britain carries a great burden of debt and suffers from a very difficult and persistent balance-of-payments problem. To keep our costs down and our prices competitive in overseas markets, domestic inflation has to be curbed, just as much as technological innovation has to be encouraged. This in turn means that the scale of domestic demand, both in the public and private sectors, and thus the rate of growth of the economy, has to be confined (or more correctly, perhaps, efforts have to be made to restrain it) within economically manageable limits. The finite amount of money available for the public sector must be used to the greatest possible effect. Hence the technological efficiency with which we spend resources in the public sector is as vital as is the choice of the projects on which public money is spent. And since the government is responsible for a vast investment in public and domestic building, in roads, in defence, in health and so on, it is also responsible for seeing that the money which goes into these fields is used as effectively as modern technology permits, and to the maximum benefit of today's and tomorrow's voters. This in turn means that modern government needs an immediate aware-ness of what is happening in scientific and technological fields, and adequate first-hand experience to respond to, and sometimes to direct, the resultant changes.

13
Technology and the Industrial Revolution

A few people still living have enjoyed a ringside view of the emergence of all the technical wonders – the automobile, the aeroplane, the telephone, the radio – which have produced the environment which we now take for granted. Some of these inventions were already there when most of those alive today were born. But over the past twenty-five years, we, too, have witnessed developments at least as far-reaching – nuclear energy, computers, control engineering, radar, and modern rocketry. The image of technology is a changing image for all of us. It is equally significant that the period about whose developments a few can talk from personal experience, is no longer than the interval of time which separated them, in their childhood, from the age of James Watt, Joseph Priestley, Matthew Boulton, Josiah Wedgwood and the other giants of England's industrial revolution of the eighteenth and early nineteenth centuries. Is the image of the technologist as one sees him today, the same as, or how does it differ from, that of the technologist of the eighteenth and nineteenth centuries? And now that the recognition of the key position of the technologist in modern society has spread to all sections of society, one also needs to ask whether it is likely to be transformed in the years ahead.

In following this train of thought, it is unnecessary to embark upon any detailed analysis of the environment in which technology flowered in the eighteenth century. As we now know well, the significant part played by commerce and manufacturing industry in economic progress had been recognized long before Adam Smith published his *Inquiries into the Nature and Causes of the Wealth of Nations*. Colin Clark[1] refers to the relationship between the two as Petty's Law, in recognition of the ideas about rates of labour productivity which Sir William Petty set out in his *Political Arithmetick*, published posthumously in 1690.[2]

At the time Petty wrote, the level of income per head in the Netherlands was higher than in other European countries; Petty concluded that the difference was due to the employment of a relatively large proportion of the population in trade and manufacture and a relatively small proportion in basic agriculture, the Dutch 'having put that Employment upon the *Danes* and *Polanders*, from whom they have their Young Cattle and Corn. Now here we may take notice', he concluded, 'that as Trades and curious Arts increase; so the Trade of Husbandry will decrease'. He went further. Since in England the wages of a seaman at 12*s*. per week were three times those of a husbandman at about 4*s*. per week and as a tradesman 'earn(s) 16*d*. a day (which is no great Wages 2*s*. and 2*s*. 6*d*. being usually given)', he 'dare affirm . . . that it would be the advantage of *England* to throw up their Husbandry, and to make no use of their Lands, but for Grass Horses, Milch Cows, Gardens, and Orchards, &c.' and concentrate on 'Trade and Manufacture'. As it turned out, concentrating on trade and manufacture was a policy Britain was to follow with singular advantage. That of abandoning the land has, however, always been a somewhat controversial political and economic issue.

Since Petty's formulation of his law, the complex historical process of technological change and industrial development has been painted in many economic analyses, as well as in studies of scientific and technological history. Technological change is not something which just occurs, the way a tree grows. 'It means,' as Landes[3] puts it – and I am drawing here in large part on his lucid account of the industrial revolution – 'the displacement of established methods, damage to vested interests, often serious human dislocations', and it will occur only when circumstances combine in a particular way – when there is a need or an opportunity to improve prevailing techniques, and when the new methods which suggest themselves 'pay sufficiently to warrant the costs of the change', and when they are enough of an improvement to ensure that the progressive producer will outprice and displace his more conventional competitors.

Circumstances in eighteenth-century Britain favoured technical innovation and industrialisation more than they did in other countries. This was partly because Britain had already started exploiting her deep coal seams, and because she already enjoyed a relatively high level of wealth and income per head, and a home market for manufactured goods, particularly woollen textiles, which was continually growing because of a multiplying population and improving communications – roads and then canals. It was also due to the fact that in that period of history Britain dominated export markets because her large merchant fleet was directed with great commercial skill in accordance with what, no doubt, some today would regard as an effective colonial and foreign policy. On the Continent, Britain's only serious competitor was Holland, but she soon failed in the race for new markets because while she was a strong sea-faring and mercantile power, she was deficient in fossil fuels, and at the time was unable to develop an industrial base for manufactured goods with which to reinforce her other advantages.

In short, eighteenth-century England was a booming country, and the making of money through manufacture and trade was a common ambition. But, equally, shortage of labour set a limit to the expansion of trade and production by old methods.

The classical illustration of these generalisations is the transformation which occurred in textile manufacture and trade during the seventeenth and eighteenth centuries. At the start the growth and prosperity of the industry was based on the yarn, mainly wool, provided by cottage spinners, and on the fabric woven on hand-looms. As production rose and demand increased, an inevitable shortage of labour resulted. This applied less to cotton, of which relatively little was then being produced, than it did to wool, but it was through the application of machine methods to the former that the problem was eventually solved.

First, the spinning-jenny was invented to help those manufacturers who were eager to increase their output, but who were constrained both by a shortage of individual spinners, and by the limitations of the old craft methods. The spinning-jenny, which increased the supply of fibre, in turn called for new mechanical methods in order to improve the raw material fed to it. And as the volume of fibre increased, the capacity of hand-looms became inadequate. Cartwright then invented his steam power-loom (1785), by which time Crompton's 'mule' (1779) had made Hargreaves's spinning-jenny (1764) obsolete. All these changes occurred within the space of some twenty years.[4]

As the 'mule' and the power-loom created the factory, the cottage spinner and weaver gradually disappeared. Increasing output generated an ever-mounting demand for raw material, which in the case of cotton could be satisfied from the New World, where the combination of a favourable climate and soil, together with slave labour, placed no apparent limit on cotton production. The increase in the supply of yarn in turn called for improvements in the quality of the textile machinery which was being manufactured, and for increases in the output of the bleaching and other chemicals which go into textile manufacture – chlorine compounds, and alkali. The technological revolution which transformed the textile industry during the course of the eighteenth century and the early nineteenth century was thus a revolution compounded of many interlocking technical changes. Through their interaction, the individual craftsmen became displaced, and the way was opened for the discipline of the factory. When the machine, and not man, became the pacemaker, economies of scale and lower prices followed.

As Landes[3] reminds us, none of the inventions concerned came to industry in 'full blown' perfection. Aside from the trial and error of creation, there were innumerable adjustments and improvements – in the articulation of parts, in the transmission of power, and in the materials employed – before the primitive contrivances worked commercially. 'The first decades of industrialisation saw a ceaseless war against breakdowns.' The process of mechanisation was also a ceaseless fight against the old and conventional, whether in the processes of production themselves, or in the social conditions to which they applied. At the start there may have been no marked exploitation of labour. At first no one regarded the multiplication of small houses for workers as anything but a good thing; urbanisation provided a better environment than the rural conditions which the new industrial population had abandoned. But soon the new urban settlements became synonymous not only with slum development, but also with the exploitation of labour; and the social forces which these in their turn generated stimulated other and vast political changes.

I have left out of this brief summary of Landes's analysis – an analysis which leads to the broad conclusion that 'it was in large measure the pressure of demand on the mode of production that called forth the new techniques in Britain, and the abundant, responsive supply of the factors that made possible their rapid exploitation and diffusion', – many things which might have been said. I have also passed over such considerations as the fact that in comparison with other European countries, Britain was favoured by freer institutions, by better banking arrangements, and by a more flexible society in which the many religious dissenters of the time were not prevented from setting up their own schools in which to cultivate the science and technology of the age. Nor have I dealt with to quite a different matter, with the influence which the agricultural revolution of the early eighteenth century, in which both Holland and England played the main part, had on the social conditions of the time. If food supplies had not been improving in Britain because of the greater productivity of its agriculture, the tempo of the industrial revolution might well have been far slower than it was. It was a concatenation of many circumstances which made Britain the home of the industrial revolution, all of them adding up to what Landes calls 'an exceptional sensitivity and responsiveness' of the British to pecuniary opportunity. 'This was a people fascinated by wealth and commerce, collectively and individually.'

The pervasive social motivation which helped bring the industrial revolution about – and without which it would not have occurred – is clear enough. But fascinating though Landes's analysis may be, I myself find the picture lacking in something – to me it lacks the gleam in the inventor's eye. Was the inspiration of the technologist really the urge to design machinery which would increase the productivity of labour, the need to devise labour-saving devices? Was it his sensitivity to pecuniary opportunity? Undoubtedly these things were part of the inspiration, particularly in the case of the small improvements which are always being made in mechanical things. But if this is all the explanation, why was it, in the words of Sir Harold Hartley,[5] that 'British engineering reached its competitive climacteric soon after 1851, when the world came to the Great Exhibition to see how it was done and establish their own industries'. Why did the technologist's response to challenge fail? Did it, in fact, fail? Somehow I cannot help feeling that the economic analysis fails to illuminate the individual's part in the process, fails to provide an adequate picture of the characters of the men who were responsible for the big technical steps forward, without whose efforts the consequent smaller changes would never have taken place. What men were they, what drove them on? In what way did they project their own personalities to create the image we have of technology as it was two hundred years ago? What men were they who, for example, made up the circle of the Lunar Society of Birmingham in the eighteenth century?

For me one man, James Watt, provides an image for the rest, a man who died at the age of eighty-three, in 1819, little more than fifty years before a few distinguished scientists and scholars still with us were born. I shall deal with only one part of the well-known story of Watt, so well told by Crowther,[6] and then only to discern the basic characteristics of one whom I see as the prototype of the great technologist, of the man who makes the big leap forwards.

After a year spent in London with a Scottish instrument maker, Watt returned to Glasgow, to become, at the age of twenty-one, mathematical instrument maker to the University, which was then at the height of its vigour. John Robison, a lecturer in chemistry, and a few years younger than Watt, drew Watt's attention to the possibility that a steam engine could be used to provide power to move the wheels of carriages, 'and for other purposes', but nothing of note came out of this initial stimulus. The spark was provided by the fact that the Department of Natural Philosophy possessed a model of a Newcomen steam engine which had been sent to London for repair, but without success. In 1763, when he was thirty-seven, the machine was then given to Watt to put in order, but try as he would, he could not make the boiler, which apparently had been made to the right scale, provide enough steam to make the engine run. Yet the full-scale Newcomen engine was a dependable machine, and while sadly inefficient in its use of fuel, was much better than the Savery fire-engine which it was in process of superseding. It was also a vitally necessary machine. Without it, the miner, because of flooding, could not go on digging deeper for his coal, or bring to the surface the non-ferrous metal ores of Cornwall.

If Watt had succeeded in making the model work, he might well have regarded the job as merely one of the chores of an instrument maker, and that would have been the end of it. But failure was an intellectual challenge. He set himself to discover why it was that so vast an amount of steam and heat produced by the fuel the engine used was wasted. He worked out where and how, and how much heat was being lost, and embarked upon a systematic study of the relations between the pressure and temperature of steam, and in the course of doing so, discovered that steam can raise to boiling point something like six times its own weight of water.

His friend, Professor Black, with whom he discussed this finding, then introduced him to the principle of latent heat, which Black had discovered a few years earlier, and Watt concluded that the inefficiency of the Newcomen engine depended on a change of state from steam to water inside the working cylinder and that 'the cylinder should be maintained always as hot as the steam which entered it'. The solution to the problem hit him

on a fine Sabbath afternoon . . . when the idea came into my mind that as steam was an elastic body it would rush into a vacuum, and if a communication was made between the cylinder and an exhausted vessel, it would rush into it and might be there condensed without cooling the cylinder . . . I had not walked further than the Golf house when the whole thing was arranged in my mind.

The 'whole thing' was a separate condenser into which steam was made to escape from the working cylinder.

Scientists who have enjoyed the thrill of discovery will know full well that at the time Watt's mind could have been filled only by his technical problem, and by the solution which had sprung to life. It is inconceivable that the urge which led him to his fundamental discovery was the knowledge that by so doing he would improve the efficiency of pumping machinery, in order to make mining operations easier, more economic, and more profitable, and himself in turn a rich man. Money must have been far from his mind that Sabbath afternoon, if, indeed, it was in his mind at all at the period, in spite of the secrecy with which he immediately started to guard his discovery.

This was the turning point. But it was also the start of ten years' hard development work before he had devised an industrial engine, and before he had made all the supplementary inventions which had to go with it – the governor to control the speed of the engine, and the indicator which he invented with the help of James Southern. Moreover, the development of a commercial engine required money, and this was a commodity which Watt did not possess. Apart from some financial help from Professor Black, his first patron was Dr John Roebuck, a physician turned industrialist-scientist, who had founded near Edinburgh the Carron Iron Works. Roebuck knew a fair amount about the shortcomings of the Newcomen engines, which were not preventing the flooding of the coal mines he had to work in order to feed his foundry. Realising the technical importance of Watt's discovery, he was ready to provide him with what monetary and other help seemed necessary. But Roebuck's other industrial activities – he was one of the most remarkable and versatile scientific figures of the eighteenth century – were getting him into financial difficulties, and the resources he could spare Watt were hardly adequate. So Watt, through the intermediary of Dr Erasmus Darwin and then of Dr William Small, whom we acclaim primarily because he was Thomas Jefferson's Professor of Mathematics and Philosophy, sought the help of Matthew Boulton, all of them being members of the Birmingham Lunar Society. Boulton, however, was unwilling to assist Watt, who was then getting into real trouble, so long as he was associated with Roebuck. It was not that Boulton lacked enthusiasm for Watt's ideas. That he had in plenty. Nor was he unfriendly to Roebuck. Presumably what he wanted to avoid was linking his fortune with Roebuck's shaky prospects, at the same time as he was unready to 'embark on any trade over which he had not a substantial share of the control'.

Watt had patented the engine in 1769 in order to protect his own interests, but in order to carry on at all, he had assigned two-thirds of the rights to Roebuck, who in return took over Watt's debts and gave an understanding to finance his future experiments. This arrangement immediately failed because Roebuck's difficulties none the less forced him out of the picture. In payment of a debt, he found himself compelled to transfer his rights in the engine, with Watt's blessing, to Boulton.

Watt then moved his machine to Boulton's Soho Works in Birmingham, where he was able to find people more technologically advanced in the fabrication of metal than were available in Scotland. In particular, Wilkinson, who had devised a new and accurate method for boring guns, was at hand to bore cylinders with a constant radius, and Boulton was there with a factory manned by men specially trained for the job.

In the end, but in as many years as it takes us today to design and produce a sophisticated aircraft, or a nuclear submarine, and after financial difficulties which hit even the rich Boulton, the first engine, with a fifty-inch cylinder, was installed in a Staffordshire colliery – and was immediately successful. In the ensuing five years some forty were to be built.

The Cornish copper and tin mines were an obvious market because of the inability of the Newcomen engine to pump out the flood water which was almost bringing their operation to an end. Watt himself installed the first of the Soho Works new engines at one of the Cornish mines, but the job was then handed over to a young engineer named Murdoch, who later became famous for the invention of coal-gas lighting. With what was then a thriving mining industry, there were a lot of bright, technically-minded spirits around in Cornwall in those days. One of them was the famous Trevithick who championed the high-pressure steam engine, and who built the first coal-fired steam locomotive railway, and with whom Watt, a low-pressure steam man, soon found himself crossing swords.

What lessons do we draw from the story of Watt? First and foremost, that however sound a big new technological idea, its transformation into successful hardware demands absolute conviction and persistence in the face of difficulties, and of difficulties which cannot be foreseen in advance. This means conviction and understanding from more than just the person who has the idea. If Watt's enduring conviction had not been shared by Black, Roebuck and Boulton, he would never have had the resources with which to achieve success.

The second lesson that emerges is that the sharing of conviction of this kind demands faith in the eventual – and 'eventual' may mean years – utility, economic or otherwise, of the invention. At the time it all started, Watt may not have been interested in money; but Roebuck and Boulton certainly were. And in the end Watt undoubtedly was.

Our third lesson is that technology can leap well ahead of the basic science from which, *post hoc*, it seems to derive. Watt knew in his bones what was wrong with the Newcomen engine, and how to cure its defects. The idea of the separate condenser came to him in 1765, and ten arduous years passed before he achieved a satisfactory working model. But it was left to Clerk Maxwell, years later, to work out the theory of Watt's governor, and in doing so to provide the start for the modern science of control engineering. Watt's methods of measuring engine power in turn started a line of experimentation and thought which eventually produced the laws of thermodynamics and led on to the quantum theory. As Crowther has rather dramatically put it: 'The effective impulse to its [i.e. quantum theory] development came from the work of Watt, and in this sense, Watt has inspired the most original part of the vast extension of physics since the achievements of Newton.'

As I see it, the social and economic background of Britain in the eighteenth century proved fertile soil for Watt's inventions, but he and others like him, and not the background, provided the image of technology from which all else has flowed. He was the engineer who had the genius to do things without understanding their conceptual basis. The fact that at the time he worked there were no laws of thermodynamics did not prevent him from making mechanical engineering into a practical, as well as a real science, as well as transforming the whole basis of society through the impulse which his discoveries imparted to the processes of industrialisation.

Moreover, success with the steam engine did not prevent Watt from turning his creative genius to other aspects of engineering, or to the problems of the chemical industry – it is said that he helped introduce to England Leblanc's process for making sodium carbonate – nor did the fascination he had for practical matters stop him from embarking on enquiries which by present-day definition we would say fell into the field of basic science. Watt was no exception in the breadth of his interests. There were other brilliant practical scientists and engineers around in Britain, focusing attention first on one thing, then on another, jealous of their achievements, ready to take big chances in their exploitation, but always driving forwards.

14
Technological Competition Today

Yet in spite of this magnificent start, we are told that by the middle of the nineteenth century, Britain had passed her industrial climacteric, that the scientific and technical drive which had characterised the industrial revolution had started to flag, that Britain had begun to be overhauled in the quality of her applied science by Germany and France. And in our own generation we are told – and we go on repeating – that while Britain remains outstanding in basic science, we fall down when it comes to applied science, that we do not accord the engineering sciences enough prestige, that we revere the pure scientist and fail to honour the technologist. Is all this true? Certainly we revere the pure scientist. But has Britain really failed in the markets of advanced technological industry because her applied scientists have let her down? Are they the ones we should blame?

To my mind the answer to this question can only be 'no'.

The industrial revolution gave England the leadership of the commercial world of the eighteenth and nineteenth centuries. That is certainly true. The conspicuous technical developments of the textile industry were paralleled by corresponding ones in innumerable other fields of industry – iron and steel, non-ferrous metals, chemicals, and communications. The railway locomotive and the steamship were enormous steps forward. The need to work to finer accuracy and greater precision led to better machine tools and to the possibility of products with interchangeable parts.

All these technological transformations inevitably stimulated the growth of Britain's industrial and economic power.

But the area of competition was expanding too. Britain's achievements in the development of new goods, in the means of mass production, in the lowering of prices, in raising the general standard of living, were not going to be allowed to go unchallenged. And challenged they very rapidly were. If 1851 is the ritual date by which we mark Britain's industrial climacteric, a year in which we practically outbid the rest of the world together in export markets, by that time our own scientific and technological successes were beginning to be matched in other countries, and in particular by German chemists whose connexions with industry appear to have been closer than those of their British opposite numbers. It was in this that a major, and what in time became a vital, difference lay. The graduates of university science departments in Germany seem to have been accustomed to seek, and to expect to find, openings in the small industrial undertakings of their country. If they failed, they either started their own firms or sought their fortunes abroad – many in England, where opportunity and riches beckoned. On the other hand, the record seems to suggest that the few graduates of the small number of British schools of science of the mid-nineteenth century were neither sought nor welcomed by British industry, which was still finding it possible to push ahead, or at least maintain its ground, on the basis of past performance. In his memoirs Hutton[1] relates that Ludwig Mond, who had thrived in partnership with Brunner after coming to England from Germany in 1862, and himself was a product of Marburg and Heidelberg,[2] was the first chemical manufacturer to take on a science graduate of a British school. Be this as it may, there is no doubt that the trend in Germany was to recruit to industry all the professionally trained men who were available, men who knew at first hand how their industrial activities related to the basic sciences, who were aware that both waste and efficiency, whether of raw materials or of the fuel used in manufacturing, could be controlled only through a scientific understanding, and who were technically competent at all levels of the business, from the initial processes of production to the final marketing. It also seems plain that the German bankers, businessmen, and managers who supported the technologists were themselves imbued with a scientific understanding of what they were backing.

What shattered the dominance of British industry was not a decline in the quality of its scientists, but the simple fact of more concentrated and more dynamic competition. By the mid-nineteenth century the pattern of most British industry had been set, and most of its resources committed, on the basis of past technological developments. And then the competition started. First it was Germany and France, and then the United States, in precisely the same way as the United States, partly by the sheer volume of its resources, has now (but if history is any guide, no doubt, only temporarily) out-stripped others in several sectors of advanced technological industry. Germany, like France, enjoyed the advantage of building on a foundation of British experience and success. Her industrialists, scientists, and technologists, and not least her sophisticated banking community, quickly realised the desirability of concentrating in large vertically integrated units, and of building their industrial complexes in places where communications and raw materials, including fuel, favoured economic production. Large-scale production demanded technical efficiency, and this could not be achieved without a full appreciation of the scientific processes concerned. In the chemical and other industries, by-products became as important a consideration as primary products. The continental and American industries which started to compete with us in the second half of the nineteenth century were also enjoying the momentum of a vastly greater rate of growth.

It was that, and perhaps a certain commercial indolence, rather than a decline in our technological competence, which were the basic causes of Britain's climacteric. From the moment we started to lose our monopoly position in textiles, chemicals, and metal goods, the situation became increasingly difficult. Britain's industrial plants, to which so much capital had been committed, had become confined, fragmented, and obsolete. As the nineteenth century wore on, the multiplication of British manufacturing enterprises to meet the mounting world demand for its products became more and more based on processes which had already proved their commercial viability, in factories which were often relatively small, and less and less on new and possibly risky technological ventures. Management did not need scientifically trained men in plants whose patterned operation had already proved its profitability.

Yet over the years we seem to have laid the main blame for the loss of our industrially dominant position on the weakness of our applied science. As I see the situation now, I think this is a gross over-simplification. Britain's main weakness lay – and may still lie – elsewhere.

Lyon Playfair,[1] who saw these things coming, and who from the mid-nineteenth century onwards campaigned for more science in British industry, uttered all the appropriate warnings, but also started some unnecessary hares. 'For a long time,' he wrote, 'practice, standing still in the pride of empiricism, and in the ungrateful forgetfulness of what science has done in its development, reared upon its portal the old and vulgar adage, "an ounce of practice is worth a ton of theory". This wretched inscription,' he went on, 'acted like a Gorgon's head, and turned to stone the aspirations of science. Believe it not! For a grain of theory, if that be an expression for science, will, when planted, like the mustard seed of Scripture, grow and wax into the greatest of trees.'

This glowing tribute to the germinal nature of scientific discovery was, and still is, fully justified. But while it and other polemics – not only from Playfair but from others who thought like him[3] – had the effect of stimulating the growth of university departments of science, they also had the effect of glorifying basic or university as opposed to applied or industrial science, at the same time as they glossed over the fact that technology, as James Watt had shown, can sometimes anticipate science. These attitudes, which are only now being dissipated, were and are totally unjustified.

There was nothing wrong with the image of the British technologist during the period when British industry found itself increasingly assailed by formidable competitors. Look at the achievements of British applied scientists during the long period when it is commonly assumed it was due to their failure that Britain's dominant industrial position was undermined. Practically every big name in the iron and steel industry of the latter part of the century was that of a British applied scientist. The basic Bessemer steel process was invented in 1856. Basic steel was invented by Sidney Thomas and his cousin in 1878; Robert Hadfield invented manganese steel in 1882; in our own century Brearley developed stainless steel. British achievements were equally rich in other fields. Roller bearings were patented by William Brown in Birmingham in 1877. In 1884 Parsons's steam turbine and generator made the biggest leap forwards in the use of power since the time of Watt. Ferranti's high voltage alternating generator of 1887 followed soon after. Even in the chemical field, where the Germans were dominant, Perkin's discoveries provided the essential seed for the German dye industry. The decline of Britain's commercial power, at the end of the nineteenth century, was certainly not associated with a decline of her technological genius. Nor, while we acknowledge the great technological innovations that have since emanated from other countries, need we feel anything but pride in British contributions to applied science in our own century. Where, without Watson Watt, would radar be; or jet engines without Whittle; or antibiotics without Florey and Chain; or, wherever computers may be now, computers without Williams and Wilkes; or, as we come to today, hovercraft without Cockerell?

One is not being chauvinistic in saying that the image of the British technologist shines today as bright as it ever did. The weakening of our competitive industrial power should not be attributed to any decline in the strength of our applied science. The explanation lies elsewhere, and properly belongs, as I have suggested, to another and complex story. I have already indicated two of its facets – first, the fact that the manufacturing industry with which Britain found itself increasingly in competition from the latter part of the nineteenth century onwards was in general more technically competent, better integrated, more concentrated and modernised than our own; and, second, what I have described as a kind of commercial indolence which, as it were, shielded British industrialists from a clear realisation of what was happening in industry overseas. Other factors were equally important and interrelated. For example, the wealth and power Britain had gained during the earlier period had made it possible to set up a worldwide Empire, and an even wider trading area, within which we were, or seemed to be, economically self-sufficient. This of itself weakened what urge there might otherwise have been to commercialise in an up-to-date way the fruits of applied science, and no doubt contributed to a view that technology was in general irrelevant to commercial success. Another factor was the complementary urge to encourage protective tariffs against other countries' manufactured goods, not only in the home market, but throughout the Empire – and later the Commonwealth – in return for the preferential treatment of their primary products. This system, which has been gradually

breaking down over recent years, undoubtedly helped to dis-
courage competitiveness in many branches of manufacturing
industry.

But these are, in the main, matters of the past. As a nation
Britain is now going through a vast process of awakening. One
of its aspects is a clearer understanding of the links that exist
between scientific knowledge on the one hand and technology
on the other, and of the critical influence which advanced technology has on industrial growth and economic welfare. The
lessons we learnt in the first world war, when England woke
to the fact that she had neglected the scientific development of
many of her industries, is as nothing to the present awakening.
What we know now is that the efficiency of modern industry,
like that of agriculture and other areas of economic activity,
necessitates a continuous scientific awareness in all stages of its
process, and that however brilliant a country's science, basic and
applied, it will fail in its exploitation if it is not backed with the
proper resources and the proper understanding. From bitter
experience we also know that alone we cannot command the
resources with which to exploit commercially expensive new
knowledge, and that even in combination with others the choice
of what to back is critically dependent on scientific as well as
commercial judgment, and not on the latter alone. Perhaps the
old jibe that England was a nation of shopkeepers helped to lull
her into a false sense of security, which made her blind to the fact
that others had evolved some sectors of industry into more
powerful scientific-commercial complexes than our own.

Today advanced technological industry is characterised mainly
by the competition between vast undertakings who between them
spend the bulk of the money which countries have available for
research and development. And in all countries these industrial
complexes appear to be operating in the same major fields – in
aviation, in electronics and computers, in chemicals, and in
machine tools. The National Aeronautics and Space Administration (NASA) of the United States alone spent until 1970–1
twice the total amount of money that goes to all research and
development in the United Kingdom. Its operations are on the
frontiers of scientific and technological knowledge, and the technical challenges which have had to be faced by those engaged in its
activities have led to the development of many new materials and

to great advances in the miniaturisation and reliability of components. The same kind of challenge is faced in all modern technologically-based industries. As they reach out into new fields, they generate new demands so that the pattern of consumption of the products of industry becomes continually transformed.

Britain's manufacturing industries have to compete not only among themselves but, in their search for overseas markets, with the corresponding industries of the rest of the world, the whole of which is gradually industrialising. In this competition we can no longer rely, as did the technologists of the industrial revolution, on the security provided by patents. Technological knowledge spreads rapidly regardless of attempted secrecy, and patents also have a restrictive influence on development.

Experience has also shown that the high quality of our research and development is not enough to secure us economic rewards, any more than the rate of a country's economic growth necessarily bears a close relation to the proportion of its own resources which it spends directly on research and development, whether measured as a fraction of gross national product or of industrial turnover. What counts for economic growth is the whole process of innovation in industry. As I remarked in an earlier chapter, this process, which includes prototype development, tooling, market research and preparatory production, may cost, on an average, nine times the technical resources, including the services of skilled manpower, as may have been spent on the initial research and development which showed how an idea could be translated into a marketable product – say, a new aero-engine or new computer.[4] The economics of modern technological industry, therefore, demand bigger and bigger units and more and more resources, if research and development is not to prove a sterile enterprise. That, quite independently of longer and more assured production runs, is one of the main reasons why Britain's closer association with Europe in a Common Market should lead to major long-term benefits for all. Europe will never be able to compete effectively with the giant technological corporations of the United States unless its industries combine their efforts in what has been called a technological community.

Essentially what the large industrial organisations do is provide the only adequate environment for the fruitful exploitation of discovery. But the basic ideas and inventions will still continue to be the brain-children of single, highly gifted individuals. And the truly creative technologist, wherever he may be, whether working alone, or in some small company as is so often the case with inventors, or as a member of the R & D staff of some large corporation, will always have to fight to bring his ideas to fruition – ideas which may produce new products or transform old processes – because the choice of what ideas should be backed by large resources will have to be decided by the combined judgment of others. The technologist will have to fight for his brain-child, just as James Watt fought, because those who dispose of the resources without which industrial innovation cannot occur are usually nervous of the insecurity which is associated with the birth of new things. Since there is always an element of gamble in the costly process of developing something which is new, small advances will always be more likely to be backed than large ones, even though it is the latter which have the more enduring effect. The creative applied scientist and technologist will always have to be ready to defy the cynical adage that nothing should ever be done for the first time.

The way manufacturing industry is going to unfold in the world in the years ahead cannot be foreseen. At this moment in time, no one can, for example, tell precisely what effects the introduction of computer technology will have in scientific work, in industrial processes, and in administration. No one can predict the developments that are likely to occur in fields of, say, gaseous metallurgy, any more than they can deny the possibilities of synthetic protein production or that the science of molecular biology will have practical applications. These things will be determined by the technological geniuses of tomorrow, in the same way as James Watt helped transform the environment of his day. And the more informed scientifically and technically becomes the population within which they work, the better aided will they be in their task. Britain did great things in the days before a deliberate effort was made to cultivate a widespread scientific awareness. Now that it is national policy to promote this aspect of education, it will do at least as well in the future – provided only that its industrial and commercial institutions adapt themselves to the world of modern technological competition.

15
Technological Forecasting

The basic issue in the exploitation of technology in private industry is to employ resources to the greatest immediate effect, and in the case of the United Kingdom, particularly in the export field, since it is the revenues that our industry and commerce earn in overseas markets that pay for the bulk of the raw materials used by our factories, and for about fifty per cent of the food we eat. Competition from other countries which export manufactured goods is increasing all the time, while countries which used to absorb the product of Britain's factories are themselves industrialising at an ever-increasing rate. Not surprisingly, the latter trend is most marked in conventional manufactures, at the same time as in a country like the United States growth is fastest in the modern science-based industries. The pattern of Britain's present industrial investment is thus of the utmost importance to its future well-being. This is where the question of technological choice becomes a matter of paramount importance. But there are no guidebooks which lead one to the correct choices. Technological forecasting, as it is now called, is still more an art than a science, and we do not enjoy the advantages either of time or of a superfluity of resources in deciding where to invest. As a nation, the United Kingdom cannot afford to repeat some of the mistakes in technological investment which have marred its post-war history.

Much has been written about technological forecasting, some in its relation to modern management techniques such as cost-effectiveness analyses; some in its still wider Washington connotation of 'Planning-Programming-Budgeting'; and some in the context of what is called 'Futurology'.[1] In so far as the intellectual techniques which may be involved in any or all of these enterprises support the general proposition that it is wiser to make judgments about possible future investment on the basis of all the facts and figures that can be marshalled in the relevant field, as opposed to simply leaping in the dark, they are clearly to be welcomed. But the welcome needs to be qualified by scientific caution, and not surcharged with the enthusiasm of ignorance. Except where it relates to the short-term, and to minor developments, technological forecasting in the private sector is a hazardous enterprise.

Charles Townes,[2] a Nobel Laureate in physics, whose work in quantum electronics was in large part responsible for the development of both the maser and laser, and who has worked in industrial as well as university laboratories, illustrates this thesis on the basis of his own experience. He reminds us that microwave spectroscopy grew out of a field of technology which emerged during the second world war, and that at the end of the war four American industrial laboratories, as well as a number of university departments, began to work on the subject. He himself was with the Bell Telephone Company, but like research workers in the three other industrial laboratories concerned, he failed to convince 'Management' that since electronics was 'their business', this new field of physics was potentially of great commercial significance. As a result, all four firms independently took the decision to stop work in microwave spectroscopy. A few years after they had done so, and after the maser and then the laser principles were demonstrated in university laboratories, they were all 'back in the game', with hundreds of scientists and engineers working in what had been shown to be a most powerful new technique of amplification. But even this step was not taken without much hesitation. Townes tells us that Bell's patent department at first refused to patent the amplifier or oscillator he and his colleague, Schawlow, had designed, because 'optical waves had never been of any importance to communications and hence the invention had little bearing on Bell System interests'. Today, business in the United States based on the exploitation of quantum electronics, not only in microwave communications, but in a host of other applications reaching all the way from metallurgy to surgery, amounts to nearly one billion dollars a year. And all this has happened in the past ten years or so!

There are, of course, contrary examples of major developments, such as the transistor, where practical and commercial benefits came from deliberate and costly efforts to fertilise and exploit a field of basic knowledge. But these are so much in the minority, as compared with stories like the laser, that one doubts whether technological forecasting, except in the short-term, is an intellectual weapon which will allow one to forecast the details of the future. ICI was much slower than some believe it need have been in developing the newer plastics, but spent some millions in rapidly but abortively developing the protein fibre ARDIL. DDT was for years in a bottle on the shelves of the Geigy Laboratories in Switzerland before Müller discovered its powerful insecticidal properties. The basic physiological and chemical knowledge for 'the Pill' was with us in the mid-thirties – but it is only within the past ten years that this powerful contraceptive technique has become a reality; whereas, to take a contrary example, thalidomide was developed and put into use, with such tragic results, within the space of a few years.

These illustrations relate to only one aspect of technological forecasting in the private sector, and particularly in manufacturing industry. There are others, which I propose only to mention and not to spell out – for example, inadequate estimation of technical difficulties, and therefore of costs, particularly in science-based industry, and conspicuously in the defence field; inadequate market analysis, or market analysis based on assumptions not borne out by the technical realities as they unfold; and an inadequate appreciation of the responses of potential competitors.

But a far more important question than the choice of the right projects to develop is whether we have yet reached a level of sophistication sufficient to allow us to foretell the impact which present and new technology is going to have on the future shape of human society. The somewhat sceptical views which I have expressed before on this subject – and which it has been suggested[3] I have derived from what has been called the 'treacherous logic of philosophical idealism' – have not been allowed to pass without challenge. But I am unrepentant. I also think it is possible to define an immediate and more modest course between what has been ambitiously called by Jantsch[4] the exploratory and normative methods of technological forecasting as it affects the future of human society, and one which could at least provide a helpful beacon as we navigate to future horizons. But to do this we must – to mix the metaphor – keep our feet on the ground. I am convinced, for example, that the giants of the industrial revolution, men like Stephenson, Watt, Wilkinson and Boulton, however much they might have seen their steam engines, pumps, and other mechanical contrivances, adding to wealth and human welfare, could never have envisaged the vast social and economic consequences of their technological developments. Crowther[3] contests this view. But I repeat it in spite of his reminder that Watt wrote in 1808 that 'the very existence of Britain as a nation seems to me, in great measure, to depend on her exertions in science and in the arts'; or that Boulton told Boswell that he sold 'what all the world desires to have – Power'. These assertions by two of the fathers of the industrial revolution are very different from some prophetic view of the likely social and political consequences of the technological developments which they were responsible for introducing into the human environment – which is what really concerns us. So far as 'computerised judgment' is concerned, both in the civil and the military spheres, my view has been, and still is, that we shall not be able to rely upon machines to replace human judgment in the really important areas of social decision. However much the machine can accelerate and extend certain human mental processes, the permutations and combinations of its operations are restricted to the 'logic' and pieces of information that have been fed into it. The machine can make precise, and probably even more certain estimations, than the unaided brain in areas of operation which have known and given dimensions. It cannot operate creatively where its terms of reference have not been precisely defined; and the capacity to do this, to my mind, is the essence of what we implicitly mean by expressions like genius and inspired social judgment.

What has happened since I first expressed these opinions[5] gives them even greater force today than they had ten, fifteen years ago, at the same time as experience has revealed the immense value of modern computer techniques as an aid to, as opposed to a substitute for, judgment. My justification for saying this derives largely from American experience.

In 1965 President Johnson decided that the cost-benefit studies which Mr Charles Hitch had introduced into the affairs of the Department of Defense during his term as Controller should be extended to other spheres of government under the name 'Planning, Programming and Budgeting System', or PPBS as it became widely known. In the words of the President, PPBS provided a means whereby national goals could be identified 'with precision and on a continuing basis', and whereby the government could 'choose among those goals the ones that are most urgent'.[6]

The far-reaching nature of this claim, deriving, as it did, mainly from the views of exponents of cost-benefit analysis and management techniques in the Department of Defense, immediately led the United States Senate Committee on Government Operations to appoint a sub-committee to examine the problem. An interim report[6] was published late in 1967. It began by pointing out that PPBS is as old as government itself – 'the problem from the outset has been to avoid an underestimation of costs and an over-estimation of benefits'. The sub-committee then went on to consider the widely-advertised success of PPBS in the US defence field, and pointed out that what success it had achieved took place during a period of rising defence expenditure. Questioning whether the 'system' would have been of much use in promoting the national interest, and of deciding what should be done, in a period of declining budgets, it also pointed to the fact that PPBS had been used to rationalise the choice of the largest single military aircraft project in history – presumably a reference to the F-111, a project which so far has been dogged with enormous bad luck, which has proved far more costly than was estimated at the start, and which after nearly ten years is not yet in operational service. In the sub-committee's view all that PPBS can provide is 'a set of sharp tools which in experienced hands and guided by sound judgment can be a helpful aid in some of the business of government. . . . It is not a statistical litmus paper, scientifically sorting good projects from bad. It may be used as easily to rationalise a decision as to make a rational choice. It is no substitute for experience and judgment.'

Above all, I myself would add, PPBS is not a system of government which helps in deciding how much should be spent on, say, education, in relation to roads, health or housing. It merely constitutes one means whereby government can decide how the resources it commits to each of these fields of public expenditure is most effectively spent. Overplaying the concept has its obvious dangers, as Charles Hitch[7] himself warns, 'including the risk of discrediting the techniques'. One should therefore see cost-benefit analyses as being of the utmost value in helping to decide between alternative methods of achieving a specified technological goal, given that all the main facts relating to the alternatives are available. But it is essential to realise that when some of the critical facts are missing from the cost-benefit equation, or when some essential technological issue is assumed, when it should have been proved, the analyses can go badly awry. As one critic has put it in somewhat exaggerated terms, the men in the Pentagon have all too often shown that they know little of costs and nothing of benefits. And as Admiral Rickover, a powerful opponent of the wider use of cost-benefit studies as carried out by US defence planners, but a brilliant manager of projects, has emphasised repeatedly, cost-benefit sums only too often exclude, as of no account, the cost of human life, or the purpose of human effort.

What we, therefore, need to learn, in the most dispassionate way possible, is how far we can go with these methods in the systematic analysis of the complicated problems of modern society. Do they let us peer with assurance into the future in order to see which way technology is transforming the environment of tomorrow? Clearly we need to remove from the concept of technological forecasting the implication of the statements of some of its bolder protagonists, that somewhere along the road politics can be eliminated from major decisions which affect the well-being of society at large. This can never be so. As the US Senate Sub-Committee puts it, in the 'making of decisions on matters of public interest, we do not propose to delegate the task to a dictator, no matter how benevolent, or to an expert, no matter how objective, or to a computer, no matter who programs it'.

Exploratory forecasting, in the terminology of Jantsch, means extrapolating present technological trends and innovations to derive a picture of the range of possibilities that are likely to open up in the future. By normative forecasting he means the definition of some desirable 'future', or some future development, and then tracking back to determine what kinds of technological path connect the predicated future with the actual present. Both are intrinsically hazardous enterprises, since they depend equally on the frail assumption that the trends and rate of technological progress experienced in the immediate past can be depended on to continue, in some form, into the future. In addition, the normative approach implies that the technological forecaster not only has the intellectual capacity, but also the authority to define the future goals of society. Even if he were competent in the first respect, it is most unlikely that he would be provided with a remit for the second. Bertrand de Jouvenel,[8] who has written extensively on these issues, has defined what can be regarded as a modest middle course. His view is that 'the presently likely future . . . should not be confused with necessity'. The utility of any long-term view 'is to show where we are going according to our present courses and values . . . this is a warning urgently required to bring some degree of correction in these courses and views'. This middle course, which takes heed of both the normative and exploratory aspects of forecasting is, in my view, the one which we should follow as we try to avoid some of the pitfalls and hazards that lie ahead of us.

16

The Social Cost of Technological Choice

But how much freedom of action has society in determining the future trends or the pace of technological advance? It used to be said that necessity is the mother of invention. But as many as eighty years ago, Ludwig Mond,[1] in a presidential address to the Society of Chemical Industry, declared that this was no longer so, since scientific knowledge kept revealing 'where, and in what direction, and how far, improvement is possible. And since,' as he put it, 'the increase in our knowledge of the properties of matter enables us to form an opinion beforehand as to the substances we have available for obtaining a desired result, we can foresee, in most cases, in what direction progress in technology will move, and in consequence the inventor is now frequently in advance of the wants of his time.'

This is certainly what is demanded of him by manufacturing industry today. The firm which is not ahead of its competitor in those technological innovations which lead to better products at lesser cost is soon at a disadvantage. Competition, as Paul Chambers[2] has said, drives firms along the road of technological advance whether they like it or not. But what determines the direction the road takes is questionable. According to Paul Chambers, it is the preference of the consumer. In his view, 'the wishes of the consumers should be the factor determining technological development of consumer goods, and so long as there is competition, those wishes will be expressed by their choice of one manufacturer's products rather than those of another'. The same view has been put equally strongly by Cadbury.[3]

This, however, is true only up to a point. Clearly it was not the consumer who dreamed up the idea of television, or supersonic transport aircraft, or antibiotics. Where totally new products are concerned, the customer has to be persuaded that he wants them. New things have to be imposed on him because of what Galbraith[4] calls 'the imperatives of technology', because of the large investments involved, because of the long period that elapses between the conception of a major new product and its appearance on the market, and because of the inflexible commitment of particular investments to particular tasks. But, as Galbraith also recognises, the consumer, in spite of the stimulation of his appetite for the new product, through advertising and other forms of sales pressure, may still fail to buy. It is because the consumer has the last word, and because modern technology has become so complex and costly, that every effort has to be made to plan not only the productive process, but also the market. The relentless progress of technology is thus as much determined by competition between producers to improve the nature and quality of their goods, that is to say by competition in technical innovation, as it is by competition to gratify the wants and stimulate the appetite of the consumer with new things. But either way, it is clear that the process is not conditioned at its start by any broad conception of what the environment of man's future should be. If supersonic flight is wanted, let there be supersonic flight – and leave the secondary problems which it will generate to be sorted out in due course. If plastic bags make the handling of fertiliser easier, use them instead of the old-fashioned sack, even if they become a kind of indestructible litter. The immediate satisfaction of the individual comes first. If the benefits are undiluted, well and good. If secondary problems arise, they have to be dealt with later.

This is the dilemma which now characterises the interaction of technology and society – and which the United Kingdom faces in an acute form. If we, as a nation, are to preserve and raise our standard of living, technology must be given its head. But when it is given its head, both the structure of society and its physical environment may be affected, usually unpredictably and often deleteriously.

This problem was clearly recognised in the well-known 1967 US Report on Technological Innovation,[5] to which I have already referred, and which accepted that 'private innovation' creates conditions which call for what it termed 'social innovation' – for example, measures to check the pollution of water and air and to improve highway safety. The American report implies that 'private innovation' means innovations in manufacturing industry brought about by private individuals using resources over which they have full command. To deal with 'social innovation' they proposed a number of measures, among them the suggestion that government should encourage private enterprise to seek 'profit-making opportunities' in the solution of the social problems brought about by the technological innovations of the private sector.

We would assess this situation somewhat differently in the United Kingdom, if for no other reason than that the UK government provides a very large part of the money which is spent in the furtherance of technology in, and indeed for, private manufacturing industry, where in certain fields, as is also the case in the United States, it calls the tune. The development of nuclear power, which by 1980 will provide about half the installed generating capacity in the United Kingdom, is one such field; the aerospace industry another. Overall, the government supports research and development in private industry to a greater extent than it contributes to its fixed capital formation. The government is also directly responsible for the whole range of defence 'R and D' which is undertaken in the United Kingdom, a range which is still very wide, partly for the reason that it is not so long since we were trying to cover the whole spectrum of military research.

The government is thus critically involved in private as well as social innovation, to use the terms of the American report, and consequently is faced by the issue of technological choice in both. With a few qualifications, to which I shall refer later, a private firm, whether it be the kind of small enterprise which provides the focused environment for a specific innovation, or a vast inter-national company, covering many areas of industrial development, is concerned only in the first, and thus has an immeasurably easier task in deciding its technological priorities than has the govern-ment. Moreover, the determination of the priorities according to which the government disposes of the scientific and tech-nological resources it commands not only constitutes a consider-able problem in the short-term, but is of even greater importance in its impact on the environment of tomorrow, both positively and negatively. Decisions to direct resources in one direction affect the future because, as I have said, they deny resources to another area. Some decisions affect the future because a favoured development, when it emerges, may generate some highly costly secondary problem, as motor traffic has done and continues to do, and as supersonic aircraft promise to do. In addition, the decisions are often constrained by economic and political considerations which seem to be peripheral to the central issue of choice. Of these secondary considerations one is always overriding. If Britain's standard of living is to rise, and the problem of its balance-of-payments kept under control, the volume of its exports must remain high, which means that the competitiveness of its manufacturing industries has to go on improving. It is essentially for this reason that the previous UK government instituted a policy of shifting R and D resources from the defence to the civil sector, and from certain long-term projects in, for example, the nuclear field, to others which have a better prospect of yielding social and economic benefits.

A strategic decision of this kind does not, however, ease the problem of deciding which projects to back and which to reject. Technological choice can never be certain. If the risk of mistake is to be lessened, deciding which projects to foster demands a sophisticated understanding, not only of the technical promise and uncertainties of the projects themselves, but also of the possible consequences of their successful completion and subsequent use. A Concorde, a new nuclear reactor, a Channel tunnel are difficult enough in themselves. But traffic control on and about airports, noise and sonic bangs; the disposal of nuclear waste when the bulk, if not all, of our electricity supply will come from nuclear power stations; and the regulation of traffic in the south of, and around, London will prove at least as difficult.

This is why Bertrand de Jouvenel's approach to forecasting is so salutary a warning. We must never confuse 'the presently likely course' along which we are driven by technology as 'the only necessary course'. Each of us could make a list of those aspects of the unfolding scene of society's physical environment which he dislikes most. Most 'civilised' people would probably agree about the worst threats to man's future well-being: environmental pollution, the loss of amenities in urban areas, the erosion of the countryside, traffic congestion, and the continued growth of vast conurbations – and at all times when we turn our thoughts to the future we need to remember that by the year 2000 the population of the United Kingdom is likely to be some ten to fifteen million more than today's figure of fifty-four million, with a larger proportion than today in the age groups below twenty.

The merits of every new technological development which might be proposed have, therefore, to be judged not only in terms of its immediate commercial utility, but also in the light of its possible impact on the transforming social scene. As Mishan[6] continues to emphasise, one has to ask whether the unquantifiable social cost of a particular contribution to economic progress may not be excessive in relation to the material and commercial benefit of the technological development itself. One ought always to be able to regard this as an essential question without running the risk of being treated as some kind of backwoodsman or economic reactionary. Man is a very adaptable creature, and over the years has tolerated and adjusted to many a deleterious consequence of technological change. We have, for example, learnt to live with a burden of DDT in our tissues; the ban on the atmospheric test of nuclear devices was a reaction to the knowledge that, as a result of such tests, young people – as well as all animals and plants – were being dangerously contaminated by radioactive fall-out; police do traffic duty at cross-roads in New York City while suffering from the inhalation of unhealthy amounts of carbon-monoxide from the exhausts of motor cars. No sensible person wants to constrain the development of useful technology, or limit the freedom of the 'technological entrepreneur'. But the pace of change is so fast that we must beware lest, in giving the entrepreneur his head, we create for the year 2000 – when world population will be at least six billion, possibly twice what it is now – and for the years after that – when some urban agglomerations in the world can be expected to number hundreds of millions of citizens – a physical environment to which it will be difficult to go on adapting. Innumerable biological species have disappeared from the face of the earth during the course of geological time because they did not have the capacity to adapt to changes in the environment in which they lived. A wood in which starlings roost may in time be destroyed by their droppings. In the years ahead more species will disappear, and more woods will be destroyed. But we ourselves should neither be the agents of our own destruction, nor the destroyers of our physical environment.

Obviously the value which society attaches to the concept of economic progress has been assessed by democratic decision.

People want the wealth of the country to increase, and the resulting benefits to be disposed more and more fairly through the community. This does not necessarily mean that the desire for greater material riches will motivate society for ever. But so long as it does, the societies of today will necessarily have to reflect the consequences of technological development, in the same way as did the societies of the neolithic period. But increasingly, we shall have to modulate, as effectively as possible, the deleterious consequences of technological progress, in the knowledge that in the final analysis we ourselves choose which developments to foster and which to suppress. General Eisenhower's 'military-industrial complex', today more correctly the 'military-industrial-scientific complex', may have provided a large part of the momentum of modern technology. But its power is not supreme. Society itself is the final arbiter of technological development; and government is its instrument. If, as one forecaster[7] suggests on the basis of present trends, pure air and water become by the year 2000 the scarcest and costliest of natural resources in industrialised societies, it will be our fault. If we cannot organise society 'in such a way as to provide a fair chance that our children will not curse technology and its aftermath' – to quote a rhetorical question put by Dr Mansholt, the Vice-President of the European Economic Community in an address entitled 'Our Accelerating Century'[8] – it will again be our fault. We shall avoid these things the more major decisions in technological matters are taken in the context of a proper appreciation of what secondary consequences might be entailed.

There has been some talk recently about the desirability of engineers taking the equivalent of the Hippocratic oath of the doctor, and forswearing participation in technical developments which could reduce social welfare. It would be far better if, as they exercise their professional responsibilities, the engineer and scientist did not stand aside from those who took the decisions. Technology, as I have said, is in the domain of politics. The more the technologist – and scientist – understands how events move in the political sphere, the more he is able to participate, either directly or indirectly, in the decisions of politics, the more society would benefit from technology and the less there would be to fear.

For if we are not vigilant there will be something to fear. The multiplying millions of the world will not be catered for unless more and more new technology is called into play to provide for their needs and desires – for example by the discovery of better pesticides and herbicides to prevent waste in food production, of new and cheaper pharmaceuticals and vaccines, of new means of transportation, better urban organisation, of more nuclear power, and so on. The present phase of competitive technology has an enormous momentum of its own, and some of its developments have already imposed a high social cost. Adding to the momentum in order to satisfy the needs of the three to four thousand million additional people who will be living by the year 2000 – only thirty years away – entails a real risk of multiplying the social cost and intensifying the threat to man's physical environment. Because the momentum cannot fail to increase, a new morality as well as better measures of technological forecasting than exist now are called for to help guide new technology into safe as well as useful directions.

Science, we all know, has no national boundaries. Technology, because of competition, has often been a divisive force. But because of its soaring costs, and because of the scale and pervasiveness of its effects, it has also promoted the growth of the international company and the sharing of the costs of very expensive projects between nations. It is also beginning to demand more and more co-operative international effort to deal with some of its deleterious secondary consequences, of which the pollution of our physical environment is the most obvious. In the end technology may well become, therefore, a unifying force between nations. It is not just the fear of nuclear annihilation that is forcing nations to get together in some kind of mutual understanding. Above all, the problems of population growth and the development of resources, which we all now face, cannot be dealt with on a purely national basis. The issues involved are mainly technical, and here at least is one place where opportunity beckons the scientist and engineer to enter the political arena, not necessarily as a politician in the narrow sense of the term, but as one who concerns himself, as does any public servant, with those secondary effects of technological innovation which are, and will increasingly be, the business of government.

17

The Transformation of the Medical Environment

Nowhere is the interaction of private and social innovation more pronounced than it is in the field of health. And hardly anywhere has the interaction shown itself more swiftly or more dramatically. British medical students who registered before the 1923 regulations of the Royal Colleges of Physicians and Surgeons came into force were able to complete their clinical studies in no more than twenty-four months before embarking on private practice in a medical world of free enterprise. In those days one served as a dresser to a surgeon, as a clerk in a physician's 'firm', and went out 'on the district' to deliver some twenty babies. So far as I can recall, that was essentially the sum total of my own clinical training, or rather of the amount of training some people, including myself, managed to get by with, and get away with. No doubt those who were really keen did better. One attended a modicum of lectures and out-patient clinics; did some sporadic duty in 'casualty'; crammed a few textbooks, and then took the 'Conjoint' examination of the Royal Colleges of Physicians and Surgeons. As a student I do not recall hearing anything of pediatrics or social medicine, and little of pathology. One visit to what was called a lunatic asylum was enough, and what I learnt in the hurried reading of a handbook – literally a handbook – on public health was all I knew of the subject. If one was going into practice, there was no obligatory year that had to be spent as a 'houseman', serving as an apprentice to one of the consultant physicians, surgeons, or obstetricians. In my time as a clinical student I even managed, like others in those days, to pass the primary Fellowship examination of the Royal College of Surgeons. Fortunately, for an unsuspecting public, I myself had no intention of ever practising medicine. And let me also confess it never occurred to me at the time that the way people were trained, or the way medical practice was organised, was not for the best in the best of all possible worlds.

Since then vast changes have taken place in the medical curriculum and in the organisation of medical practice. It is enough to say that for a possible minimum of twenty-one months of hospital study, we now have to read three years, as well as an obligatory pre-registration year as a 'houseman'; that in place of a system in which medical care, to say the least of it, was sporadic in its distribution, in which most patients paid the doctor according to their means, and in which the poor were looked after by a hospital system sustained by a patchwork of grants, workmen's compensation schemes, National Health Insurance and charity, Britain now has a comprehensive National Health Service financed by the state out of revenues provided mainly by general taxation, and at the flanks of which the remnants of private medical practice continue to thrive; and that in place of a chemist's shop on the corner, we now have a powerful pharmaceutical industry, which, by means of a spate of advertising literature, instructs the medical profession every day through the post, as well as in other ways, about new drugs and new cures.

It is against the background of the vast changes that have taken place since I became a student that I find myself asking where medicine now stands in relation to the community, and where it is likely to stand tomorrow, with the speed of social and technological change now vastly greater than it was when I became a university student.

One basic thing will, I believe, never change. Whatever progress is made in fields of preventive and social medicine, the quest of the individual for medical care will be at least as demanding tomorrow as it is today. I should expect it to be even more demanding because of the vast developments that have been taking place, and that are still taking place, in medical treatment. The time is long past since people were prepared to resign themselves to their ills as an affliction from on high. Health, disease and death may still remain a mystery, but antibiotics, asian-flu vaccines, kidney machines, heart transplants, and 'the pill' – with all the publicity by which these things were heralded, and by which they are still promoted – have encouraged most people to believe that their medical troubles, if not avoidable, are certainly curable ills, provided they get into the right hands for the right treatment. Tuberculosis kills no more than a fraction of its victims as compared with the situation when I was a student; pneumonia is not the lethal disease it used to be; one hardly hears the name of poliomyelitis any more, and in the United Kingdom typhoid is a rare and largely imported affliction; and the prevalent belief is that even cancer will one day be cured, as indeed it often is now. Clearly if modern medicine does not promise immortality, at least it does promise a long life free from pain – provided, of course, one does the right things, and the resources are there.

This, to my mind, unchangeable individual view of what medical science and practice can and should provide to some extent also reflects a communal view. The British National Health Service was introduced in 1948, not only in order to alleviate distress and to spread the boon of medicine to poor as well as rich, but also because of the belief that the healthier the population as a whole, the better it was for the state. These are the two sets of considerations which for centuries have impelled improvements in health services. 'Ill-health is to a large extent the results of mistakes which could be avoided, given greater knowledge and care', as a 1937 PEP volume[1] on the British Health Services optimistically put it. Whatever medical schools, hospitals, district nurses, and other community services cost the nation, it was never as much as what the state lost through sickness and ill-health. The humanitarian motive was assuredly the driving force which brought the British comprehensive national health service into being – the Bill[2] placed 'a general duty upon the Minister of Health to promote a comprehensive health service for the improvement of the physical and mental health of the people . . . and for the prevention, diagnosis, and treatment of illness'; but it was the powerful sense – reinforced by the wartime experience of dealing with casualties of the 'Blitz', – that the cost of ill-health to the nation, both in direct payment and in value of work lost, had become so great that forced the pace with the Parliament of the day.

That the British National Health Service has fulfilled its promise – even if not all that some expected from it – is no longer disputed in any quarter. The annual reports of the Chief Medical Officer of the Ministry of Health on the State of the Public Health provide evidence enough of the benefits that have accrued from it, or which have been associated with the period of its existence.

This is not to say that the service is perfect – far from it. Administratively it may undergo significant changes following on the recent publication of a series of far-reaching reports on different aspects of its organisation, and all of which are concerned to improve the links between the three branches of the service – the public health or community services, the hospital services and the family doctor services. Many of these institutional matters will no doubt be the subject of lively debate before they, or some amended scheme, are put into effect. But they are clearly less interesting to the man in the street than the possibility that new miracle cures and new miracle treatments will make his medical lot even easier in the future than it has been made over the past twenty years or so.

The most manifest sign of the general improvement in the nation's health is to be found in figures for the average expectation of life. The changes which have taken place over the past fifty years, and particularly in the post-war years, are dramatic by any standard. Sixty years ago, British children aged ten had on average a further expectation of about fifty to fifty-five years. Today the figure is nearer sixty-five. People in their twenties could expect to live on average to about sixty-five. Today the figure is about seventy-five. It is not so much that the aged live longer than did their forbears, but rather that more of them reach old-age. There are differences between the sexes in the expectation of life; but it is the broad picture which matters. And what it shows is that there has been an incredibly dramatic change, and that a large part of it has taken place in the postwar years.

The essential reason for the continuing improvement in the average expectation of life is that medical advances and better public health measures have reduced mortality rates in both sexes, and in every age group, but particularly the younger ones, and especially infants in the first years of life. In general the decline in a wide category of infectious diseases has more than offset an increase in death-rates due to such conditions as coronary disease and cancer of the lung on the one hand, and motor accidents on the other. For people of my generation it is amazing to think that in the United Kingdom illnesses like measles, whooping cough and diphtheria were each responsible for between 5,000 and 10,000 deaths a year in the earlier part of this century, and that today they are responsible for all but none. Scarlet fever I remember as a communicable disease which was frequently fatal. Today it claims hardly a victim. Tuberculosis was a scourge. Today large hospitals devoted to TB patients no longer exist, and as a cause of death TB has become relatively insignificant. One could go on endlessly with illustrations of the sub-causes in the decline in mortality rates.

We can take as obvious that the improvement in the spectrum of disease has not only made life more tolerable for the individual, but that in those sectors in which it has had its greatest impact, it has also considerably reduced the costs, direct and indirect, of disease to the state. But in saying this I have implicitly posed two questions. To what do we owe the decline in the incidence and virulence of the communicable diseases – to the Public Health Service and the work of the medical profession, or to what? And can we expect the trend to continue? A clear answer to these two questions, were one possible, would do much to ease the problems of choice in medical policy in the future.

Before I attempt to face these two questions, let me turn briefly to the issue of the volume of resources one could legitimately expect to go to the medical services. Today the Health and Welfare Services cost the British Exchequer roughly five per cent of our gross national product. We have no figure for the amount that is spent in the private medical sector – it can hardly be more than a fraction of the public figure; nor do we know how much was spent on medical care in the 1930s, before the institution of the National Health Service. Needless to say, the institution of the service has meant a more equitable distribution within the population of the resources that are available for medical care. But is there any reason why these resources should not be double what they are, or half their present volume?

For quite different reasons they could be neither. The level at which the health budget now stands has been determined by the countervailing demands on the public purse of all forms of public expenditure – roads, schools, the armed services, social security, as well as health. It is hardly likely, therefore, that the health services would be provided in any one year with a significantly higher proportion of national resources than they have been receiving – there are too many other claims, many unfulfilled, on the public purse. Correspondingly, the Government and White-hall are not going to be able to say to the electorate that the medical services are getting too much of our total resources, or that the state of health of the nation has improved so greatly over recent years that we can reduce the amount going to the National Health Service to, say, three quarters of its present level. Public demand for medical care will continue to be insistent however many diseases are eliminated and whatever improvements occur in medical practice. While man remains mortal, and so long as pain and distress remain his lot, he will continue to demand that there be doctors and hospitals – as well as improvements in both – in numbers as well as quality.

A former Minister of Health, Enoch Powell, has put the case very clearly.[3] Demand for medical care is for all practical purposes unlimited. 'Every advance in medical science creates new needs that did not exist until the means of meeting them came into existence, or at least into the realm of the possible. For every heart-lung machine or artificial kidney in operation, there must be many times that number of cases to which the treatment would be applicable.' Correspondingly, the individual is capable of absorbing any amount of medical care, as he cannot, let us say, food and drink, in the same way as there are no limits to improvements in the potential quality of medical care – a feature in which medicine differs in its impact on the public purse from, for example, education, where it is possible to lay down criteria on such matters as the curriculum, school-leaving age, size of class and so on. Demand being in theory infinite, it is only by rationing supply that governments can prevent the Health Services, through their own growth, denying resources to other forms of national enterprise. In recent years the annual rate of increase in the resources going to Health and Welfare Services has been about three per cent at constant prices, the total volume of money voted, now about £2,000 million, being apportioned by the Minister of Health to the development and servicing of the hospitals and associated Welfare Services of the country, and to the remuneration of medical practitioners outside the hospitals – together with, of course, that part of the secondary costs of medical care, drugs and so on, for which the state pays out of the monies that are raised through general taxation. But as Mr Powell emphasised in his book, whatever is done, whatever the resources given to the Health Services, medical care has to be rationed. This shows itself in the waiting lists of hospitals, which stand at the same figure year after year, and which would probably do so if the annual rate of growth of the resources going to the NHS were doubled or trebled; or in the queue at the general practitioner's surgery, whose length is determined not so much by the numbers of doctors inside as by the amount of time each doctor can give a patient.

In the final analysis the community cannot enjoy more medical service than it can afford. This, of course, is not to say that the more favoured amongst us cannot go outside the national service to buy from the private practitioner or consultant what care and treatment we can pay for. But even if one were to assume that everyone could do this, either directly out of his pocket or on the basis of some private insurance scheme, we would again be in trouble. For with demand for medical attention in effect limitless, one could then in theory visualise the market mechanism stimulating a growth of medical resources out of all proportion to the total volume of resources available to the community, with the latter declining as less went into more productive channels of national enterprise, such as manufacturing industry, until chaos – if that is the right word – once again supervened on the medical scene.

18

The Consequences of Medical Progress

Not even the USA, the centre of free enterprise, and the richest country in the world, can any longer afford a health service that operates just by the market mechanism. What then is the likely future of our medical environment? Six sets of considerations are clearly important when one tries to delineate the trends which will determine the medical future. They are, first, medical education – which for present purposes can be regarded as applying not only to those who dispense medical services, but also to the patients of the future, and also the organisational changes which could help make the Health Service work more smoothly; second, dramatic developments in medical science and practice; third, further spectacular developments in the pharmaceutical field; fourth, the disappearance of scourges by which we are still beset – and the possible emergence of new ones; fifth, the preponderance of the degenerative diseases which are associated with an ageing population; and sixth, the kind of social world in which we shall be living in the future.

The transformation of the educational picture can be seen under three broad heads – the education of medical and ancillary professional staff; the education of the public; and the transformation of the National Health Service on the basis of experience.

There can hardly be a medical school in the United Kingdom which, in the postwar years, has not made deliberate efforts to adjust its medical curriculum to take account, first, of the emergence of new medical knowledge and techniques; second, of the increase in specialisation; and third, of changes in the demands of the public for medical service. In 1946 when I left Oxford to go to Birmingham University, medical undergraduates (who, it was assumed, had already taken preliminary courses in biology, chemistry and physics) had to devote two whole years, of their total of five as a student, to anatomy and physiology, a large part of the time being spent in the dissecting room. In the recognition that anatomy, while still the means whereby the student learns about the structure of the body, had become increasingly functional in its interests – so much so that in many areas it was difficult to draw a dividing line between it and physiology – I and my physiological colleague devised an integrated course of anatomy and physiology in which a student completed his structural anatomy in three instead of the five customary terms, the course being trimmed of all unnecessary detail to make this possible.[1] I believe that Birmingham pioneered this change, which today is accepted in most medical schools in the United Kingdom. But it was none of our concern to see that changes were made in the clinical curriculum, which for many years was unaffected by the presumedly revolutionary step we had taken in the preclinical departments. I am mentioning this purely as a piece of history. The British medical schools now have before them the report of the Todd Commission on Medical Education.[2] This deals with all five years of a medical student's educational career, and provides a renewed stimulus to all schools to adjust their syllabuses and methods to modern needs. Correspondingly, changes are being introduced, as necessary, in the training curriculum of those other professional people whose services are essential to the practice of modern medicine – the nurses, physicists, biochemists, radiologists, who work hand in glove with their clinical colleagues in a modern health service. Improvements are also being made in the service itself on the basis of the experience of the past twenty years. It seems generally accepted that we are moving into an era in which doctors will no longer work in isolation, but in which there will be group practice linked to properly staffed and equipped health centres associated with district hospitals.

One of the major developments to which we now have to accustom ourselves is, of course, the electronic computer, which has now made it possible to collect, store and retrieve clinical information on a vast scale. As a result, we may eventually reach the point when there will be immediately available an up-to-date history of the people who pass through the hands of the medical profession, and a store of knowledge which should be immensely potent from the point of view both of diagnosis and treatment. The possibilities of improving the health of the nation by an effective recording system which relates symptoms to diagnosis, diagnosis to treatment, and treatment to results, as well as making it possible to understand more about the genetic and occupational background of disease, was recognised long before the electronic computer became a piece of equipment in everyday use. But the opportunities are now different. We are at the beginning of the computer revolution of society. And I myself have no doubt that the potentialities of the machine could be realised as quickly in the medical field as in any other. Computerisation is already widely used for repetitive work such as immunisation schedules and appointments, and will obviously improve the efficiency of our public health services in other ways, and so the field of preventive medicine, making early diagnosis more effective than it now is.

These changes would, of course, be pretty one-sided were it not for the fact that as the medical profession itself, and the services on which it depends, become more modernised, the public is becoming increasingly aware of, and indeed frank about, the facts of physiology and disease. The mysteries of the workings of the body are far less opaque now than they were ten, twenty years ago. When I was a medical student I seem to remember that most people referred to all infective agents as 'bugs'. There can be few today who do not break the class of bugs down into at least bacteria and viruses, and who do not know that while some bacteria are susceptible to treatment by antibiotics, others are not; and that while we are still plagued by many viruses, others such as the polio virus have been dealt with by means of vaccines. For well over a hundred years the word 'vaccination' related only to smallpox, as indeed it still does etymologically. In the past twenty the term has, however, become applied to active immunisation against several kinds of infective disease, and this is something which the layman well understands.

Obviously the public is not yet as well informed about medical matters as it might be. But that it is more enlightened today than it was twenty, thirty years ago seems to me unquestionable, and I myself believe that the position in this respect is improving all the time, however gradually. Television is playing a major part in this change.

My own picture of the next thirty years, therefore, includes a vision of an increasing improvement in the practice of medicine, partly through the better orientation of the curriculum of the professionals who service the machine, and partly through the introduction of new techniques, of which computers are only one; I also see an increasing appreciation by the public at large of what illness constitutes, of the causes which bring it about, and possibly of the limits of help which the medical practitioner can give to his patient. And I expect an increasing improvement, in the light of experience, in the administrative arrangements whereby public health is safeguarded and private illness treated.

There is nothing very prophetic about this picture. It is merely a projection of the trends by which the character of medical service is being transformed at the present moment. But when I turn to possible developments in medical knowledge and in the applications of such knowledge, I can really start speculating. The postwar years have already seen such vast and dramatic developments in, for example, fields such as immunology and transplantation surgery, that no one could imagine that the years which carry us to the end of our century will not see others equally far-reaching in their significance. Enthusiasts already tell us that it will not be long before new methods of controlling immunological reactions will make possible the transplantation of animal hearts and other organs to man, and when 'spare-part surgery' will become a normal part of medical practice. Let us hope they are right. These things are certainly within the realms of possibility; others which have been mooted in the popular press strike me as too fanciful to deserve mention. When people start talking about transplantation of brains, or parts of brains, they no longer speculate from any platform of real knowledge.

One must, however, consider the emergence of new far-reaching ideas in medical practice from another point of view – that of priorities. Kidney machines, attempts at heart transplantations, even some aspects of bio-engineering, are immensely costly in resources. The Planning Unit of the British Medical Association[3] tells us, for example, that though renal transplantation costs about £6,000 a patient, it is 'a better investment than long-term dialysis'. Whether the Association is right in this view, or indeed justified in using the term 'investment' I do not know. But I myself cannot envisage a National Health Service being encouraged to grow at a rate which could cater for these developments on any wide scale. Difficult though the task, urgent though the demand from the patient, and even if, as the BMA Planning Group writes, the relief of suffering cannot be measured in financial terms, the Minister of Health and his advisers must always have a sense of priorities in the distribution of the resources which go to medicine. Someone will have to decide whether, for example, a comprehensive computerised recording service, which will help in early diagnosis and which could assist in the unravelling of the background of disease, should come before startling developments of the kind heart transplantations represent. Obviously medical skill is something to be encouraged and admired, but it must not be encouraged to the point when, to quote an observation made by Lord Platt[4] in his Harveian Oration of 1967, it is used 'all too often' to keep alive 'those who by any possible standard would be better dead'.

It thus also becomes necessary to ask whether developments in medical practice of the kind major organ replacement represents could have more than a marginal effect on the improvement of the general state of public health. The average expectation of life for all ages and for both sexes has improved so greatly in our modern society - if not as yet in every part of the world – that one could well ask whether we have not already reached the end of the road from this point of view. Is it conceivable that man's average natural span could be raised from, say, eighty years to ninety years? Could a dog's life which usually comes to an end between the ages of ten and fifteen years, be extended to twenty? I myself doubt it. The average duration of life in an animal species, including our own, is as much a characteristic of the species as are the anatomical and physiological characteristics by which the species is defined, and which emerged in the process of its evolution. There may be a genetic explanation for the fact that the members of some families are very long lived; and it is conceivable, I suppose, that some process of selection might help spread long life through a community. It is also possible that regional differences which occur in the expectation of life might one day be ironed out. But in general the figures in the Registrar General's 1961 Life Tables do not encourage the belief that there is likely to be any significant change in the average expectation of life for people of old age. For the majority of males in England and Wales we seem to have got stuck somewhere around 'three score years and ten', females enjoying an additional five years. Actuaries enjoy what Comfort[5] calls a 'well-justified assurance' that 'an annuitant will die between the likely ages of seventy and ninety *regardless of any* foreseeable advance in the care or prevention of specific disease'. This does not seem to be something that is likely to be changed simply by spending more money on medical research, a point on which Comfort is, however, more optimistic than I am. If this were otherwise, how is it that the average expectation of life in the United States which spends relatively far more per head of population on medical research than the United Kingdom does, is decidedly lower than our own?

This brings me to my third point – that there may be spectacular developments over the next two or three decades in the pharmaceutical field. In his 1967 Harveian Oration, Lord Platt pointed out that in spite of the development of departments of academic medicine, and in spite of the vogue for clinical research, these departments have not in general been responsible for the major changes which have transformed man's health over recent years. 'The phenomenal success of modern medical treatment seems to have depended,' so he writes, 'almost wholly on non-clinical, often non-medical, scientists frequently working in, or in close collaboration with, the pharmaceutical industry.' To illustrate his point he refers to the origins of modern anaesthetics, tranquillisers, vitamins, anti-malarials, anti-histamines, hypotensives, sex hormones and oral contraceptives. Not one of these developments, he points out, originated in a department of academic medicine or therapeutics. Another clinical authority, Professor Henry Miller,[6] the Chairman of the BMA's Planning Unit, not so long ago declared that 'the new drugs for serious mental illness represented the greatest medical advance since penicillin'. Both Lord Platt's and Professor Miller's observations have, of course, to be seen in perspective. Had there not been enquiring clinicians to point the way, the chemist and physiologist, not knowing where to look, could hardly have succeeded in the way they have.

In the light of the transformations which the pharmaceutical industry has helped bring about in the treatment of disease and in improving public health services, we can obviously expect it to do more in the remaining years of our century. Even if new developments do not change the limits of man's natural span, the treatment of illness should certainly continue to improve, with more people surviving into old age. There is, of course, another side to the coin. Risks are entailed in new pharmaceutical practices; the thalidomide tragedy remains a grim warning. Many of the new drugs which have been introduced in the postwar years, and which have had so remarkable a therapeutic effect, have not yet been in use long enough for us to be sure that some of them may not be associated with latent and undesirable secondary effects.

This brings me to my fourth point: the disappearance of scourges and the possible emergence of new ones. The pharmaceutical industry is a specialised part of the chemical industry which, particularly in the development of new pesticides and herbicides, is also transforming our biochemical environment. I have already referred to the fact that we all now carry a load of DDT in our tissues, as indeed do most wild creatures as well. Even if no ill-effects of this change – which is very much associated with the second half of our century – have been recognised, it is beginning to cause enough disquiet for the use of DDT to be banned in some parts of the world. The utmost vigilance is called for on the part of the public authorities, as well as of industry, lest some new chemical which comes into widespread use does rapidly become a real danger. I know of no such case at the moment, whereas I could point to a few which have been averted through official action.

The transformation of the story of the communicable diseases over the past three to four decades is also very encouraging. Some diseases, such as measles and scarlet fever, have declined in virulence for no very clear reason. Others, such as diphtheria and tuberculosis, have been suppressed as a result of active measures. In general, the fight against infectious diseases has been so successful over the past twenty-five years, with the virtual elimination of the main killing diseases of the first half of our century, that it is difficult to imagine the tide being turned in the years ahead. I well remember the fears that were expressed in the immediate postwar years, when malaria – before one of the worst 'killers' in the world – was brought under control, that it would not be long before we would be back where we had started through the emergence of a DDT-resistant mosquito. This has happened in isolated instances, which have then had to be tackled by new insecticides, and there have been recent major reverses in Ceylon and India which necessitated new anti-malarial campaigns. But I am confident that the vigilance of national and international public health authorities will see to it that setbacks such as these are contained. The day will assuredly dawn when the World Health Organisation programme for complete malaria eradication will have been achieved, even though we may have to wait until those backward parts of the world, which are still plagued with the disease, have provided themselves with the basic health services, trained personnel and communications to make this possible. Epidemics, even pandemics, of new virus infections, against which the population would have limited resistance from previous experience, could obviously still occur, but here too we are safe-guarded by the activities of an increasingly effective World Health Organisation. Drug addiction is also something which is within our power to decrease, however much the tide may still be flowing the other way.

So successfully has the fight against communicable disease been waged that in his 1968 report[7] on the State of the Public Health, the Chief Medical Officer of the British Department of Health and Social Security was able to write that it was not to the further suppression of these diseases that one should look for further significant improvements in health. In his view, 'the abolition of cigarette smoking would be the greatest single contribution to the improvement of the public health still open to us.' This state-ment, on which there is no need to comment, is a remarkable reflection of the transformation which has already occurred in the spectrum of disease, and which we have every right to suppose will continue in the years ahead.

This brings me to my fifth point – an increase in the incidence of degenerative disease in a population the members of which can increasingly expect to survive into old age. I do not know what the right definition of degenerative disease is, nor do I know how important the issue is. We all have to die sometime, and presumably we all have to die of something. Cancer and cardio-vascular disease can strike at any age, but begin to have their most powerful impact in middle life. Are they degenerative diseases? Should we be surprised if their relative incidence as fatal diseases goes up as the incidence of other killing diseases declines?

Degenerative diseases of the central nervous system also emerge in old age, but fortunately they are still relatively rare. But whichever way we define the degenerative diseases of old age, I think that we shall have to accept as a consequence of the general improvement in the health of the nation that more and more medical attention will automatically be focused in the years ahead on the disabilities of the aged, with a parallel increase in research into the maladies with which they contend. I can imagine improvements in the early diagnosis and treatment of cancers, and the development of new psychotropic drugs to counter the degenerative disorders of the central nervous system. I foresee dietary modifications that may prolong the useful life of the cardiovascular system and of the pancreas, and the development of new ways of combating auto-immune diseases. But in the end I cannot imagine that medical science will ever be able to banish the diseases which are responsible for bringing man's natural span of life to an end.

And what of the shape of the world in which medical services and the community of tomorrow will exist at the end of the century? This is my final point. By then the population of the world could be double what it is today – well over six thousand million as opposed to three and a half thousand million people. The population of the United Kingdom is then likely to be close to seventy millions, with a somewhat different age distribution from what it has today. Urbanisation is almost certain to have increased in scale, with the density of population in the South of England, and the Southeast in particular, growing significantly in spite of attempts to direct population to other parts of the country. This will be occurring in parallel with increasing urbanisation in all parts of the world, in a few of which there are likely to be by the turn of the century conurbations numbering between a hundred and five hundred million people. Our present traffic problems could conceivably have been solved – but more likely than not they will still be with us, and could be even worse than they are now. The social costs of technological advances are likely to be far more apparent tomorrow than they are today. Noise will be a worse nuisance. The deleterious and indeed dangerous effects of environmental pollution – pollution of our rivers, of the air, and of the land – are likely to be more widespread, unless the most strenuous efforts are made to intensify the measures which have already been successfully applied in reducing pollution. So far as the ordinary life of the U.K. citizen is concerned, in my view it would be unreal to suppose that as a nation we shall need to strive over the next few decades any less than we do now in order to 'pay our way' and maintain, leave alone raise, our standard of living.

In other words, the social environment in which our medical services will have to operate ten, twenty, thirty years ahead is unlikely to be easier, and could be more difficult, than the one of which they are at present a part. The strains which now underlie some kinds of illness are, I think, still going to be with us, if indeed they do not become worse. In short, I myself cannot envisage a sort of civilised technological paradise in which we shall be able to lean back and enjoy the fruits of modern medical science. Our health services will have to adapt as skilfully as they can, and with the utmost of understanding on all sides, to a world which is likely to embody many of the features against which people of imagination now protest.

The alleviation of distress caused by illness is bound to improve, but unless someone can show that it is possible to increase what seems to be the natural span of human life, I think that we have to accept that we are moving into a phase where the *average* health of the community can be only marginally improved. If I were to seek support for this view, I would again repeat what the Chief Medical Officer has said – that if we want to do better than we are doing, the most important single thing left to us to do would be to put an end to cigarette smoking.

I have heard it said that we spend less in the United Kingdom on health than do most other developed countries. I do not know the figures on which this statement is based, and I am unaware that statistics comparable to our own exist in other countries which do not have a state health service. I can well understand, however, why the Planning Unit of the British Medical Association should urge members of the profession to press 'unceasingly' for more financial resources for the Health Service. On the other hand, as I have already pointed out, we have to accept that the rate of growth of the health services is constrained by the availability of trained staff and by other pressures on the national purse; and I cannot see how this could change with time. Moreover, if it is a fact that some countries spend relatively more than we do on health, it can only mean that they spend less in other fields, say, education or defence; or that they tax relatively more; or that they generate much more resources per head of population than we do. I realise that constraints on the health budget could imply a conflict between what is possible in practice and the belief that the medical practitioner is, as it were, impelled by his Hippocratic Oath to do the utmost that can be done in order to alleviate the ills of his patient, and in the extreme, to fight to keep alive, even if only for the space of a few weeks or months, aged patients whom incurable disease has brought to the point of death. This belief clearly needs to be set in a modern frame. The world of today is not that of 2,000 years ago; nor is the world of tomorrow going to be the same as that of today. No country can plan for the future without laying down priorities within the limit of the resources it has available. The social value of highly costly clinical developments which circumstances will confine to a few will have to be balanced against the benefits which all will enjoy if common ailments by which we are all plagued, such as colds and backaches, are made less troublesome than they now are, and if measures of what has been called 'environmental sanitation' are devised to deal with all present-day and future pollutants. The state of the public health in the year 2000 will, in my view, therefore be determined every bit as much by the general measures which have brought it to its present high standard, as it will be by the future efforts of the individual medical practitioner. There is still much to expect from both sources even when we forget about isolated dramatic developments.

19

The Possibility of Priorities

I have already remarked that the pattern of distribution of the resources which now go to the advancement of science and technology in the United Kingdom seems more like a series of unrelated decisions taken in the past, than the reflection of a conscious assessment of present and emerging social needs. Such an observation, I imagine, could apply equally to the scientific effort of most, if not all countries. I also briefly contrasted the criteria that are implicitly used in deciding the relative merits of different projects which seek support in the basic sciences, with those that apply in the field of technological development, arguing that the final decisions about the deployment of the bulk of our scientific resources are inevitably taken outside the scientific field. These are very broad generalisations, and the topic deserves a closer look if there is to be a better understanding than now exists of the difficulties which impede attempts to get the priorities of science and technology more in line with the potential and assumed social needs of tomorrow.

Because the fruits of technology have always seemed to result in an easier and richer way of life, and although there have been occasional short-term setbacks due to the immediate social dis- locations they have caused, most people have usually regarded technology as a 'good thing'. This has been true all over the world. Indeed the better life which modern technology makes possible is everywhere eliminating differences in traditional modes of living, and thus paradoxically helping to unify human aspirations in a period when disputes between nations, deriving from past history, still remain acute. In so far as new scientific knowledge has also promised material rewards, it, too, has generally been welcomed whenever and wherever it has emerged. Only when the pay-off seemed non-existent, and the new knowledge was in clear conflict with some ruling dogma – as in the case of Galileo – has there been any organised attempt at its suppression. Indeed, if the search for 'useless' new scientific knowledge could be conceived of as something that was pursued without any risk of the results 'spilling over', no doubt it might always have been tolerated as the mark of a harmless cult whose existence affected no one but its disciples.

One can only speculate why the system of scientific method which rules basic science, what in this book I have called private science, and which has now swept the world in a way no single religious or political system has ever done, should have emerged in the seventeenth century rather than in some earlier age, and in the culture of medieval Western Europe rather than in, say, China or Greece or some corner of Islam. But what cannot be doubted any longer is that today the practical repercussions of private science almost inevitably do spill over into the domain of politics, which to an ever-increasing extent becomes concerned with the social consequences of the technological transformations new knowledge keeps bringing about. What I described as 'public science' is the link between politics and private science, and a major problem today is to discover how scientists – obviously not all of them, but at least more than today – can become better equipped, and readier than they now are, to help deal with the social problems for which their activities are ultimately responsible. There is little merit in scientists and engineers, secure in their laboratories and workshops, proclaiming that the priorities of scientific effort are misconceived, and crying woe as they witness science being 'misused', and the environment of to-morrow destroyed. Nor as matters stand, is there much hope of individual scientists and engineers abandoning a particular search lest it ultimately has some undesirable result. When it comes to the test, each scientist has his own views about what is worth pursuing; and the potential goodness or badness of ideas becomes forgotten in the heat of the chase. As I have already said, the best chance scientists could have of influencing the events which flow from their discoveries, would be by engaging, in one capacity or other, in the controversies which decide industrial, social, and political action, and by entering the debate on the platform where these things are resolved, in the knowledge that the rules by which they are decided are not those which theoretically govern the search for objective truth. The effort would be worthwhile even if it were beset by endless frustrations. Fortunately, in spite of the individualistic nature of discovery, the pattern of scientific activity today is more favourable from the point of view of helping 'to get our priorities right', than it has ever been.

First, scientists are much more organised than they were twenty-five years ago. Those of us who started our scientific careers before the second world war can appreciate this fact only too readily. Second, much more research and development is now carried out by teams of research workers, sometimes big teams, than by individuals. Third, though we borrow each other's techniques, we have also tended to become more specialised. And fourth, technological developments have not only made more science possible, but on average, very much more expensive per research worker employed. For example, there can be few areas in science in which computers have not made it possible to undertake researches which could never have been dreamed of before. But, compared to the kind of equipment scientists enjoyed in the thirties, computers cost big money. So do radio telescopes and particle accelerators and space vehicles.

An immediate consequence of all this is that however considerable, in terms of actual money, the resources that are now made available to scientists, whether pure or applied, there are never enough, and their allocation calls increasingly for rational decision. Hard experience of budgetary constraints is forcing this fact home on scientists, and with it a realistic appreciation of the need to achieve agreement about our priorities. On the other hand, it is difficult to conceive of a conscious balance of effort over the whole field of science when the latter is always changing, and always becoming more variegated; and even more, when so large an amount of the money that is made available for research and development now comes from defence budgets, and when a great deal of other work which is carried out by scientists is shrouded in secrecy.

For in addition to the distinction between what I have called private science on the one hand and public science on the other, there is another which in practice is also highly significant – the world of open science and that of closed or secret science. The open world is mainly concerned with the secrets of nature which are laid bare by the researcher. In the closed world are the secrets which have to be guarded because of national or commercial considerations. Hardly any scientist would question the proposition that certain kinds of information must be protected in the interests of national security. This kind of secrecy is necessary, often vital. But the fact that so much work has to be carried out behind locked doors impedes the formulation of a scale of priorities across the whole board of scientific and technological activity.

Moreover, work which is done in secret almost always suffers in quality because it is not exposed to the full blaze of scientific criticism. Before scientific journals began to appear in the latter half of the seventeenth century, the small number of scientists who were alive at any one time kept each other informed about the work they were doing by way of a direct and critical exchange of their information and views. Journals provided an easier and wider method of communication, and eventually a means whereby the individual scientist could satisfy his desire to proclaim his discoveries to the world, in an effort to 'get in first'. The fear that one's incipient discoveries might be pre-empted from some unknown quarter is both an urge to secrecy when a piece of work is in progress, and a spur to publication when it is completed. But in spite of the understandable impulse which may lead a scientist to suppress information about some brain-child of his until he feels the time is ripe to disclose it, secrecy hardly plays a useful or enduring part in the open world of science, whereas communication and uninhibited criticism certainly do.

We are no longer in the days of, say Lavoisier, when because of the small numbers of scientists in the world, it might have been expected that discoveries would usually be the product of only one mind, and that they would emerge at one particular moment in time. Scientists, who were once numbered in their tens, are now counted in their tens of thousands. We all base ourselves on a common pool of knowledge. We all know the general form of the 'hot' problems in physics, or chemistry, or genetics. When we exclude the small number of absolutely novel discoveries or hypotheses which constitute the foundation stones of the body of scientific knowledge, and which are added to only rarely, we need not be surprised if in these days the same ideas are formulated more than once, in different parts of the world, and often about the same time. It is almost inconceivable that a Mendel could today report the basic law of genetics, and that no one would pick it up till thirty years later. What is more likely is that we would find that more than one Mendel had been thinking along the same lines, and that two, three, or four of them were about to publish their results at about the same time – and much the same results. In the pursuit and exploitation of new concepts, we almost always seem to find several laboratories pursuing similar courses, checking and comparing results, arguing about them, and learning from each others' successes and mistakes. This, for example, was the case in the elucidation of the double helix form of the molecule of DNA, about which I spoke in an earlier chapter. We can also recall only too well how much parallel development of the same projects occurred in England and America on the one hand, and Germany on the other, during the course of the second world war.

The effect of secrecy is also transient rather than permanent. One of the supposedly best technical secrets of all time was the work which led to the development of the nuclear bomb. At its start it was hardly a secret at all. It was certainly not a military secret. The scientists in whose minds the idea was born themselves decided, as a corporate voluntary act, to curtail open publication of any information which might point in the direction of a bomb. When the idea of a nuclear weapon became an officially defined project, government administrators, in both the UK and the US found themselves in a quandary because of the number of refugee scientists from enemy countries who were involved. But in spite of the administrators' opposition – I quote from the official British History[1] of the subject – 'the greatest of all the wartime secrets was entrusted to scientists excluded for security reasons from other war work.' Later, officials in the USA and UK argued about the manner and extent to which security should be maintained, and at the end of the war the British authorities expressed strong opposition, on grounds of security, to the publication by the US of Dr Smyth's celebrated report of the US Manhattan Project, the code name for the work which led to the 'Bomb'. Here the British authorities were almost certainly too cautious. Both Niels Bohr, whose intervention in the politics of nuclear affairs had enjoyed a better reception at the hands of President Roosevelt than at those of Mr Churchill, as well as Sir James Chadwick, the scientist who discovered the neutron, believed that the mechanics of the bomb could not be held secret for long, and for this reason had urged 'the international control of the atom' well before the end of the second world war – and to the best of my knowledge well before the British Prime Minister and American President of the day did. Their hopes that this would come about were not realised, and even though every effort was made to prevent the spread of information about the design and construction of the Bomb, and the construction and operation of plants producing fissile material, other governments – and not just the USSR – did find out. And many who have not yet revealed a knowledge of the subject probably know its secrets, which no doubt they would already have put to use had they judged it in their political interest to do so, and had they had the resources, scientific and financial, which the enterprise would have demanded. Hence the significance which sensible people attach to the non-proliferation treaty, which has recently come into force.

What then was gained by the imposition of secrecy in this case? The main prize was obviously time. And essentially this is probably all that security ever gains in any scientific field. In the end, in most cases sooner rather than later, we can expect our opponents to discover what we know. The purpose of security in technical matters is to prolong the time it takes them to learn, and so to add to their costs. In the case of the bomb the prize was at first priceless, as it might be with any military secret. It is a moot point, however, whether the additional military security which we can attribute to the nuclear secrecy of more recent years has not been counterbalanced by the political problems which it has also generated.

Security, of course, also plays a powerful role in the commercial world. It is indeed difficult to conceive of an industrial undertaking which has diverted its own resources to research on some particular project, revealing to its competitors knowledge which it may have gained at great expense. But it is reasonable to ask how far commercial scientific secrecy should be pressed. There are some who declare that it would pay to publish everything, in the hopes that doing so would be more likely to confuse than benefit a rival firm or country, which would otherwise be focusing its intelligence efforts in trying to find out what *really* mattered. This is clearly an extreme view, but a contrary policy of publishing little or nothing can go too far. In any event, no commercial secret lasts for long, and there are considerations much more important than secrecy which now affect the assessment of the value of the results of industrial research and development. Secrecy relates to commercial value, but as the mounting concern over the spoliation of our physical environment makes only too plain, commercial value and social value are not necessarily synonymous. When the consumer contributes as much as he does to the cost of industrial research – and in the end he contributes, one way or the other, 'the lot' – he has the right to urge that social values should not be subjugated to short-term commercial advantages.

If the international and national secrecy which characterises what is by far the larger part of the field of scientific effort magnifies the task of deciding rationally the priorities of science, the subdivision of the scientific world into its multifarious interests does not make it any easier. The vast growth of science over the past two to three decades has made it all but impossible for anyone to keep up with what is published, even in the open world of science. We are involved in what has been called a 'crisis in communication'. So much is published that, secrecy or no secrecy, the average scientist might sometimes be ignorant of published observations which could help galvanise his own research in his own narrow field. When one adds to this the fact that the research worker often fails to realise the significance of one or more of his own observations, it becomes all the more important that there should be no unnecessary barriers to information which someone else can provide. A trivial thought, captured from anywhere, from some printed sentence, from the storehouse of memory, can suddenly illuminate what has been obscure, and by so doing bring about a revolution in understanding. Modern computer systems can, of course, be used to codify and process the mounting flood of new scientific information, and then to reassemble it as required. But this is not going to get us over the difficulties of communication. For whatever can be done by modern bibliographical methods to draw a scientist's attention to a piece of information which might be critical to his work, we have to recognise, as Fox[2] so rightly says, that 'machines cannot distinguish good papers from bad ones ... nor can they answer those often crucial questions ... the ones the enquirer does not know how to ask'.

Nothing is ever static in science – neither fields of interest nor methods, techniques or what you will. Molecular biology began, as it were, yesterday; radio astronomy, which took off from radar, the day before that; as the involvement of European countries in overseas colonial territories declines, their interest in systematic helminthology and parasitology and tropical diseases wanes; nuclear physics increased the number of atomic elements, and radiochemistry revivified organic chemistry; lasers emerge and find a potential use in highly different fields ranging from tele-links in weapon systems to ophthalmic surgery. As the techniques of one branch of science become applied to another, new border-line subjects emerge, and these then become established as disciplines of their own. The changing pattern of science is thus not only like a view through a turning kaleidoscope; it is one seen through an expanding kaleidoscope, the beads and bits in which are added to hourly, and in an unpredictable way. As the pattern changes, so does the intellectual stimulus of its different parts. At the same time the potency of any piece of knowledge which derives from the pursuit of basic science can never be assessed at the moment of its emergence. At no time can anyone be certain about the ultimate outcome, for good or bad, of any particular change in, or of any particular advance of, knowledge.

In spite of all these difficulties, a considerable intellectual effort has been made in different countries to agree on the principles which should dictate the proportion of public expenditure which should go, first, to the whole of research and development; second, to basic as opposed to 'mission-orientated' or applied research (in a different terminology 'curiosity-directed' as opposed to 'need-directed' research); and third, to separate fields of science. We are still far from agreement on any of these matters. I have already indicated my own scepticism about our chances of ever finding a set of universal principles which will tell us how much support pure research should receive, whether we accept as a working assumption that the cultivation of basic science should be regarded as an 'overhead' cost to the economic exploitation of scientific knowledge in general; whether it is something which should be supported as one of man's cultural activities; or whether the justification is a mixture of both these propositions. In financial terms, the problem is fortunately not very important relative to other questions of priorities in the scientific field, since basic research consumes only a small fraction of the total of R & D resources which any nation makes available for scientific activity. In the United Kingdom, the figure today can hardly be more than a few per cent, perhaps ten, of some £1,100 millions. It reached this level from at most one to two millions which it was up to the end of the second world war, merely as a consequence of the increase in all scientific activity, and particularly of scientific education. But in any event money is hardly the most important consideration in the advance of basic knowledge. Brains and ideas are the final limiting factor.

Scientists do not decide the global sum of money which is provided at any given moment for basic research. But as a professional group they would be more likely than would non-scientists to be imbued with a sense of the whole changing pattern of science, and so to judge wisely about the value of new ideas and of work in progress, and therefore to decide how the money should be allocated. However poorly they might do the job, no one could do it better, whatever the criteria by which the relative claims of different fields of work are judged, whether of possible utility or intellectual merit – or in the final analysis, even from the point of view of the possible anti-social effects of some piece of scientific work.

Needless to say, the resources which are set aside for basic science are, for all practical purposes, totally deployed at any given moment, and as I have already said, proposals to move them around are not unnaturally always resisted by those who might suffer in the process. Moreover, while one sometimes reads about fixed research budgets being adjusted, and of dying points in research giving way to growing points, one seldom hears about deliberate efforts to bring about the demise of a project once it has been started. The tendency is for a piece of research to go on till it dies a natural death because of intellectual, leading eventually to financial, inanition. Nonetheless, the new and inexpensive good research worker usually gets what he wants after the quality of his ideas and the excellence of his performance have been endorsed by the more experienced scientists who are usually called upon to act as judges by money-giving institutions. This happens even for scientists belonging to countries where very little is spent on science, for if a dedicated and talented man cannot get at home what he feels he needs in order to pursue his researches, he usually finds a way of obtaining it from some other source.

The situation is very different when big money is wanted for some major new departure in basic science, say, for the provision of a new radio telescope. In these circumstances, the men who advise in the national interest on the quality and promise of scientific ideas have to agree among themselves that the resources which are being sought would be better spent on the new scheme than on some other expensive work to which they may already be devoted; and it is very difficult either to get agreement to such a decision or to implement it if one is reached. Equally if new money can be raised, the 'referees' would have to agree that it would be better spent on the new scheme than on any of, say, a half-dozen other schemes in different areas of science which are also 'on the table' awaiting decision. And someone else would have to agree that the new money could, in fact, be provided. The bitter controversies which characterise this kind of situation are now commonplace in the scientific communities of advanced societies.

One also sometimes hears it said that if less money were devoted to, say, space research, more could be spent on finding a cure for cancer – or whatever happened to be the topic of interest in the discussion. On occasion this might be true. But it is far from being generally true. What *is* true, however, is that the provision of vast resources to one sector of scientific and technical endeavour tends to set a powerful fashion which diverts attention from other fields of actual or potential interest. I imagine that most working scientists would join me in attributing the broad outlines of the present pattern of interests in basic science to the interaction of the inertia of past decision, and the play of present fashion. And no doubt many would cynically add that decisions about the allocation of resources for basic science are largely determined by a combination of chance, advocacy and other intangibles.

So far, I have been discussing basic science in accordance with the strictest meaning of the term – that is to say in the sense of advances and changes in the structure of fundamental scientific knowledge. Within this framework there is no hierarchy of importance between different subjects, whatever differences there may be in the cost of their cultivation, or in the potential value of their application. For example, the enduring transformation of our understanding of the living world brought about by Darwin through his theory of evolution cost nothing by modern standards, no more say, than what it would take to keep a research student in some chemical laboratory happy for a few years, as he pursued some relatively insignificant idea with a commercial pay-off far greater than Darwin's hypothesis. Einstein's revolutionary ideas, which have had enormous practical applications, cost no more than the pen and paper it took to write down his thoughts; and the Cavendish Laboratory in Rutherford's day, the day of the most spectacular and far-reaching advances that have ever been made in nuclear physics, cost what it costs to run the laboratories of one of our modern schools. Research into the mechanisms of the brain, or into the control of embryological development, or into molecular biology, that gateway to a new understanding of living processes, costs but a fraction of what it takes to mount a new departure in particle physics. Cost is clearly no criterion in assessing the intellectual importance of different fields of basic science, although clearly if more costly fields are promoted, less is available for others.

The most expensive science today is undoubtedly what is called space science, but most of the resources which go to it are in fact consumed by the engineering work, based on established scientific principles, necessary to put space vehicles into orbit, and on the design of the vehicles themselves. Communications satellites, TV satellites, 'spy-in-the-sky' satellites, are applications of space technology again all based on known principles, and hardly count as 'space science'. In the final analysis only a small part of the total expenditure on space could be regarded as implying a direct attempt to advance basic scientific knowledge. The rest of the effort in effect provides the platform from which such knowledge could be gained.

It is inconceivable that the vast resources committed to this new field of endeavour would have been agreed by the democratic decision of a national, still less an international caucus of scientists. The plea would have been immediately made, as it still is in the United States, that the cost was incommensurately great in relation to any conceivable scientific gain, and that given the same resources, there were other far more fruitful and far less costly fields of science worth cultivating. But the decision to go into 'space' was not a scientific one; as is generally acknowledged in the case of the Americans, it was a political resolve, largely based on the issue of national prestige. 'Space' is the most prominent illustration there is of the way politics can intrude – and in the minds of many scientists wrongly intrude – in the determination of the priorities of basic science. There are others.

On the other hand, political and commercial considerations are expected to be paramount when it comes to choosing alternatives of action in fields of applied science, particularly in the case of big and costly projects. Here we are in an area of choice where judgment implies some prophetic view of the usefulness of, and demand for, the tangible things which may materialise from the proposed work, in the kind of world which will exist, say, ten years hence. The concept of utility, is however, always a relative one because the future usually turns out differently from what one imagined; and we also know that when it comes to utility, some other line of approach to the same general end, of which we might be unaware, may turn out to be better than the one we have pursued. This applies just as much in the national confines of secret defence research, as it does in areas of commercial secrecy. Utility is moreover only one consideration when it comes to decisions about providing resources to a particular technological development. National prestige is another; the power of vested industrial interest a third; social considerations, by which one has hitherto mainly meant the problems of the labour market, a fourth; the demands of international co-operation, a fifth – and so on. The particular consideration, or combination of considerations, which becomes paramount in determining the issue varies from project to project; but in every instance, as in the case of James Watt's steam engine, or von Braun's space rocket, the germ of the whole enterprise must be someone's technological idea, presented with enough conviction to infect others with the same sense of mission – the industrialists, the bankers, the administrators, and the politicians, without whose endorsement the project could never leave the drawing board. The development of nuclear energy for civil purposes, of nuclear propulsion for vessels of war, of a supersonic aircraft like the Concorde, or, to move to the less expensive end of the scale of technological development, of some new synthetic textile or drug, demands the commitment of such vast, or relatively vast resources, that the final responsibility for going ahead must lie with governments or boards of companies – persuaded in the first instance, of course, by the technical man or men who originated the idea.

The subdivision of responsibility in the sequence of steps which leads to the final decision is both inevitable and unfortunate. It is inevitable because those who originate the ideas hardly ever command the resources. And it is unfortunate because those who can and do commit the resources are rarely people who have any first-hand knowledge of the scientific and technological issues and difficulties which are involved. The men who promote the scheme in the first place are usually so enthusiastic, and so concerned that it goes ahead, that they underestimate the difficulties, and so the costs. And those who are persuaded then find themselves endorsing a project which may cost five, ten times the resources which they were assured were all that was required in order to bring the project to a successful and profitable conclusion. The commitment could become so great as to affect a country's entire economy, and so its political life – even though, to take as illustration an example to which I have already referred, it does not follow that if the United States were not supporting space science and technology at a cost of several billion dollars a year, the same resources would have been made available, say, to resurrect decaying cities or to institute a national health service or to develop some other field of science, pure or applied.

Since the big technological projects which are in train at any given moment absorb so considerable a proportion of the total R & D resources a country can afford to deploy, and since such projects are usually decided case by case, and often secretly, one can hardly expect much correspondence between the actual pattern of deployment of technological resources, and some ideal pattern based upon a close assessment of possible technological alternatives related to agreed social needs. I myself doubt if a close correspondence could ever be achieved. There will always be differences of view about social priorities; while the inevitable setbacks that occur in the course of the evolution of a technological project can be relied upon to separate conception from achievement, and to disrupt carefully-laid plans, however well conceived in relation to desirable social needs. On the other hand, there are signs, however vague, that the actual pattern of deployment of scientific resources is beginning to move gradually in a direction which accords more closely with some broadly-conceived view of the way they should be deployed in the best interests not only of society's present, but also future well-being.

As I have already pointed out, in the United Kingdom the

responsibility for deciding what technological developments should be promoted essentially rests with industry on the one hand, and with separate government departments on the other, the understanding being that in the latter case every minister with executive powers has the right to use part of his budget for such scientific enquiries and technological developments as he judges necessary for the proper discharge of his responsibilities to Parliament. If practice were fully in accord with this under-standing, it would in theory be possible for a minister in charge of a department with a large budget to pre-empt scarce scientific and technological resources, and so make it impossible for another department to undertake scientific work which it regarded as essential for its purposes. Fortunately, this does not happen. In the public sector, there has to be a measure of 'across-the-board' planning in the use of professional scientific manpower. If this were not the case, it would be impossible for the government to implement a policy of shifting R & D resources from the defence to the civil sector, or to embark on any new policy demanding large R & D resources. In the year 1958-9, for example, defence R & D in the United Kingdom accounted for about seventy per cent of a total of £320 million of direct government expenditure on science and technology.[3] Five years later, in 1964-5, the figure was fifty-seven per cent of £455 million.[4] Today it is forty-three per cent of £550 million.[5] The decline partly reflects the reduction that has been taking place over the years in the UK's total 'spend' on defence. But it is also the result of a deliberate decision to achieve a much-needed reinforcement of the R & D effort of various civil departments without at the same time increasing the total numbers of professional scientists employed within the government machine. In addition to increasing the R & D budget of the departments concerned, and holding back that of the defence departments, resources can thus be transferred by restraining the rate of new recruitment of scientists in the defence sector, and by 'rationalising', sometimes by amalgamation, the work of defence R & D establishments with similar fields of interest. And here it is worth noting that despite the considerable increase in the numbers of scientists and engineers turned out by university institutions over the past twenty-five years, and of signs that there may be no numerical shortage of professionally-trained men in the country, there is never any decrease in the demand for the services of the more talented among them. When it comes to assuring the success of a piece of research, or a project of development, the quality of the scientists and engineers engaged is far more important than their numbers.

Within the public sector, the priorities of the projects on which scientists and technologists are employed can thus be gradually adjusted in accordance with some conscious overall plan, by changing the allocation of R & D resources between departments within a total manpower allocation, given, of course, a ceiling to government expenditure. But although government is still the largest single employer of professional R & D manpower in the United Kingdom, this is only one part, and indeed the simplest part, of the problem of 'getting our priorities right'. A far larger number of scientists and technologists are engaged on research and development, in an unknown number of units, in private industry. We live in a competitive world, and success in technological innovation is synonymous with commercial success; in the same way as commercial success, particularly in overseas markets, is a precondition of a healthy state of the British economy. Because the pattern of immediate demand of the market, that is to say current fashion, plays so powerful a part in determining the acceptibility of the goods produced, it seems highly improbable that there could ever be a scale of R & D priorities in the private sector which accorded with any set of values other than the general criterion of the profitability of the resources employed. But again, as in the public sector, another kind of regulatory influence is beginning to become evident. Innovation has to be checked when it is established that the commercial and other benefits it yields are outweighed by secondary consequences which are deleterious to society as a whole. The banning of a certain variety of food-additives is perhaps the most direct example. In the USA[6] the statutory limitation of the venting of the exhaust gases of motor-cars is another. The increasing concern now shown in almost all industrialised countries about the pollution of the environment suggests that this factor could in time become powerful in restraining the socially indiscriminate growth of technology, and a force which could help to get the priorities of scientific development in the private sector more aligned with the prospective well-being and demands of society than has always been the case in the past.

Pollution, on the other hand, has always been with us, and the process is bound to be slow. Action to prevent specific kinds of pollution which has been taken on a national basis over the years has already achieved much, even though it has at times failed to prevent some disastrous tragedies – for example the present state of Lake Erie in North America. Much more action is clearly possible on a national basis. But in the end the protection of the environment of our globe depends, to a critical extent, on international agreement and action. The seas around us, and the air we breathe, are affected by what happens in every part of the earth, not just in the British Isles. And the pollution for which we are responsible affects other countries. Moreover, preventing or reducing the pollution which results from industrial processes costs money, and no country is likely to take unilateral action which will add to the cost of its production, and so price itself out of the markets of today, in order to assure the physical well-being of those of tomorrow. Against this it can be argued that the scale of the pollution problem is now increasing at least as fast as, and almost certainly faster than, the rate of growth of the world's total industrial output; and that the problem is also being inevitably exacerbated by the vast growth of population which is now occurring throughout the world, and which while affecting the underdeveloped countries to a greater extent, is also making a considerable mark on the developed countries. For these and other reasons, the concern with the whole problem of the environment which is now being voiced – in some countries for the first time – is bound to grow. There can hardly be a forum of international discussion which has not already put the matter high on its agenda.

Whatever remedial action results because of this international concern, and however slowly it takes place, it is likely to bring societal and commercial goals closer together as the objective of technological innovation, and as a result to influence the scale of scientific priorities in industrialised societies. Knowledge of what is at stake must be spread rapidly, and spread in all countries – whether overdeveloped, developed, or under-developed. There are many useful precedents on which to build in seeking international agreement in the task of bringing the criteria of long-term social welfare to bear on technological choice. The World Health Organisation is one. The international control of traffic in narcotics another. But more important than these from the point of view of pollution are two more recent agreements, the first about the international control of the pollution of the seas with oil, and the second, which was implicitly recognised in the 1963 partial test-ban treaty, about tolerable levels of background radiation. Common dangers tend to lead to uniform standards of control, and concern about other aspects of environmental pollution will undoubtedly lead to further measures of international agreement. It may be too early to think of an agreed International Code of Industrial Practices covering the whole field of industry, (although the growth of the 'international company' may help bring this about); and too soon to imagine that the national institutions which several advanced countries have set up in order to safeguard their populations against impure food and against dangerous drugs, or against the misuse of certain kinds of herbicides and pesticides, or against atmospheric pollution, will be joined together in a single organisation under the United Nations. But in the long term these things are not impossible, and in the long-term they are likely to prove essential. The concern that is being voiced in several countries about the possible anti-social effects of supersonic passenger-traffic already indicates that the world is hardly likely to slip once again into a situation in which a technological development such as the motor-car could be introduced onto the scene without any thought about the way it was likely to transform the organisation of society, and without any idea of the collateral costs in roads, in traffic-control systems, in pollution, in accidents and so on – all of which the public has had to pay in exchange for the advantages the internal-combustion engine was able to provide the individual traveller.

The concern which is being voiced about the deterioration of the quality of our physical environment, and equally, about the consequences of the unrestrained growth of the world's population, thus makes it possible to visualise a situation in which the priorities of technological activity in general, and not just those of the public sector, which is controlled by governments, would be changing rationally in a direction which could bring them more and more closely into line with what informed people would judge to be the prospective needs of the world of tomorrow. But if the change is not to be dangerously slow, the number of scientists and engineers who are concerning themselves seriously with these matters will have to multiply fast. This is a field in which scientists have a special and responsible part to play – not just inside, but outside their laboratories. As I have said, they should in practice be far better informed than others about the possible deleterious side-effects which certain otherwise beneficial technological developments might engender, and also far better trained to take a balanced view of the risks which might be entailed. But if scientists are to exercise, and exercise in an effective way, the authority of their special knowledge in preventing what is often too loosely called the misuse of science, they will have to do so in the world of action. The more they are prepared to learn at first hand how this world operates, the greater the assurance that man's lot will be safeguarded for the good of all. While there may be some satisfaction in shouting from the sidelines in an effort to prevent harm resulting from new scientific and technological knowledge, it is undoubtedly more effective to try and see that the right things are done where the final decisions are taken. And what is more – the controversies which surround these decisions, even though very different in kind, are often as stimulating as those which enliven the forum where pure scientific knowledge is distilled.

Appendix

The History of Apes and Monkeys as Objects of Enquiry

Monkeys, apes and man are classified together in an 'order' of mammals called the Primates. This consists of two suborders, the one, the Prosimii, which comprises our very distant cousins, the lemurs, lorises, galagos, and *Tarsius*; and the other, the Anthropoidea, in which are classified the New and Old World monkeys and the great apes, with whom we usually also classify the gibbons. The total number of recognised species in the suborder Anthropoidea is about 400, of which about 150 are species of New World monkey, which are indigenous only to Central and South America, and 230 are species of Old World monkey, which are widely distributed in Africa and Asia. Man is included with the apes in the 'super family' Hominoidea of this suborder. There are four species of Ape, the Gorilla and Chimpanzee, whose homeland is central Africa, the Orang-utan, which comes from Borneo and Sumatra, and the Gibbon, of which there are several species, with a fairly extensive distribution in Southeast Asia. Monkeys and Apes were much more widely spread over the world in geological epochs which preceded the present one.

The classification of the Primates reflects the recognition by countless generations of scholars that man has a special zoological affinity with the monkeys and apes. John Bell,[1] the elder brother of Charles Bell, a distinguished anatomist of the early nineteenth century, and himself also an eminent anatomist and surgeon, wrote in 1825 that Hippocrates, the Father of Medicine, who lived between the years 460 and 377 BC, had already realized this relationship.

It has long been a matter of debate, [John Bell writes] whether the ancients were, or were not, acquainted with anatomy, and the subject, with its various bearings, has been much and keenly agitated by the learned. If anatomy had been much known to the ancients, their knowledge would not have remained a subject of speculation. We should have had evidence of it in their works; but, on the contrary, we find Hippocrates spending his time in idle prognostics, and dissecting apes, to discover the seat of the bile. If more of anatomy had been known than could be seen through the skin, or discovered from a skeleton found on the seashore, it would not have been left an imperfect and nearly unknown science. The ancients had no opportunity of becoming acquainted with the formation of the human body, except what might be the result of accident.

Aristotle,[2] who came on the scene after Hippocrates (384–322 BC), also knew that 'some animals share the properties of man and the quadrupeds, as the ape, the monkey, and the baboon.' So did Galen of Pergamum, whose period was nearly five hundred years later, and to whom we owe our earliest useful knowledge of anatomy. He based much of his description of human structure on dissections of baboons and of the so-called Barbary Ape, a tail-less monkey best known from the few specimens which still live on the Rock of Gibraltar in a state of semi-domestication. There is also a suspicion that he studied one of the great apes as well. In his famous work[3] entitled *On Anatomical Procedures* we read that 'now of all living things the ape is likest man in viscera, muscles, arteries, veins, and nerves, as in the form of the bones. From the nature of these it walks on two legs and uses its fore-limbs as hands, and has the flattest sternum of all quadrupeds.' And he instructed his students to choose for their anatomical studies 'those apes likest man, with short jaws and small canines. You will find other parts also resembling man's, for they can walk and run on two feet. Those, on the other hand, like the dogfaced baboons, with long snouts and large canines, far from walking or running on their hind-legs, can hardly stand upright. The more human sort have a mainly erect posture.' The reason why Galen resorted to the dissection of monkeys was that in his time the dissection of the human body was heavily frowned upon. Accurate enquiries into human anatomy, and then only on a limited scale, did not begin till about the thirteenth century – and then in Western Europe.

Galen learnt a great deal from the writings, now lost, of two earlier anatomists called Herophilus and Erasistratus, both of whom flourished in Alexandria between 300 and 250 BC. The latter is believed to have carried out experiments on the living animal. So did Galen; what is more, he almost certainly used monkeys, as well as a variety of other animals, in living experiments. He was either the first, or one of the first, to study the effects of such surgical procedures as dividing the spinal cord, or cutting the phrenic nerve, the nerve which supplies the diaphragm. He also reports, among others, an operation which he carried out on a muscle of the shoulder called the trapezius. He tells us that when the nerve to the muscle is divided, the shoulder of the side affected cannot be lifted, whereas movements of the head are unimpaired. But in his *Anatomical Procedures*,[3] he also warns those who wish to follow him in the investigation of the living animal to use 'pigs, because there is no advantage in having an ape in such experiments and the spectacle is hideous'. This is the first occasion of which I know in which expression is given to this sentiment. It occurs frequently in later literature in which writers express their anguish when witnessing the reactions of a wounded monkey.

I have made no deep search, but to the best of my knowledge there is no record of monkeys being used in any other experimental or in any critical anatomical work until we come to the period of Vesalius,[4] who lived from 1514 to 1564, and the perfection of whose anatomical work will never cease to astonish. Vesalius devoted a part of his effort to a comparative study of the structure of monkeys and man in order to prove that Galen had been describing not human but simian anatomy. A hundred and fifty years or so after him, Tyson,[5] the dissector of the chimpanzee (which he called the 'orang-outang'), also brought his criticism to bear on Galen, this time for choosing monkeys rather than apes as his model for describing human anatomy.

The last chapter of Vesalius' great work is entitled 'On the dissection of living animals'.[6] Here we are given descriptions of systematic experiments which reveal what had been discovered about the function of the different systems of the body up to his period, including Galen's discoveries. But Vesalius' writings provide no evidence that he himself ever experimented on a monkey ('a tail-less ape'), or that he added anything significant to what was already known about the physiology, as opposed to the structure, of the body.

Indeed, we have to wait until the dawn of the nineteenth century before Galen's observations on the spinal cord and spinal nerves and on the functional effects of their interruption were bettered. Until then, as William Osler[7] in his Harveian Oration of 1906 put it so eloquently, 'the dead hand of the great Pergamite [Galen] lay heavy on all thought, and Descartes had not yet changed the beginning of philosophy from wonder to doubt.'

In 1811 Charles Bell,[8] who was the most famous of all British anatomists of the early nineteenth century, came upon the scene with his studies of the function of the two roots by which each spinal nerve is attached to the spinal cord. His observations were made on the horse, ass, calf and dog, and he argued convincingly that the ventral (anterior) roots were motor in function. There is some question as to whether he, or Magendie[9] in 1822, was responsible for the proof that the dorsal (posterior) roots of the spinal nerves, to which the spinal ganglia are attached, are sensory in function. The dispute occurred probably because Bell was best known, not by his monograph of 1811, but by his more famous work *The Nervous System of the Human Body*[10] published in 1830.

It was not until the 1870s that experimental work on the nervous system was extended to the monkey. The person responsible was Professor David Ferrier, a physician of King's College Hospital in

London, where he was also Professor of Forensic Medicine. Ferrier's studies were stimulated on the one hand by the discovery, published by Fritsch and Hitzig in 1870,[11] that the outer layer, or cerebral cortex, of the brain of the dog reacts to stimulation by means of a galvanic current, and on the other hand, by the brilliant clinical work of Dr Hughlings Jackson.[12] It is to the latter that we owe both the concept of higher and lower levels of control within the central nervous system, and the first recognition of the fact that epileptiform convulsions are due to abnormal and mechanical stimulation of a particular part of the cerebral cortex. It is to him, too, that Ferrier dedicated his celebrated monograph on *The Functions of the Brain*,[13] which was first published in 1876, the year in which he also delivered the Croonian Lecture on the same subject to the Royal Society of London.[14]

Ferrier's first important paper on the monkey appeared in the *Proceedings of the Royal Society* of 1874[15] under the title of 'Localisation of Function in the Brain', following a preliminary report published the year before in the West Riding of Yorkshire Lunatic Asylum Medical Reports.[16] It is interesting and fascinating to read both these papers today. How different they are from the modern scientific paper! There was no need for the author to begin by referring to the work of anyone else – for the good reason that no one else had worked on the monkey brain before him. He plunges straight into his subject, describes the experiments he carried out, and states precisely and simply what he observed. His Croonian Lecture covers more than fifty pages of quarto print, describing a variety of experiments. Yet it ends with only one half-page of conclusions, all of a non-controversial kind, and some remarkable for their far-reaching character. Ferrier was the first to discover that damage to a specific area of the outer layer (cortex) of the brain causes paralysis of muscles of the opposite side of the body, and he was also the first to report that 'after removal both of the frontal and occipital lobes an animal still retains its faculties of special sense and the powers of voluntary motion'. These lobes, which make up the front and back of the cerebrum, had always been supposed to be critical to the proper functioning of the brain. Ferrier's book on *The Functions of the Brain* is just as straightforward as his Croonian Lecture, and ends in as precise a fashion, with a chapter in which he considers the extent to which the human and simian brains resemble each other.

If we forget Galen and Vesalius, who worked before the days of anaesthesia and antisepsis, it is Ferrier more than anyone else who turned the monkey into an experimental animal. In 1884 Horsley, in collaboration with Schäfer,[17] extended Ferrier's experiments on the cerebral cortex of the monkey, and then in 1890 published the first paper which described an experiment in which one of the great apes was used as the subject for investigation. This was a report of an experiment he carried out with Dr Charles Beevor to observe the effects of 'electrical excitation of the so-called motor cortex and internal capsule in an orang-outang'.[18] This paper was published in abstract form in the *Proceedings of the Royal Society*, and in full in the *Transactions*.[19]

In their extended report in the *Transactions*, Horsley and Beevor referred to the expense of their experiment as the reason why they were publishing observations made on only one animal. They were quite right about the expense. Only occasional experiments on apes were done in the course of the next twenty-six years, at the end of which, in 1917, C.S. Sherrington, working in collaboration with A.S.F. Leyton[20] in Liverpool, published a major study on the excitability of the cerebral cortex. Well before then, in 1874, the excitability of the human cerebral cortex to faradic stimulation had been established in the United States by R. Bartholow,[21] who was then on the Medical Faculty of the University of Cincinnati. His paper describing the effects of electrical stimulation of the cortex was the only one he did on this particular subject. The patient had a fungating cerebral tumour, and it was this which Bartholow explored with faradic stimulation.

Sherrington, one of the greatest names in the history of neurophysiology, and to many the greatest British physiologist since William Harvey, published his first experimental paper on monkeys in 1889.[22] It dealt with the degeneration of nerve tracts, following experimental lesions of the cerebral cortex of monkeys. It was followed in 1893 by his famous monograph on *The Distribution of the Posterior Roots of Some Spinal Nerves*.[23] These and other studies led to his classical work, *The Integrative Action of the Nervous System*.[24]

Sherrington's big study of the ape brain was published in 1917 and dealt with 'the excitable cortex of the chimpanzee, orang-utan and gorilla'. This is how the paper[20] opens.

> The investigation the results of which are here recorded arose from an observation, which chance opportunity afforded us, of examining by stimulation the cerebral cortex of a chimpanzee. That anthropoid species had not at that time come under experimental examination. On faradising the cortex we found, contrary to our expectation, that, although the gyrus centralis anterior yielded motor responses readily, we obtained none such from gyrus centralis posterior. A second similar opportunity arising, we repeated our experimental tests, and the results confirmed our former ones. Obtaining then a specimen of gorilla, an anthropoid also not previously experimented on, results were again met confirmatory of our first. It was therefore decided to carry out an enquiry into the motor cortex of the anthropoid apes, more especially from the 'localisation' aspect. The following paper is based on the experimental examination of twenty-two chimpanzees, three gorillas, and three orang-utan. The methods employed have included both stimulation and ablation, but chiefly the former.
>
> At the time our observations were begun the only recorded experiment on the

cerebral cortex of the anthropoid ape was one of stimulation of the cortex of an orang by Beevor and Horsley (1890). The results they arrived at will be referred to later in the present paper; an excellent diagram summarising them is given by Schäfer in his *Text-book of Physiology* (1900). More recently, observations on localisation in the anthropoid have been (taking them in the successive order of date of publication) two preliminary Notes by ourselves; observations on the orang by Roaf and Sherrington, and by the Vogts; on the gibbon by Mott, Schuster, and Sherrington; on the chimpanzee by T. Graham Brown and Sherrington; and on the chimpanzee by T. Graham Brown. Individual reference is made to these subsequently in the text.

This paper will probably stand as the record for all time as the single report of related physiological experiments in which the largest number of great apes were studied.

The late nineteenth century experimental work on the brain of the monkey, in which we can include Beevor and Horsley's 1890 study of the orang, provided what is still the hard core of our knowledge of the functional localisation of the cerebral cortex. Indeed, there are some who might say that since then we have been merely dotting the 'i's' and crossing the 't's' of the subject, and that we have added little of real significance. These nineteenth-century studies, as a by-product, also provided a start for experimental work on the reproductive cycle of Primates.

The observation that the reproductive rhythm of monkeys follows the same pattern as the human had been recorded by several writers before the nineteenth century, as had, also, the fact that in many monkeys the skin around the external genitalia undergoes cyclical changes either of coloration or swelling, or both. The first to make systematic observations on these matters was John Bland-Sutton,[25] who in 1886 published a short paper on the menstrual cycle of the rhesus monkey and the Chacma baboon. As a contribution to scientific knowledge it had no particular merit. Nor was it, strictly speaking, an experimental paper. All Bland-Sutton did was kill rhesus monkeys and baboons during the phase of uterine bleeding in order to determine whether the bleeding was associated with destruction of the inner lining (= mucosa) of the uterus. His answer was wrong, and I mention him only for historical and sentimental reasons. Sir John Bland-Sutton, as he later became, was chairman of the Selection Board which appointed me to my first research post – anatomist to the Zoological Society of London.

In 1891, a few years after Bland-Sutton's paper of 1886, Langley and Sherrington used the term 'sexual skin' in a paper on pilo-motor nerves,[26] to describe the area of the upper part of the thighs, lower part of the back and tail of the female rhesus monkey, which reddens and swells during the course of the menstrual cycle. In 1893,[23] in his celebrated study of the posterior roots of the spinal nerves, Sherrington described this cutaneous area in greater detail. He was the first to investigate it with any scientific precision.

His interest was, however, confined to problems of the nervous system, and did not extend to reproductive mechanisms. The man who really laid the first foundation stone of modern knowledge of the menstrual cycle of monkeys was Walter Heape, of Trinity College, Cambridge. Heape spent the years 1888 and 1889 in India collecting large numbers of entellus langurs and rhesus monkeys, which he killed at different stages of the menstrual cycle, and whose reproductive tracts he then studied histologically. Heape's main concern was to describe the wave of growth and degeneration of the uterine mucosa, and to correlate the uterine changes with ovulation.[27] He was soon followed, in 1905 and 1906, by Dr Maria van Herwerden[28]; of Utrecht, who did much the same thing for the common macaque of the Dutch East Indies as Heape had achieved for the two monkeys of India.

In the same period, monkeys started being used in experimental studies of disease. Routine observations of the illnesses from which they succumbed in captivity had, of course, been made, and recorded, before then. In the case of the Zoological Society of London they began about 1830.

I have not made as exhaustive search as is possible, but so far as I can make out, Dr Lebert of Breslau must have been one of the first, if not the first, to use monkeys in work of this kind. The results of his studies, which started about 1869, were published in 1876.[29] His particular interest was tuberculosis. The main materials for his investigation were the cadavers of monkeys which died in the Zoological Gardens at Breslau, of which the Director at the time was Dr Schlegel. In addition to his pathological descriptions, Lebert also describes two monkeys which were inoculated with material from a tuberculous lesion. Since this was probably the first experimental study of its kind, it is not surprising that it hardly measures up to the critical standards which would be imposed today in a corresponding investigation. An equally crude experiment on the transmissibility of tuberculosis to monkeys was reported by Imlach in 1884.[30] It was about this time that establishments such as the Institute of Experimental Medicine in St Petersburg (Leningrad today, where Pavlov, of conditioned reflex fame, worked) were equipped to use monkeys in a routine way.[31]

Some ten years after the start of these early studies of tuberculosis, a corresponding but much more extensive series of investigations was made into the transmissibility to monkeys and apes of what subsequently became recognised as the spirochaete of syphilis. An account of these experiments, most of which were conflicting or inconclusive in their results, is given by Metchnikoff,[32] who himself, some time before 1900, used chimpanzees as subjects in these experiments. Among those who took part in this wave of work were Klebs, Martineau and Hamonic, Sperk, Mosse, and Krishaber, Fournier, and Barthelemy. Between them, they used a large variety of different genera and species of sub-human Primates. Metchnikoff himself tried to discover whether the lesions produced as a result of inoculating experimental animals with extracts from a natural syphilitic lesion themselves contained some factor which could be transmitted to a second experimental animal.

By the turn of the century, Landsteiner in Vienna[33] was using monkeys in studies on the transmissibility of poliomyelitis – in the production of a vaccine against this disease in children many more monkeys have since been sacrificed than could ever have been used in all experiments ever carried out on these animals. About the same time, monkeys started to be used in work on enteric and scarlet fever and measles. The first paper of which I know which describes the use of these animals in the investigation of the latter diseases is that of Grünbaum, published in 1904.[34] His experiments were carried out mainly on chimpanzees and were completely abortive.

In the earlier years of this century, the scene of the experimental investigation of monkeys and apes shifted, almost overwhelmingly, to the United States. The distinction of being the first American to write about monkeys would seem to be J. Jeffries, who in 1825 published an account of the dissection of an 'ourang outang' in the *Boston Journal of Natural Philosophy and Arts*.[35] Later there were the two well-known papers by Savage and Wyman on the African great apes,[36-37] and Wilder's observations on the musculature of the chimpanzee[38] to mention only a few of several American studies on primate anatomy. So far as I can make out, the first truly experimental papers on monkeys published in an American journal was one by Sanger Brown[39] in 1888, and another in which he collaborated with W.G. Thompson in 1890[40] on sensory localisation in the cerebral cortex. Brown had worked on monkeys with Schäfer in England before joining the University of New York.

The American work of this period which had the most lasting significance in increasing our knowledge of monkeys and apes was not, however, pursued in these more conventional fields of biological enquiry but in the analysis of monkey behaviour. With few exceptions, animal psychology in the nineteenth century was largely anecdotal in character, and given to facile comparisons of animal and human behaviour of the kind with which we have been once again made familiar by some recent vulgarisations which have dealt with such subjects as human aggression and sexual behaviour. Towards the end of the century the tide started to turn, first in England, through the work of Romanes and Hobhouse, to name two scholars whose writings are still well worth reading, and then in America, when in 1901

E.L. Thorndike published a magnificent monograph on *The Mental Life of the Monkeys*.[41] Thorndike was followed in 1902 by A.J. Kinnaman with a paper on the behaviour of two captive rhesus monkeys.[42] G.V. Hamilton also referred to monkeys in his noteworthy 1911 paper on trial and error reactions.[43] Then came Robert M. Yerkes who in 1915 published a paper on the maternal instinct of monkeys.[44] His powerful interest in the biology of monkeys and apes continued unabated throughout his life, and had a major influence on the development of the whole subject. His was the vision which led to the establishment of the Department of Psychobiology in Yale University, and to the foundation of the Anthropoid Experimental Station in Orange Park, Florida, joint institutions which in their time provided much information about the behaviour of the great apes. He was also for years the chairman of the Committee for Research in Problems of Sex of the National Research Council in Washington, a committee which helped sponsor, *inter alia*, the distinguished researches into the physiology of reproduction of rhesus monkeys of Dr George Corner[45] of the late Dr Edgar Allen,[46] and of Dr Carl Hartman[47] to name the outstanding leaders of a phase of experimental work to which I have already referred, and the zest of which, during the late twenties and thirties, it is difficult to recapture, except as a memory of an overwhelmingly exciting period in which discovery piled on discovery.

As I indicated in chapter 3, I was fortunate to participate in this pre-war wave of scientific endeavour. I also enjoyed nearly two of the early years of the laboratory of neurophysiology established in the Yale Medical School by the late Dr John F. Fulton,[48] in parallel with Dr Yerkes' laboratory. As a result of Dr Fulton's drive and influence, more experimental researches were carried out over a period of some fifteen years into various aspects of primate neurophysiology than ever before or since, both in his own laboratory and in others which were inspired by his successes to undertake work on monkeys and apes. The physiological basis for Moniz's brain operation to deal with a certain type of mental disorder was largely provided by Fulton's work on two female chimpanzees, familiarly known as Becky and Lucy.

This burst of laboratory work in the thirties was backed both by field studies into the behaviour of sub-human Primates in the natural habitat, of which those carried out by Bingham,[49] by Nissen,[50] and by Carpenter,[51] were outstanding examples, and by a variety of experimental enquiries into the natural and learning abilities of monkeys and apes, following on the pioneer studies of Köhler[52] and Kohts.[53] In my view, the most distinguished and enduring work by which this phase of behavioural research will be remembered is Kluver's *Behavior Mechanisms in Monkeys* published in 1933.[54] It is a scholarly study, not only rich in its account of the behavioural capacities of these animals, but also more penetrating in its analysis of their perceptual and other mental processes than any other work of which I know.

This historical catalogue which is not taken beyond the start of the second world war in 1939, should end with a cautionary note. With the vast increase in higher education and in the volume of scientific research which has occurred over the past two decades in most countries of the world, monkeys are being increasingly used in experimental studies of almost every aspect of physiology, pharmacology, virology, haematology, experimental medicine, as well, and as always, in enquiries into comparative psychology. So extensively are they being used that the result has been a wholesale traffic in monkeys from India and Africa to other parts of the world. The first major stimulus to this trade, as we all know, was the discovery of the poliomyelitis vaccine. But there have been many others. And there is a real danger now that man's exploitation of the other members of the Order of Mammals to which he belongs, both for utilitarian purposes and for the satisfaction of his intellectual curiosity, may prove as powerful a factor in bringing about their extinction, as will the more direct menace of man's spread into the remote forests and plains which still provide the natural habitat for those species of monkey and ape which still survive.

References

PREFACE   (pages ix to x)

1   Liberty in an age of Science (1959). Nature, 184.
2   *Scientists and War* (1966). London. Hamish Hamilton.

INTRODUCTION   (pages 1 to 7)

1   Smith, John Maynard (1969). The conscience of the scientist. *Listener*, August 7, 178–180.
2   Peierls, R.E. and Frisch, O.R. (1940). On the construction of a 'super-bomb', based on a nuclear chain reaction in uranium, in *Britain and Atomic Energy* 1939–45 by Margaret Gowing (1964). London. Macmillan.
3   Williams, Francis (1961). *A Prime Minister Remembers. The War and Post-War Memoirs of The Rt. Hon. Earl Attlee.* London. Heinemann.
4   Zuckerman, S. (1959). Liberty in an age of science. (Commemoration Address, Cal. Inst. Tech.) *Nature Lond. 184,* 135.

THE SEARCH FOR OBJECTIVE TRUTH   (pages 11 to 21)

1   Popper, Karl R. (1963). *Conjectures and Refutations.* London. Kegan Paul.
2   Tarski, Alfred (1956). *Logic Semantics, Metamathematics.* (Section on The Concept of Truth in Formalized Languages). Translated by J.H. Woodger. Oxford. Clarendon Press.
3   Lewis, C.I. (1967). *Mind and the World Order.* London. Dover Constable.
4   Huxley, T.H. (1863). Reprinted in *Darwiniana*, p. 463. London. Macmillan.
5   Huxley, T.H. (1854). Reprinted in *Lay Sermons, Addresses and Reviews*, p. 85. 1871. London. Macmillan.
6   Watson, James D. (1968). *The Double Helix.* London. Weidenfeld and Nicolson.
7   Medawar, P.B. (1967). *The Art of the Soluble.* London. Methuen.

215

References

8   Myrdal, Gunnar (1968). *The Problem of Objectivity in Social Research.*
New York. Pantheon Books. Also *Objectivity in Social Research*
(1970). London. Gerald Duckworth.

A STORY ABOUT MAMMALIAN EGG-CELLS (pages 22 to 34)

1   Zuckerman, S. (1965). The Natural History of an Enquiry.
Ann. Roy. Coll. Surg. Eng. 37, 133–148.

2   Zuckerman, S. (1930). The Menstrual Cycle of the Primates.
Part 1. General nature and homology. *Proc. Zool. Soc. Lond.*
1930. 691–754.

3   Stockard, C.R. and Papanicolaou, G.N. (1917). The existence of a
typical oestrous cycle in the guinea-pig – with a study of its
histological and physiological changes. *Am. J. Anat. 22*, 225–283.

4   Waldeyer, W. (1870). *Eierstock Und Ei.* Leipzig. Engelmann.

5   Evans, H.M. and Swezy, O. (1931). Ovogenesis and the normal
follicular cycle in adult mammalia. *Mem. Univ. Calif. 9*, 119–224.

6   Allen, E. (1923). Ovogenesis during sexual maturity. *Am. J. Anat.*
31, 439–481.

7   Zuckerman, S. and Parkes, A.S. (1932). The menstrual cycle of the
primates. Part 5. The cycle of the baboon. *Proc. Zool. Soc. Lond.*
1932. 139–191.

8   Zuckerman, S. (1937). Inhibition of menstruation and ovulation
by means of testosterone propionate. *Lancet* 1937, 676–680.

9   Green, S.H. and Zuckerman, S. (1947). A comparison of the
growth of the ovum and follicle in normal Rhesus monkeys and in
monkeys treated with oestrogens and androgens. *J. Endocr. 5*,
207–219.

10   Breward, M.M. and Zuckerman, S. (1949). The reaction of the
body to multiple ovarian grafts. *J. Endocr. 6*, 226–234.

11   Lipschütz, A. (1925). Dynamics of ovarian hypertrophy under
experimental conditions. *Br. J. exp. Biol. 2*, 331–346.

12   Mandl, A.M. and Zuckerman, S. (1949). Ovarian autografts in
monkeys. *J. Anat. 83*, 315–324.

13   Everett, N.B. (1943). Observational and experimental evidences
relating to the origin and differentiation of the definitive germ
cells in mice. *J. exp. Zool. 92*, 49–91.

14   Mandl, A.M. and Zuckerman, S. (1950). The numbers of normal
and atretic ova in the mature rat. *J. Endocr. 6*, 426–435.

15   Mandl, A.M. and Zuckerman, S. (1951a). The effect of destruction
of the germinal epithelium on the numbers of oocytes. *J. Endocr.*
7, 103–111.

16   Mandl, A.M. and Zuckerman, S. (1951b). Numbers of normal and
atretic oocytes in unilaterally spayed rats. *J. Endocr. 7*, 112–119.

17 Arai, H. (1920a). On the cause of the hypertrophy of the surviving ovary after semi-spaying (albino rat) and on the number of ova in it. *Am. J. Anat. 28*, 59–79.

18 Arai, H. (1920b). On the postnatal development of the ovary (albino rat), with especial reference to the number of ova. *Am. J. Anat. 27*, 405–462.

19 Jones, E.C. and Krohn, P.L. (1960). The effect of unilateral ovariectomy on the reproductive lifespan of mice. *J. Endocr. 20*, 129–134.

20 Mandl, A.M. and Zuckerman, S. (1951c). The relation of age to numbers of oocytes. *J. Endocr. 7*, 190–193.

21 Jones, E.C. and Krohn, P.L. (1959). Influence of the anterior pituitary on the ageing process in the ovary. *Nature, Lond. 183*, 1155–1158.

22 Jones, E.C. and Krohn, P.L. (1961b). The relationships between age, numbers of oocytes and fertility in virgin and multiparous mice. *J. Endocr. 21*, 469–495.

23 Talbert, G.B. (1968). Effect of maternal age on reproductive capacity. *Am. J. Obstet. Gynec. 102*, 451–477. Jones, E.C. (1970). The ageing ovary and its influence on reproductive capacity. *J. Reprod. Fert.* Suppl. *12*, 17–30.

24 Mandl, A.M., Zuckerman, S. and Patterson, H.D. (1952). The number of oocytes in ovarian fragments after compensatory hypertrophy. *J. Endocr. 8*, 347–356.

25 Mandl, A.M. and Zuckerman, S. (1951d). The reaction of the ovaries and adrenal glands of female rats to ovarian and muscle homografts. *J. Endocr. 7*, 344–348.

26 Mandl, A.M. and Zuckerman, S. (1951e). The time of vaginal opening in rats after ovarian autotransplantation. *J. Endocr. 7*, 335–338. Mandl, A.M. and Zuckerman, S. (1951f). Ovarian hypertrophy after unilateral hysterectomy. *J. Endocr. 7*, 339–343. Mandl, A.M. and Zuckerman, S. (1952). Factors influencing the onset of puberty in albino rats. *J. Endocr. 8*, 357–364.

27 Zuckerman, S. (1951). The number of oocytes in the mature ovary. *Recent Prog. Horm. Res. 6*, 63–109.

28 Swezy, O. (1933). *Ovogenesis and its Relation to the Hypophysis.* Science Press. Lancaster, Pa.

29 Ingram, D.L. (1953). The effect of hypophysectomy on the number of oocytes in the adult albino rat. *J. Endocr. 9*, 307–311.

30 Jones, E.C. and Krohn, P.L. (1961a). The effect of hypophysectomy on age changes in the ovaries of mice. *J. Endocr. 21*, 497–509.

31 Ingram, D.L. (1958). Fertility and oocyte numbers after x-irradiation of the ovary. *J. Endocr. 17*, 81–90.

References

32 Ingram, D.L., Mandl, A.M. and Zuckerman, S. (1958). The influence of age on litter-size. *J. Endocr.* *17*, 280–285.

33 Krohn, P.L. (1962). Review lectures on senescence. 2. Heterochronic transplantation in the study of ageing. *Proc. Roy. Soc. B* *157*, 128–147.

34 Talbert, G.B. and Krohn, P.L. (1966). Effect of maternal age on viability of ova and uterine support of pregnancy in mice. *J. Reprod. Fert.* *11*, 399–406.

35 Beaumont, H.M. and Mandl, A.M. (1962). A quantitative and cytological study of oogonia and oocytes in the foetal and neonatal rat. *Proc. Roy. Soc. B* *155*, 557–579.

36 Ioannou, J.M. (1964). Oogenesis in the guinea pig. *J. Embryol. exp. Morph.* *12*, 673–691.

37 Baker, T.G. (1966). A quantitative and cytological study of oogenesis in the rhesus monkey. *J. Anat.* *100*, 761–776.

38 Hughes, G.C. (1963). The population of germ cells in the developing female chick. *J. Embryol. exp. Morph.* *11*, 513–536.

39 Baker, T.G. (1963). A quantitative and cytological study of germ cells in human ovaries. *Proc. Roy. Soc. B, 158*, 417–433.

40 Ioannou, J.M. (1967). Oogenesis in adult prosimians. *J. Embryol. exp. Morph.* *17*, 139–145. Anand Kumar, T.C. (1968). Oogenesis in lorises; *Loris tardigradus lydekkerianus* and *Nycticebus coucang.* *Proc. Roy. Soc. B* *169*, 167–176.

HORMONES AND HUMOURS (pages 35 to 45)

1 Addison, T. (1855). *On the Constitutional and Local Effects of Disease of the Supra-renal Capsules.* London. Highley.

2 Bayliss, W.M. and Starling, E.H. (1904). The chemical regulation of the secretory process. *Proc. Roy. Soc. Lond., 73*, 310–322.

3 Starling, E.H. (1905). The chemical correlation of the functions of the body. *Lancet, 11,* 339.

4 Berthold, A.A. (1849). Transplantation der Hoden. *Arch. Anat. Physiol. Lpz.* 42–46.

5 King, T.W. (1836). Observations on the thyroid gland; with notes on the same subject by Sir Astley Cooper, bart. *Guy's Hosp. Rep. 1,* 429–446.

6 Cooper, A. (1836). Notes on the structure of the thyroid gland. *Guy's Hosp. Rep. 1,* 448–456.

7 Brown-Séquard, E. (1856a). Recherches expérimentales sur la physiologie et la pathologie des capsules surrénales. *Arch. gén. Med.* 8, v^e série 11, 385, 572. Brown-Séquard, E. (1856b). Recherches expérimentales sur la physiologie et la pathologie des capsules surrénales. *C.r. Acad. Sci., Paris. 43*, 422–425, 542–546.

8 De Bordeu, T. (1775). Recherches sur des maladies chroniques.

Part 6. Analyse medicinale du sang. Reprinted in *Oeuvres complètes de Bordeu*, tome 11, 1818. Paris. Caille et Ravier.

9   Hutchinson, J. (1856). Bronzed skin and disease of the supra-renal capsules. *Med. Times Gaz.* N.S. 12, 233–236, 281.

10 Hutchinson, J. (1884). *The Pedigree of Disease*. London. Churchill.

11 Singer, C. (1925). *The Evolution of Anatomy*. London. Kegan Paul.

12 Meyer, A. (1937). The tradition of ancient biology and medicine in the vitalistic periods of modern biology and medicine. *Bull. Inst. Hist. Med. John Hopkins Univ.* 5, 800–821.

13 Singer, C. and Rabin, C. (1946). *A Prelude to Modern Science*. Cambridge University Press.

14 Singer, C. (1942). *Vesalius on the Human Brain*. London. Oxford University Press.

15 Swedenborg, E. (1882). *The Brain considered anatomically, physiologically and philosophically*. Edited by R.L.Tafel. London, Speirs, Vol. 1. (Vol. 2 1887).

16 Willis, T. (1664). Cerebri anatome, nervoriemque descriptio et usus. Reprinted in *Opera Omnia*. Amsterdam. Henricum Wetstenium. 1682.

17 Lower, Richard (1672). *De Catarrhis*. Together with a Bibliographical analysis by Richard Hunter and Ian Macalpine (1963). London. Dawsons of Pall Mall. See also Rolleston, H. (1936). *The Endocrine Organs in Health and Disease with an Historical Review*. London. Oxford University Press.

18 Vieussens, R. (1685). *Neurographia universalis*. Leyden. Joannem Certe.

19 Lieutaud, J. (1742). *Essais Anatomiques*. Paris. Pierre-Michel Huart.

20 De Bordeu, T. (1751). *Recherches anatomiques sur la position des glandes et sur leur action*. Paris. Quillan.

21 Riolano, J. (1649). *Encheiridium anatomicum et pathologicum*. Leiden. Adrian Wyngaerden. Riolanus, J. (1657). *A Sure Guide: or, the best and nearest way to physick and chyrurgery: that is to say, the arts of healing by medicine, and manual operation*. 1st Ed. Translated from the Latin by Nicholas Culpeper. Printed by John Streeter, London.

22 Cumston, C.G. (1926). *An Introduction to the History of Medicine from the Time of the Pharaohs to the End of the XVIIIth Century*. London. Kegan Paul.

23 Wenzel, J. and Wenzel, C. (1812). *De Penitiori structura cerebri hominis et brutorum*. Tubingen, Cottam.

24 Luschka, H. (1860). *Der Hirnanhang und die Steissdrüse des Menschen*. Berlin. Reimer.

References

THE NEW SECRETIONS OF THE BRAIN (pages 46 to 60)

1 Oliver, G. and Schäfer, E.A. (1895). On the physiological action of extracts of pituitary body and certain other glandular organs. *J. Physiol. Lond. 18*, 277–279.

2 Howell, W.H. (1898). The physiological effects of extracts of hypophysis cerebri and infundibular body. *J. exp. Med. 3*, 245–258.

3 Magnus, R. and Schäfer, E.A. (1901). The action of pituitary extracts upon the kidney. *J. Physiol. Lond. 27*, ix–xP.

4 Dale, H.H. (1906). On some physiological actions of ergot. *J. Physiol. Lond. 34*, 163–206. Dale, H.H. (1909). The actions of extracts of the pituitary body. *Biochem. J. 4*, 427–447.

5 Teel, H.M. and Cushing, H. (1930). The separate growth-promoting and gonad-stimulating hormones of the anterior hypophysis: an historical review. *Endokrinologie 6*, 401–420.

6 Cushing, H. and Goetsch, E. (1910). Concerning the secretion of the infundibular lobe of the pituitary body and its presence in the cerebrospinal fluid. *Am. J. Physiol. 27*, 60–86.

7 Cushing, H. (1933). Posterior pituitary activity from an anatomical standpoint. *Am. J. Path. 9*, 539–547.

8 Gersh, I. (1939). The structure and function of the parenchymatous glandular cells in the neurohypophysis of the rat. *Am. J. Anat. 64*, 407–443.

9 Karplus, J.P. and Kreidl, A. (1909). Gehirn und Sympathicus. 1. Mitteilung, Zwischenhirnbasis und Halssympathicus. *Arch. ges. Physiol. 129*, 138–144.

10 Camus, J. and Roussy, G. (1913). Hypophysectomie et polyuria experimentales. *C.R. Soc. Biol., Paris, 75*, 483.

11 Fisher, C., Ingram, W.R., Ranson, S.W. (1938). *Diabetes Insipidus and the Neuro-hormonal Control of Water Balance: a Contribution to the Structure and Function of the Hypothalamo-hypophyseal System.* Ann Arbor: Edwards.

12 Verney, E.B. (1947). The antidiuretic hormone and the factors which determine its release. (Croonian lecture). *Proc. Roy. Soc. B. 135*, 25–106.

13 Noble, R.L., Plunkett, E.R. and Taylor, N.B.G. (1950). Factors affecting the control of the pituitary gland. *Recent Prog. Horm. Res. 5*, 263–304. Ed. G. Pincus. New York, Academic Press.

14 Taylor, N.B.G., and Noble, R.L. (1950). Appearance of an antidiuretic substance in the urine of man after various procedures. *Proc. Soc. exp. Biol. N.Y. 73*, 207–208.

15 Harris, G.W. (1951). Neural control of the pituitary gland. I. The neurohypophysis. *Brit. med. J.* ii, 559–563.

16 Bayliss, W.M. and Starling, E.H. (1904). The chemical regulation

of the secretory process. (Croonian Lecture). *Proc. Roy. Soc. Lond.*
73, 310–322.

17 Harris, G.W. (1948a). Electrical stimulation of the hypothalamus
and the mechanism of neural control of the adenohypophysis.
J. Physiol. Lond. 107, 418–429.

18 Clark, W.E. Le Gros, McKeown, T. and Zuckerman, S. (1939).
Visual pathways concerned in gonadal stimulation in ferrets.
Proc. Roy. Soc. Lond. B, 126, 449–468.

19 Thomson, A.P.D. (1951). Relation of retinal stimulation to oestrus
in the ferret. *J. Physiol. Lond. 113*, 425–433. Thomson, A.P.D.
(1954). The onset of oestrus in normal and blinded ferrets. *Proc.
Roy. Soc. Lond. B 142*, 126–135.

20 Harris, G.W. (1948b). Neural control of the pituitary gland.
Physiol. Rev. 28, 139–179.

21 Popa, G. and Fielding, U. (1930). The vascular link between the
pituitary and the hypothalamus. *Lancet* 1930 (2), 238–240.

22 Wislocki, G.B. and King, L.S. (1936). The permeability of the
hypophysis and hypothalamus to vital dyes, with a study of the
hypophyseal vascular supply. *Am. J. Anat. 58*, 421–472.

23 Green, J.D. and Harris, G.W. (1949). Observation of the hypophysio-portal vessels of the living rat. *J. Physiol. Lond. 108*,
359–361.

24 Barrnett, R.J. and Greep, R.O. (1951a). The direction of flow in
the blood vessels of the infundibular stalk. *Science, 113*, 185.

25 McCann, S.M., Dhariwal, A.P.S. and Porter, J.C. (1968). Regulation of the Adenohypophysis. *Ann. Rev. Physiol. 30*, 589.

26 Zuckerman, S. (1955). The Possible Functional Significance of
the Pituitary Portal Vessels. In *Ciba Foundation Coll. Endocrin.*,
8, 551–586.

27 Vincent, D.S. and Anand Kumar, T.C. (1969). Electron microscopic studies on the pars intermedia of the ferret. *Z. Zellforsch.*,
99, 185–197.

28 Holmes, R.L. and Zuckerman, S. (1959). The blood supply of the
hypophysis in Macaca mulatta, *J. Anat., Lond., 93*, 1–8. Holmes,
R.L. (1967). The vascular pattern of the median eminence of the
hypophysis of the macaque. *Folda primat., 7*, 216–230.

29 Herbert, J. (1969). The pineal gland and light-induced oestrus in
ferrets. *J. Endocrin. 43*, 625–636.

30 Anand Kumar, T.C. and Knowles, F.G.W. (1967). A system linking the III ventricle and the pars tuberalis of the rhesus monkey.
Nature, 215, 54–55. Anand Kumar, T.C. (1968). Sexual differences
in the ependyma lining the III ventricle in the area of the anterior
hypothalamus of adult rhesus monkeys. *Z. Zellforsch. 90*, 28–36.
Knowles, F.G.W. and Anand Kumar, T.C. (1969). Structural

changes, related to reproduction, in the hypothalamus and in the pars tuberalis of the rhesus monkey. *Phil. Trans. Roy. Soc. Lond. 256*, 357–375. Knowles, F.G.W. (1969). Ependymal Secretion, especially in the Hypothalamic Region. *J. Neuro-Visceral Rels. IX*, 97–110.

ART AND SCIENCE IN ANATOMICAL DIAGNOSIS
(pages 61 to 74)

1 Dawson, C. and Woodward, A.S. (1913). On the discovery of a palaeolithic human skull and mandible in a flint-bearing gravel overlying the Wealden (Hastings beds) at Piltdown, Fletching (Sussex). With an appendix by G.E. Smith. *Q. J. geol. Soc. Lond. 69*, 117–151. Dawson, C. and Woodward, A.S. (1914). Supplementary note on the discovery of a palaeolithic human skull and mandible at Piltdown (Sussex). With an appendix by G.E. Smith. *Q. J. geol. Soc. Lond. 70*, 82–99.

2 Smith, G. Elliot (1927). *Essays on the evolution of man*. 2nd ed. Oxford University Press.

3 Hdrlîcka, A. (1922). The Piltdown Jaw. *Am. J. phys. Anthrop. 5*, 337–347.

4 Hrdlîcka, A. (1923). Dimensions of 1st and 2nd lower molars with their bearing on the Piltdown jaw and on Man's phylogeny. *Am. J. phys. Anthrop. 6*, 195–216.

5 Waterston, D. (1913). In Appendix to Dawson, C. and Woodward, A.S. (1913). On the discovery of a palaeolithic human skull and mandible in a flint-bearing gravel overlying the Wealden (Hastings beds) at Piltdown, Fletching (Sussex). *Q. J. geol. Soc. Lond. 69*, 117–151.

6 Miller, G.S. (1915). The jaw of the Piltdown man. *Smithson. misc. Collns. 65 no. 12*, 1–31. Miller, G.S. (1918). The Piltdown jaw. *Am. J. phys. Anthrop. 1*, 25–52.

7 Boule, M. (1923). *Fossil Man*. Edinburgh. Oliver and Boyd.

8 Gregory, W.K. (1920). The origin and evolution of the human dentition: a palaeontological review. Part 4. The dentition of the higher primates and their relationships with Man. *J. dent. Res. 2*, 607–717.

9 Frasetto, F. (1927). New views on the dawn man of Piltdown. *Man 27*, 121–124.

10 Weidenreich, F. (1943). The skull of *Sinanthropus pekinensis*: a comparative study on a primitive hominid skull. *Palaeont. sin.* n.s.D., *no. 10*, 1–485.

11 Keith, A. (1925). *The Antiquity of man*. Vols. 1 and 2. London. Williams.

12 Keith, Sir A. (1939). A resurvey of the anatomical features of the

Piltdown skull, with some observations on the recently discovered Swanscombe skull. Part 2. *J. Anat. 73*, 234–254.

13　Marston, A.T. (1950). The relative ages of the Swanscombe and Piltdown skulls, with special reference to the results of the fluorine estimation test. *Br. dent. J. 88*, 292–299.

14　Oakley, K.P. (1950). Relative dating of the Piltdown skull. *Advanc. Sci. Lond. 6*, 343–344.

15　Weiner, J.S., Oakley, K.P. and Clark, W.E. Le Gros (1953). The solution of the Piltdown problem. *Bull. Br. Mus. Nat. Hist. Geol. 2*, 141–146.

16　Broom, R. (1950). Summary of a note on the Piltdown skulls. *Advanc. Sci. Lond. 6*, 344.

17　Marston, A.T. (1954). The Piltdown 'hoax'. *Dent. Rec. 74*, 1–14.

18　Osborn, H.F. (1922). Hesperopithecus, the anthropoid primate of Western Nebraska. *Nature, 110*, 281–283.

19　Woodward, A.S. (1922). A supposed ancestral man in North America. *Nature 109*, 750.

20　Gregory, W.K. and Hellman, M. (1923). Notes on the type of *Hesperopithecus haroldcookii* Osborne. *Am. Mus. Novit. 53*, 1–16.

21　Gregory, W.K. and Hellman, M. (1923). Further notes on the molars of *Hesperopithecus* and of *Pithecanthropus*. *Bull. Am. Mus. Nat. Hist. 48*, 509–530.

22　Gregory, W.K. (1927). Two views of the origin of Man. *Science 65*, 601–605.

23　Black, D. (1927). On a lower molar hominid tooth from the Chou Kou Tien deposit. *Palaeont. sin.* n.s.D, no. *7* (1), 1–26. Black, D. (1930). On an adolescent skull of *Sinanthropus pekinensis* in comparison with an adult skull of the same species, and with other hominid skulls, recent and fossil. *Palaeont. sin.* n.s.D, no. *7* (2), 1–145.

24　Zuckerman, S. (1933). *Sinanthropus* and other fossil men: their relations to each other and to modern types. *Eugen. Rev. 24*, 273–284.

25　Zuckerman, S. (1953). Chapter in: *Evolution as a process*, (edited by Huxley, *et al.*) London. Allen & Unwin p. 300.

26　Morant, G.M. (1926). Studies of palaeolithic man. *Ann. Eugen. 1*, 257–276.

27　Keith, A. (1931). *New discoveries relating to the antiquity of man*. London. Williams and Norgate.

AFRICAN COUSINS　(pages 75 to 94)

1　Broom, R. and Robinson, J.T. (1952). Swartkrans ape-man, *Paranthropus crassidens*. *Transv. Mus. Mem. 6*, 1–123. Broom, R. and Robinson, J.T. (1950). Further evidence of the structure of the

References

Sterkfontein ape-man *Plesianthropus. Transv. Mus. Mem. 4*, 11–83. Schepers, G.W.H. (1950). The brain casts of the recently discovered *Plesianthropus* skulls. *Transv. Mus. Mem. 4*, 89–117. Broom, R. and Schepers, G.W.H. (1946). The South African fossil apemen: the Australopithecinae. *Transv. Mus. Mem. 2*, 1–272.

2 Dart, R.A. (1925). *Australopithecus africanus:* the man-ape of South Africa. *Nature 115*, 195–199.

3 Clark, W.E. Le Gros (1947). Observations on the anatomy of the fossil Australopithecinae. *J. Anat. Lond., 81*, 300–333.

4 Clark, W.E. Le Gros (1962). *The Antecedents of Man* (2nd ed.). Edinburgh. University Press.

5 Dart, R.A. (1957). The osteodontokeratic culture of *Australopithecus prometheus. Transv. Mus. Mem. 10*, 1–105.

6 Ashton, E.H. (1950). The endocranial capacities of the Australopithecinae. *Proc. zool. Soc. Lond. 120*, 715–721.

7 Ashton, E.H. and Spence, T.F. (1958). Age changes in the cranial capacity and foramen magnum of Hominoids. *Proc. zool. Soc. Lond. 130*, 169–181.

8 Zuckerman, S. (1933). *Functional Affinities of Man, Monkeys and Apes.* London. Kegan Paul.

9 Holloway, Ralph L. (1970). New endocranial values for the Australopithecines. *Nature 227*, 199–200.

10 Clark, W.E. Le Gros (1950). New palaeontological evidence bearing on the evolution of the Hominoidea. With an appendix, diagnoses of East African Miocene Hominoidea. *Q. J. geol. Soc. Lond. 105*, 225–264.

11 Ashton, E.H. and Zuckerman, S. (1951). Some cranial indices of Plesianthropus and other primates. *Am. J. phys. Anthrop.* n.s. 9, 283–296.

12 Robinson, J.T. (1958). Cranial cresting patterns and their significance in the Hominoidea. *Am. J. phys. Anthrop.* n.s. *16*, 397–428.

13 Ashton, E.H. and Zuckerman, S. (1952a). Age changes in the position of the occipital condyles in the chimpanzee and gorilla. *Am. J. phys. Anthrop.* n.s. *10*, 277–288. Ashton, E.H. and Zuckerman, S. (1956a). Age changes in the position of the foramen magnum in Hominoids. *Proc. zool. Soc. Lond. 126*, 315–325.

14 Biegert, J. (1957). Der Formenwandel des Primatenschädels und seine Beziehungen zur ontogenetischen Entwicklung und den Phylogenetischen Spezialisationen der Kopforgane. *Morph. Jb. 98*, 77–199.

15 Zuckerman, S. (1954b). *In Evolution as a Process* (edited by Huxley *et al.*), p. 300. London. Allen and Unwin.

16 Ashton, E.H. and Zuckerman, S. (1956b). Cranial crests in the Anthropoidea. *Proc. zool. Soc. Lond. 126*, 581–634.

17 Robinson, J.T. (1954a). The Australopithecine occiput. *Nature Lond.*, *174*, 262–263.
18 Robinson, J.T. (1954b). Nuchal crests in Australopithecines. *Nature, Lond.*, *174*, 1197–1198.
19 Robinson, J.T. (1950). The evolutionary significance of the Australopithecines. *Yearb. phys. Anthrop.* *6*, 38–41.
20 Ashton, E.H., Oxnard, C.E., Spence, T.F. and Zuckerman, S. (1967). The functional significance of certain features of the innominate bone in living and fossil primates. *J. Anat.* 1967, *101*, 608.
21 Oxnard, Charles E. (1969). Mathematics, Shape and Function: a study in Primate Anatomy. *Amer. Scientist, 57*, 1, 75-96. Oxnard, Charles E. (1969). Evolution of the Human Shoulder: Some Possible Pathways. *Am. J. Phys. Anthrop.*, *30*, 319–332.
22 Oxnard, C.E. and Neely, P.M. (1969). The descriptive use of neighbourhood limited classification in functional morphology: and analysis of the shoulder in primates. *J. Morphol.*, *129*, 127–148.
23 Campbell, Bernard, G. (1968). Inspiration and controversy: motives for research. *S. Afric. J. Sci.*, 60–63.

CONVENTION AND CONTROVERSY (pages 95 to 102)

1 Osler, William (1906). *The Growth of Truth*, London, Henry Frowde. (The Harveian oration delivered at the Royal College of Physicians, London, October 18, 1906.)
2 Koestler, Arthur (1965). Evolution and revolution in the history of science. *Encounter*, vol. 25, no. 6. 32–38.
3 Yates, F. (1968). Theory and practice in statistics. *J. Roy. Stat. Soc.*, *A 13*, part 4.
4 Machlup, Fritz. (1965). Why economists disagree. *Proc. Amer. Philos. Soc.*, *109*, 1.
5 De Jouvenal, Bertrand (1967). *The Art of Conjecture*. London. Weidenfeld and Nicolson.

SCIENCE AND POLITICS (pages 105 to 111)

1 Cmnd. 9230 (1918). *Report of the Machinery of Government Committee of the Ministry of Reconstruction*. Chairman, Viscount Haldane of Cloan. London. Her Majesty's Stationery Office.
2 Cmnd. 6824 (1946). *Scientific Manpower* – Report of a Committee appointed by the Lord President of the Council. Chairman, Sir Alan Barlow. London. Her Majesty's Stationery Office.
3 Cmnd. 7465 (1948). *First Annual Report of the Advisory Council on Scientific Policy*. London. Her Majesty's Stationery Office.
4 Cmnd. 2538 (1964). *Annual Report of the Advisory Council on*

References

Scientific Policy, 1963-4. London. Her Majesty's Stationery Office.
5 Cmnd. 2171 (1963). *Committee of Enquiry into the Organisation of Civil Science.* Chairman, Sir Burke Trend. London. Her Majesty's Stationery Office.
6 Cmnd. 3007 (1966). Council for Scientific Policy. *Report on Science Policy.* London. Her Majesty's Stationery Office.

THE SCOPE FOR ADVICE (pages 112 to 117)

1 Cmnd. 6824 (1946). *Scientific Manpower* – Report of a Committee appointed by the Lord President of the Council. Chairman, Sir Alan Barlow. London. Her Majesty's Stationery Office.
2 Cmnd. 8561 (1952). *Report from the Committee on Scientific Manpower.* In Fifth Annual Report of the Advisory Council on Scientific Policy, 1951–2. London. Her Majesty's Stationery Office.

THE CRITERIA OF SCIENCE POLICY (pages 118 to 128)

1 Committee on the Management and Control of Research and Development (1961). Report. Chairman, Sir Solly Zuckerman. London. Her Majesty's Stationery Office.
2 U.S. Department of Commerce (1967). *Technological Innovation: Its Environment and Management.* Washington, D.C.: Superintendent of Documents, U.S. Government Printing Office.
3 Quinn, J.E. (1967). Discussion on impact of government policy on technology and economic growth. In *Technology and World Trade: Proceedings of a Symposium.* United States National Bureau of Standards, Miscellaneous Publication 284.
4 *Technological Innovation in Britain.* Report of the Central Advisory Council for Science and Technology (1968). London. Her Majesty's Stationery Office.
5 Skolnikoff, E.B. (1966). Scientific advice in the State Department. *Science, 154,* 980–985.
6 Handler, Philip (1967). Federal science policy. *Science, 155,* 1063–1066.

TECHNOLOGY AND THE INDUSTRIAL REVOLUTION
(pages 137 to 146)

1 Clark, Colin (1951). *The Conditions of Economic Progress.* London. Macmillan.
2 Petty, Sir William (1899). *The Economic Writings of Sir William Petty.* Edited by C. H. Hull. Cambridge University Press.
3 Landes, David S. (1965). In *The Cambridge Economic History of Europe,* vol. vi, ed. by H.J. Habakkuk and M. Postan. Cambridge University Press.

4 Heath, H.F., and Hetherington, A.L. (1945). *Industrial Research and Development in the United Kingdom*. London. Faber and Faber. Bernal, J.D. (1965). *Science in History*. London, Watts. Third edition.

5 Hartley, Sir Harold (1965). *The Contribution of Engineering to the British Economy*. Oxford University Press.

6 Crowther, J.G. (1962). *Scientists of the Industrial Revolution*. London, Cresset Press.

TECHNOLOGICAL COMPETITION TODAY
(pages 147 to 154)

1 Hutton, R.S. (1964). *Recollections of a Technologist*. London. Isaac Pitman and Sons Ltd.

2 Cohen, J.M. (1956). *The Life of Ludwig Mond*. London. Methuen.

3 See Cardwell, D.S.L. (1957). *The Organisation of Science in England*. London. Heinemann.

4 U.S. Department of Commerce (1967). *Technological Innovation: Its Environment and Management*.

TECHNOLOGICAL FORECASTING   (pages 155 to 161)

1 Shonfield, Andrew (1969). Thinking about the future. *Encounter*, *32*, 15.

2 Townes, Charles H. (1968). Quantum electronics, and surprise in development of technology. *Science, 159*, 699.

3 Crowther, J.G. (1968). *Science in Modern Society*. New York. Schocken Books.

4 Jantsch, Erich (1966). *Technological Forecasting in Perspective*. Organisation for Economic Co-operation and Development.

5 Zuckerman, S. (1950). The mechanism of thought: the mind and the calculating machine. In *The Physical Basis of Mind*. Compiled by Peter Laslett. Basil Blackwell. Oxford. Zuckerman, S. (1962). Judgment and control in war. *Foreign Affairs, 40*, 196–212.

6 *Planning-Programming-Budgeting: Initial Memorandum: Committee on Government Operations*. United States Senate. U.S. Government Printing Office, 1967.

7 *Planning-Programming-Budgeting: Selected Comment. Committee on Government Operations*. United States Senate. U.S. Government Printing Office, 1967.

8 De Jouvenel, Bertrand (1967). *The Art of Conjecture*. London. Weidenfeld and Nicolson. De Jouvenel, Bertrand (1968). Notes on Social Forecasting. In *Forecasting and the Social Sciences*, ed. Michael Young. London. Heinemann.

References

THE SOCIAL COST OF TECHNOLOGICAL CHOICE
(pages 162 to 168)

1 Cohen, J.M. (1956). *The Life of Ludwig Mond.* London. Methuen.
2 Chambers, Sir Paul (1969). Technology and the profit motive. *J. Roy. Soc. Arts, 117,* 188.
3 Cadbury, G.A.H. (1969). *Our Technological Future.* The 1969 Viscount Nuffield Memorial Paper. London. Maxwell, Love & Co. Ltd.
4 Galbraith, John Kenneth (1967). *The New Industrial State.* London. Hamish Hamilton.
5 U.S. Department of Commerce (1967). *Technological Innovation.* U.S. Government Printing Office.
6 Mishan, E.J. (1967). *The Costs of Economic Growth.* London. Staples Press.
7 Perloff, Harvey S. (1967). Towards the year 2000. *Daedalus, Proc. Amer. Acad. Arts. & Sci., 96,* 789.
8 Mansholt, S.L. (1967). *Our Accelerating Century.* Royal Dutch Shell Lectures on Industry and Society.

THE TRANSFORMATION OF THE MEDICAL ENVIRONMENT
(pages 169 to 175)

1 *The British Health Services* (1937). Political and Economic Planning. London.
2 *National Health Service Bill* (1964). H.M.S.O. London Cmnd. 6761.
3 Powell, J. Enoch (1966). *Medicine and Politics.* London. Pitman Medical Publishing Co. Ltd.

THE CONSEQUENCES OF MEDICAL PROGRESS
(pages 176 to 186)

1 Gilding, H.P. and Zuckerman, S. (1953). The integration of physiology and anatomy as a single subject in the curriculum. Chapter in *First World Congress on Medical Education. Proceedings.* Ed. H. Clegg, London. Oxford University Press.
2 Royal Commission on Medical Education. *Report.* (1968). Cmnd. 3569. Her Majesty's Stationery Office. London.
3 Priorities in Medicine (1969). B.M.A. Planning Unit. *Brit. Med. J. 1,* 106–108.
4 Platt, Lord (1967). Medical Science: Master or Servant? (Harveian Oration delivered to the Royal College of Physicians of London on 18th October, 1967). Reprinted from *Brit. Med. J. 4,* 439–444.
5 Comfort, A. (1969). Longer life by 1990? *New Scientist,* 11 December, 1969, 549–551.

6 Miller, Henry (1968). Psychiatry and the health service. *The Listener*, *80*, 257–258.

7 Department of Health and Social Security. (1968). *On the State of the Public Health*. The annual report of the Chief Medical Officer of the Department of Health and Social Security. London. Her Majesty's Stationery Office.

THE POSSIBILITY OF PRIORITIES (pages 187 to 204)

1 Peierls, R.E. and Frisch, O.R. (1940) in *Britain and Atomic Energy* 1939–45 by Margaret Gowing (1964). London. Macmillan.

2 Fox, Theodore (1965). *Crisis in Communication*. London, Athlone Press.

3 Annual Report of the Advisory Council on Scientific Policy 1959–60. London. Her Majesty's Stationery Office.

4 *Statistics of Science and Technology* (1968). Department of Education and Science, Ministry of Technology. London. Her Majesty's Stationery Office.

5 Estimates for the year ending 31st March, 1970. Memorandum by the Financial Secretary to the Treasury. London. Her Majesty's Stationery Office.

APPENDIX (pages 205 to 214)

1 Bell, John (1825). *Observations on Italy*. Edinburgh. William Blackwood.

2 Aristotle (1910). *Historia Animalium*. Translated into English by D'Arcy Wentworth Thompson; edited by Smith, J.A. and Ross, W.D. Volume 4 of Ross, W.D., ed. *The Works of Aristotle*, Oxford, Clarendon Press.

3 Galen (1956). *On Anatomical Procedures*. Trans. by Charles Singer, London, Oxford University Press.

4 Ball, J.M. (1910). *Andreas Vesalius, the Reformer of Anatomy*. St Louis, Medical Science Press, 1910.

5 Tyson, Edward (1699). *Orang-utang, sive Homo sylvestris; or The Anatomy of a Pygmie compared with that of a Monkey, an Ape, and a Man. To which is added, A philological essay concerning the pigmies, the cynocephali, the satyrs, and sphinges of the ancients; wherein it will appear that they are all either apes or monkeys, and not men, as formerly pretended*. London. Thomas Bennet.

6 Translated in Clendening, Logan. *Source Book of Medical History* (1942). London. Hoeber. 142–150.

7 Osler, William (1906). *The Growth of Truth*. London. Henry

References

Frowde. (The Harveian oration delivered at the Royal College of Physicians, London, October 18, 1906.)

8   Bell, Charles (1811). *Idea of a New Anatomy of the Brain submitted for the Observations of his friends*. London. Strahan and Preston.

9   Magendie, F. (1822). Expériences sur les fonctions des racines des nerfs rachidiens. *J. Physiol. exp. 2*, 276–279. Magendie, F. (1822). Expériences sur les fonctions des racines des nerfs qui naissent de la moelle épinière. *J. Physiol. exp. 2*, 366–371.

10 Bell, Charles (1830). *The Nervous System of the Human Body*. London. Longmans.

11 Fritsch, G. and Hitzig, E. (1870). Ueber die elektrische Erregbarkeit des Grosshirns. *Arch. Anat. Physiol. wiss. Med.* 1870, *37*, 300–332.

12 Jackson, John Hughlings (1931–1932). *Selected Writings of John Hughlings Jackson*. London. Hodder and Stoughton. 2 vols.

13 Ferrier, David (1876). *The Functions of the Brain*. London, Smith, Elder.

14 Ferrier, David (1875). Experiments on the brain of monkeys (2nd series). (Croonian lecture). *Phil. Trans. Roy. Soc. 165:* 433–488.

15 Ferrier, David (1874). The localization of function in the brain. *Proc. Roy. Soc. 22*, 229–232.

16 Ferrier, David (1873). Experimental researches in cerebral physiology and pathology. *West Riding Lunatic Asylum Med. Rep. 3*, 30–96.

17 Horsley, V. and Schäfer, E.A. (1884). Experimental researches in cerebral physiology. *Proc. Roy. Soc. 36*, 437–442.

18 Beevor, C.E. and Horsley, V. (1890). A record of the results obtained by electrical excitation of the so-called motor cortex and internal capsule in an orang-outang (*Simia satyrus*) *Proc. Roy. Soc. 48*, 159–160.

19 Beevor, C.E. and Horsley, V. (1891). A record of the results obtained by electrical excitation of the so-called motor cortex and internal capsule in an orang-outan (*Simia satyrus*) *Phil. Trans. Roy. Soc. B. 181*, 129-158.

20 Leyton, A.S.F. and Sherrington, C.S. (1917). Observations on the excitable cortex of the chimpanzee, orang-utan, and gorilla. *Q. J. exp. Physiol. 11*, 135–222.

21 Bartholomew, R. (1874). Experimental investigations into the functions of the human brain. *Am. J. Med. Sci. 67*, 305–313.

22 Sherrington, C.S. (1889). On nerve-tracts degenerating secondarily to lesions of the cortex cerebri. *J. Physiol. Lond. 10*, 429–432.

23 Sherrington, C.S. (1893). Experiments in examination of the peripheral distribution of the fibres of the posterior roots of some spinal nerves. *Phil. Trans. Roy. Soc B, 184*, 641–763.

24 Sherrington, C.S. (1906). *The Integrative Action of the Nervous System*. London. Constable.

25 Bland-Sutton, J. (1886). Menstruation in monkeys. *Brit. Gynaec. J.* 2, 285–292.

26 Langley, J.N. and Sherrington, C.S. (1891). On pilo-motor nerves. *J. Physiol. Lond.* 12, 278–291.

27 Heape, W. (1894). The menstruation of *Semnopithecus entellus*. *Phil. Trans. Roy. Soc.* 185, 411–471. Heape, W. (1897). The menstruation and ovulation of *Macacus rhesus*, with observations on the changes undergone by the discharged follicle. Part 2. *Phil. Trans. Roy. Soc.* 188, 135–166.

28 Herwerden, M.A. van (1905). *Bijdrage tot de Kennis van menstrueelen Cyclus en Puerperium*. Akad. Proefschr. (Geneesk.) Utrecht. Leiden, E.J. Brill. Herwerden, M.A. van (1906). Bijdrage tot de kennis van den menstrueelen cyclus. *Tijdschr. med. dierk. Vereen.* (2nd ser.) 10, 1–140.

29 Lebert, Prof. Dr (1874). Die tuberculösen Erkrankungen der Affen. *Dt. Arch. Klin. Med.* 12, 42–63, 332–355.

30 Imlach, F. (1884). Report on the transmissibility of bovine tuberculosis through milk to young animals. *Br. med. J.* 2, 175-176

31 The Imperial Institute of Experimental Medicine in St Petersburg (1892). *Lancet* 1892 (1), 1319.

32 Metchnikoff, E. and Roux, E. (1903). Études expérimentales sur la syphilis. *Annls. Inst. Pasteur*, Paris 17, 809–821.

33 Landsteiner, K. and Popper, E. (1909). Uebertragung der Poliomyelitis acuta auf Affen. *Z. ImmunForsch. exp. Ther.* 2, 377–390.

34 Grünbaum, A.S. (1904). Some experiments on enterica, scarlet fever, and measles in the chimpanzee. *Br. med. J.* 1904 (1), 817–819.

35 Jeffries, J. (1825). Some account of the dissection of a *Simia satyrus*, Orang-outang, or wild man of the woods. *Boston J. Philos. Arts* 2, 570–580.

36 Savage, T.S. (1843–1844). Observations on the external characters and habits of the *Troglodytes niger*. And on its organisation by J. Wyman. *Boston J. nat. Hist.* 4, 362–386.

37 Wyman, J. (1850). A description of two additional crania of the Engé-ena, (*Troglodytes gorilla*, Savage), from Gaboon, Africa. *Am. J. Sci.* 2nd ser. 9, 34–45.

38 Wilder, B.G. (1863). Contributions to the comparative myology of the chimpanzee. *Boston J. nat. Hist.* 7, 352–384.

39 Brown, S. (1888). Experiments on special senses localisations in the cortex cerebri of the monkey. *Med. Rec.*, N.Y. 34, 113–115.

40 Thompson, W.G. and Brown, S. (1890). The centre for vision: being an investigation into the occipital lobes of the dog, cat and monkey. *Researches Loomis Lab.*, *med. Dep. N.Y. Univ.* 1, 13–37.

References

41 Thorndike, E.L. (1901). The mental life of the monkeys. *Psychol. Monogr. 3* (5), 1–57.

42 Kinnaman, A.J. (1902). Mental life of two *Macacas rhesus* monkeys in captivity – 1. *Am. J. Psychol. 13*, 98–148, 173–218.

43 Hamilton, G.V. (1911). A study of trial and error reaction in mammals. *J. Anim. Behav. 1*, 33–66.

44 Yerkes, R.M. (1915). Maternal instinct in a monkey. *J. Anim. Behav. 5*, 403–405.

45 Corner, G.W. (1923). Ovulation and menstruation in *Macaca rhesus Contr. Embryol., Carneg. Instn. 15*, 73–101.

46 Allen, E. (1926). The menstrual cycle in the monkey; effect of double ovariectomy and injury to large follicle. *Proc. Soc. exp. Biol. Med., N.Y. 23*, 434–436.

47 Hartman, C.G. (1932). Studies in the reproduction of the monkey *Macacus (Pithecus) rhesus*, with special reference to menstruation and pregnancy. *Contr. Embryol. Carneg. Instn. 23*, (134), 1–161.

48 John Farquhar Fulton memorial number (1962). *J. Hist. Med. 17*, 1–51.

49 Bingham, H.C. (1932). Gorillas in a native habitat. Report of the joint expedition of 1929–30 of Yale University and Carnegie Institution of Washington for psychobiological study of mountain gorillas (*Gorilla beringei*) in Parc National Albert, Belgian Congo, Africa. *Publs. Carneg. Instn. 426*, 1–66.

50 Nissen, H.W. (1931). A field study of the chimpanzee: observations of chimpanzee behavior and environment in Western French Guinea. *Comp. Psychol. Monogr. 8* (1), 1–122.

51 Carpenter, C.R. (1934). A field study of the behaviour and social relations of howling monkeys (Alouatta palliata). *Comp. Psychol. Monogr. 10* (2), 1–168.

52 Kohler, Wolfgang (1925). *The Mentality of Apes*. London. Kegan Paul.

53 Kohts, Nadia (1928). Adaptive motor habits of the *Macacus rhesus* under experimental conditions. A contribution to the problem of 'Labour Processes' of Monkeys. *Sci. Mem. Mus. Darwinianum*.

54 Kluver, H. (1933). *Behaviour Mechanisms in Monkeys*. Chicago. University of Chicago Press.

Glossary of Selected Technical Terms

Acetabulum: The socket on either side of the pelvis into which the knob-like head of the femur (thigh bone) fits.

Adenohypophysis: The name applied to the anterior part of the pituitary gland (=hypophysis) (q.v.).

Adrenal (suprarenal) glands: A pair of hormone-producing glands which lie on the upper poles of the kidneys within the abdominal cavity. The central part of the gland is called the adrenal medulla, and the peripheral part, the adrenal cortex.

Androgen: The technical term for the male sex hormones produced by certain 'internally-secreting' (q.v.) cells of the testis. The principal male hormone is called 'testosterone'.

Aneurism: A dilatation of an arterial vessel due to a weakening of its wall.

Anoestrum: The period of sexual quiescence in the female of seasonally breeding mammals.

Antidiuretic hormone: A hormone produced by the posterior part of the pituitary gland and which reduces the secretion of urine.

Atresia: The name given to the process whereby oocytes (q.v.) (= egg cells) degenerate naturally within the ovary.

Atretic oocytes: Oocytes (=egg cells) which have degenerated.

Autograft: A graft of any tissue taken from one part of the body and transplanted elsewhere in the same individual.

Autonomic effects (functions): Bodily changes not under immediate voluntary control, e.g. heart-rate, intestinal action.

Axon: A fibrillar extension of a nerve cell (or 'neuron'), along which impulses are conducted away from the cell-body.

Cerebral cortex: The convoluted surface cellular layer of the brain.

Chemo-transmitter: Presumed chemical substances produced by the nuclei of the hypothalamus (q.v.) and conveyed down the pituitary-portal vessels (q.v.) into the anterior lobe (adenohypophysis) of the pituitary gland.

Compensatory hypertrophy: The term applied to a process whereby one of a pair of organs increases in size when the other is removed.

Glossary of Selected Technical Terms

Corpora lutea: (singular – corpus luteum). The secretory structure into which an ovarian follicle (q.v.) is transformed after the liberation of its egg-cell, and which produces the female sex-hormone progestogen (q.v.).

DNA: Abbreviation for deoxyribonucleic acid, the chemical substance which constitutes the genetic (hereditary) material of the cell.

Ductless gland: A gland producing a hormone(s) (q.v.).

Electromyographic patterns: The pattern of recordable electrical changes which occur when a muscle contracts.

Endocrine organ: A hormone-producing ductless gland (q.v.).

Ependymal cells: The layer of cells which lines the cavities within the brain, and the central canal of the spinal cord with which the cavities communicate.

False pelvis: The space enclosed by the flared iliac blades (q.v.) of the two innominate bones (q.v.) which make up the front and sides of the pelvis.

Fauces: The arch which separates the back of the mouth from the throat (pharynx).

Foramen magnum: The large hole in the base of the skull through which the brain-stem continues into the spinal cord.

Germinal epithelium: The layer of cells which covers the surface of the ovary.

Gestation: Pregnancy.

Glenoid fossa: The shallow depression on either side of the base of the skull into which the mandible (=jaw bone) fits, and forms a joint.

Gluteus maximus: The largest and most superficial muscle of the buttock.

Gluteus medius: The muscle of the buttock which lies immediately under the gluteus maximus.

Gluteus minimus: The deepest muscle of the buttock.

Gonadal hormone: A hormone produced either in the ovary or the testes.

Gonadotrophic hormone: (=gonadotrophin). This is the generic term applied to those secretions of the adenohypophysis (q.v.) which control the secretions of the ovaries or testes.

Gonads: The ovaries in the female, the testes in the male.

Granulosa cells: The cells which surround the female egg cell (=oocyte) in the ovary and which line the ovarian follicle (q.v.).

Histological: The adjective pertaining to histology, the microscopic study of tissues.

Homograft: A transplant of tissue from one animal to another of the same species.

Hormone: Hormones are chemical substances produced by a small number of glandular structures (called endocrine organs) in the body. The endocrine glands do not have ducts but pass their secretions directly into the blood stream.

Hypertrophy: Increase in the size of tissue, due to enlargement of its individual cells or fibres.

Hypophysectomy: The operation of removing the pituitary gland.

Hypophysis: (=pituitary gland). A small gland which is attached by a stalk to the hypothalamic region of the base of the brain. A gland consisting of a posterior lobe or neurohypophysis (q.v.) and an anterior lobe or adenohypophysis (q.v), producing secretions which control the activity of other endocrine (=hormone producing) glands of the body.

Hypothalamus: A minute part of the base of the brain from which the pituitary gland is suspended by means of a stalk. The hypothalamus constitutes the wall of the lower part of the third ventricle of the brain and consists of a number of discrete groups of nerve cells called nuclei.

Iliac blade: The upper flared part of the ilium.

Ilium: The ilium is one of the three bones which together constitute the innominate bone.

Incisors: The four front teeth in each jaw.

Infundibulum: The uppermost part of the stalk of the pituitary gland.

Inion: The most salient point at the back of the skull where the nuchal crests (q.v.) of the two sides meet in the midline.

Innominate bone: A bone forming the sides and anterior (front) wall of the pelvis, and consisting of the ilium, ischium and pubic bones. The innominate bones of the two sides meet in front at the symphysis pubis, and are separated behind by the sacrum, the latter and the two innominate bones forming the pelvis.

Internal secretion: A hormone, produced by a ductless or endocrine organ which passes directly into the blood stream.

Ischium: One of the three constituent bones of the innominate, and lying below the ilium and behind the pubic bone.

Lesion: Natural or artificial damage of tissue.

Lymph: A body fluid.

Marsupials: Primitive mammals which possess an abdominal pouch in which the young are carried.

Median eminence: A minute swelling in the floor of the third ventricle of the brain from which the pituitary (hypophysial) stalk begins. The median eminence is usually regarded as being the uppermost part of the neurohypophysis.

Milk teeth: The teeth which erupt in an infant and which are replaced by the permanent teeth.

Nares: Nostrils.

Neurohypophysis: The posterior lobe of the pituitary gland. It consists of the median eminence in the floor of the hypothalamus above (q.v.), the pituitary stalk, and a swollen lobe, the neural process or infundibular lobe, below.

Nuchal crest: (ridge, shelf). A crest of bone at the back of the skull which forms the upper limit of attachment of the nuchal muscles.

Nuchal muscles: Muscles of the back of the neck which are inserted into the back of the skull.

Nuclei supraopticus and paraventricularis: Two nuclei of the hypothalamus whose functions are closely linked with those of the neurohypophysis of the pituitary gland.

Nucleus: Term used to denote a collection of nerve cells.

Occipital condyles: Two rounded articular knobs by which the skull articulates with the first (=atlas) of the neck vertebrae.

Oestrogen: One of the two main sex hormones secreted by the ovary.

Oocyte: The female egg cell.

Oogenesis: The process whereby egg cells are formed.

Oogenetic, Oogonial tissue: Embryonic tissue from which egg cells are formed.

Organ-specific: When any foreign tissue is implanted into the body a 'defence reaction' occurs as a result of which the tissue is 'rejected'. This constitutes what is called an immunological response of the host tissue. An organ-specific immunological response would be a response developed not just against foreign tissue in general, but also against the kind of tissue which is implanted.

Ovarian follicles: Minute cysts in the ovary containing the female egg-cells.

Oxytocic hormone: A secretion of the posterior lobe of the pituitary gland which causes the uterine muscle to contract.

Palaeontology: The study of fossil animals and plants.

Pars distalis: The pars distalis is the main secretory part of the adenohypophysis (=the anterior lobe of the pituitary gland).

Pars intermedia: An indistinct layer of cells which intervenes between the pars distalis of the adenohypophysis and the neural process of the neurohypophysis.

Pars tuberalis: A collection of cells belonging to the adenohypophysis and adherent to the median eminence (q.v.) to which the pituitary stalk is attached.

Pilo-motor nerves: Nerve fibres which innervate the minute muscles of the hair follicles.

Pineal gland: A small cone-shaped structure projecting from the brain behind the third ventricle.

Pituitary gland: (See Hypophysis).

Pituitary-portal vessels: Minute vessels beginning in a vascular network in the median eminence and pars tuberalis above, and passing down the stalk of the pituitary gland into the anterior lobe of the pituitary gland below.

Pituitary stalk: A band of nerve fibres which connects the hypothalamus with the neural process of the neurohypophysis.

Pressor hormone: A hormone produced by the posterior lobe of the pituitary gland which causes the minute vessels of the body to contract, thus raising the blood pressure.

Progestogen, Progesterone: One of the two main sex hormones produced by the ovary.

Pubic bone: One of the three bones forming the innominate bone, lying below the ilium and in front of the ischium.

Sacroiliac Joint: The joint connecting the sacrum and the innominate bones.

Sacrum: A triangular bone consisting of fused vertebrae which forms the back of the pelvis, and which articulates on either side with the innominate bones.

Sagittal crest: A longitudinal bony crest in the midline of the skull formed by the fusion of the two temporal lines, which mark the upper limit of origin of the temporal muscles from the sides of the skull.

Sella turcica: The cavity in the base of the brain-case within which lies the pituitary gland.

Simian: Apelike.

Sinusoid: A minute blood space.

Spermatogenesis: The name applied to the process whereby spermatozoa are formed.

Splenius capitis: A muscle lying in the back of the neck and connecting the upper vertebrae with the skull.

Sternocleidomastoid: A straplike muscle which lies on the side of the neck, and which connects the mastoid process behind the ear, with the sternum (breast bone) and clavical (collar bone).

Superior cervical sympathetic ganglia: A large collection of nerve cells on the upper part of the sympathetic nervous trunk in the neck.

Symphysis pubis: The joint between the two pubic bones of the pelvis.

Taxonomic: Adjective pertaining to taxonomy, the study of animal classification.

Temporal muscle: A large triangular muscle of mastication connecting the head of the jaw-bone (mandible) below with the side of the skull above.

Thyroid gland: A hormone-producing gland (it secretes 'thyroxine') which lies in the neck.

Trapezius muscle: A large flat muscle which lies superficially at the back of the thorax, and which extends up the back of the neck to be attached to the skull.

Glossary of Selected Technical Terms

Tuber cinereum: A minute part of the floor of the hypothalamus, the central part of which forms the median eminence (q.v.) from which the pituitary stalk begins.

Uterine horn: One of the pair of tubular structures which constitute the major part of the uterus in most mammals.

Vascular bed: A network of minute spaces containing blood.

Vas deferens: The excretory duct of the testicle, transporting the semen to the penis.

Ventricle: The name applied to four cavities in the substance of the brain, two laterally and two, the third and the fourth, in the midline below.

Visceral function: (=autonomic function) (q.v.).

X-irradiation: The irradiation of any tissue of the body by means of a beam of X-rays.

General Index

General Index

Author Index

(Index numbers refer to the page on which an author's work is discussed. Full bibliographic information can be found in the references to that page at the end of the book.)

Author Index